Towards Anti-Racist
Educational Research

Towards Anti-Racist Educational Research

Radical Moments and Movements

Edited by
Delane A. Bender-Slack
and Francis Godwyll

LEXINGTON BOOKS
Lanham • Boulder • New York • London

Published by Lexington Books
An imprint of The Rowman & Littlefield Publishing Group, Inc.
4501 Forbes Boulevard, Suite 200, Lanham, Maryland 20706
www.rowman.com

86-90 Paul Street, London EC2A 4NE

Copyright © 2022 by The Rowman & Littlefield Publishing Group, Inc.

All rights reserved. No part of this book may be reproduced in any form or by any electronic or mechanical means, including information storage and retrieval systems, without written permission from the publisher, except by a reviewer who may quote passages in a review.

British Library Cataloguing in Publication Information Available

Library of Congress Cataloging-in-Publication Data

Names: Bender-Slack, Delane A., editor. | Godwyll, Francis, editor.
Title: Towards anti-racist educational research : radical moments and movements / Edited by Delane A. Bender-Slack and Francis Godwyll.
Description: Lanham : Lexington Books, [2022] | Includes bibliographical references and index.
Identifiers: LCCN 2021053796 (print) | LCCN 2021053797 (ebook) | ISBN 9781666900132 (cloth) | ISBN 9781666900156 (paperback) | ISBN 9781666900149 (epub)
Subjects: LCSH: Racism in education—Research—United States. | Multicultural education—United States. | Educational equalization—United States.
Classification: LCC LC212.2 .T69 2022 (print) | LCC LC212.2 (ebook) | DDC 371.829/96073—dc23
LC record available at https://lccn.loc.gov/2021053796
LC ebook record available at https://lccn.loc.gov/2021053797

Contents

Introduction   1
Delane A. Bender-Slack

1. Curriculum and Social Movement: Combating White Supremacy in Education   9
Dominique M. Brown

2. Creating an Equitable Learning Community for Preservice Early Childhood Teachers   21
Angela Miller-Hargis and Helene Arbouet Harte

3. Toward a Pedagogy of Anti-racist Professional Discernment in Elementary Literacy Learning: Swords to Ploughshares   37
Kerry Alexander and Jimmy McLean

4. Seeing Myself in the Curriculum: Engaging Black Students through Technology Usage and Culturally Responsive Teaching   57
K. Milam Brooks and Amari T. Simpson

5. Ten Years Later: Toward a Reconceptualization of the Racial Framework of Teacher Candidates   73
Nicole V. Williams

6. The Value of Gathering Unofficially at Predominately White Institutions: Meet Me in the Third Space   89
Jennifer K. Shah

7. Disrupting Institutional Racism in Higher Education: Beyond the Cultural Keeping in Curriculum   103
Vanessa M. Rigaud and Jody Googins

8	Anti-racist Research in Teacher Education: Creating Critical Online Communities *Lauren Angelone, Romena M. Garrett Holbert, and Joanne Baltazar Vakil*	123
9	One Man's Journey as a Black and White Educational Researcher: Self-determination through a Biracial Perspective *Brett A. Burton*	141
10	Children's Literature: Guiding Change *Teresa Young, Vanessa M. Rigaud, and Sara Fitzgerald*	159
11	Preservice Teachers' Understanding of Culturally Responsive Teaching and Learning: Fears of Working in a Diverse Classroom *Winston Vaughan*	175
12	Moving toward an Anti-racist Feminist Global Lens *Delane A. Bender-Slack*	189
13	When Silence Is Not an Option: Creating Spaces for Marginalized Voices *Francis Godwyll*	209
Index		225
About the Editors		231
About the Contributors		233

Introduction
Delane A. Bender-Slack

From radical moments to radical movements, educational research can be an integral part of the journey to create an anti-racist world. Schools play a critical role in perpetuating the status quo, labeling and categorizing students in ways that limit possibilities. As Nieto (2017) reminds us, "Public education, though a noble ideal, rather than 'level the playing field,' often served to exacerbate inequalities particularly around race, ethnicity, social class, language, and other differences" (pp. 23–24). Moreover, these aforementioned inequalities are often created subtly. For example, with regard to such pedagogical tools as classroom conversations, viewed as democratic because everyone has an opportunity to contribute, "recitation is by far the predominant mode of classroom discourse in American secondary schools, where it has been an idiosyncratic part of schooling for well over a century" (Nystrand et. al., 1997, pp. 5–6). Quite often teachers control the discourse, and scripted programs have added to that inequity. Another example, perhaps more obvious, would be those who profit from dark suffering (injuring students of color) such as the testing, prison, and textbook industries as well as charter schools and the superpredator corporate school reformers (Love, 2020).

Universities have been coconspirators in perpetuating the status quo, producing research that often does not challenge current injustices, due to the fact that professors engaging in educational research in the United States often look and sound like K-12 teachers, that is, primarily White, middle class, and female. Consequently, advancing diversity and inclusion in higher education is currently a common goal among universities. According to ACE's (2021) report on the race and ethnicity of postsecondary faculty and staff in higher education, only one-fifth are People of Color. Moreover, the majority of full-time faculty were White, with People of Color being more likely to be instructors, lecturers, and faculty with no academic rank. This is significant because in higher education, full-time faculty are provided with the resources (time, support, guidelines, and rewards) to engage in educational research. If the only means to oppose racism is to regularly identify and describe racism so that we can then dismantle it, our roles as educational researchers are no exception. The demographics of the academy, as well as what we do, must change.

This book is a call for educational researchers of all races to engage in the work needed to be anti-racist. There is no place for neutrality when it comes to race. As Kendi (2019) writes,

> One endorses either the idea of a racial hierarchy as a racist, or racial equality as an antiracist. One either believes problems are rooted in groups of people, as a racist, or locates the roots of problems in power and policies, as an antiracist. One either allows racial inequities to persevere, as a racist, or confronts racial inequities, as an antiracist. (p. 9)

The authors of this book strive for racial equity, locating the roots of problems in power and policies, in order to confront racial inequities. As we continue to grapple with our role in radical moments and movements—from our various identities, perspectives, and positionalities—we strive to identify our work in our research, and in this writing, as anti-racist. Striving to define what it could mean to be anti-racist in our research methods, projects, and agendas, we are full of questions: How do we ask anti-racist research questions? How do we create anti-racist curricula? How do we design anti-racist policies? What does it mean to be racially humanizing educational researchers? How do we intentionally work toward racial justice?

As educational researchers, we must turn the gaze on ourselves, and we believe doctoral students and early career faculty, who are both insiders and outsiders of the academy, may be able to guide us, which is why we include many of their voices in these chapters. What do they perceive as racist and anti-racist as they learn how to be educational researchers? Moreover, the various written and unwritten policies we abide by in higher education must be interrogated. "A racist policy is any measure that produces or sustains racial inequity between racial groups. An antiracist policy is any measure that produces or sustains racial equity between racial groups" (Kendi, 2019, p.18). We want our work to do the latter. From IRBs and research methodologies to the peer review process of publications, educational research is fraught with those unwritten and written rules, guidelines, practices, and protocols that would be included in the term *policy*. And for far too long, they are gatekeepers, or rather locks on the gates, disallowing a truly inclusive academy.

Doctoral students and early career faculty are expected to assimilate into the academy, and it is the role of their faculty mentors to make sure this occurs. Like racial assimilationist ideas, according to Kendi (2019), these expectations to assimilate are racist ideas. As we train new doctoral students and faculty, we require them to assimilate into the academy, which is a White, patriarchal construct. This includes teaching the *right* ways to research, the *accepted* methods, and setting the bar so that only those who assimilate well can succeed. This "has been—and still is—a White-led and White-dominated field and, therefore, should not surprise anyone that the logic of analysis and methods used to investigate racial matters reflect this social fact" (Bonilla-Silva & Zuberi, 2008, pp. 16–17). The traditional patriarchal, hierarchical, and objective structures allow space for some, while they limit or exclude others. "If learning does not strengthen our bonds, does not move us in the direction of equity, does not improve our chances of living healthy, fulfilled lives, then why do it" (Bender-Slack, 2020, p. 1)? It is past time to collaboratively, seriously, and consistently interrogate the policies and power of higher education to address those procedures that are racist.

"There are a host of critical issues in education today, and therefore, the intellectual and practical work we do in and out of schools and universities throughout the world matters" (Bender-Slack, 2020, p. 1). The critical issues of racial inequality, white supremacy, educational policies and practices, third spaces, and identities provide us places to investigate so that our work—as educational researchers—matters.

This edited volume grew out of a virtual panel discussion of the Mid-Western Educational Research Association entitled: *Racism and Anti-Racism in the Academy and K-12 Schooling: Multiple Perspectives.* The scholars in this book represent diverse backgrounds and interests. Some of the authors are willing to confront their own complicity in White supremacy, which is the "racist ideology that is based upon the belief that white people are superior . . . and that therefore . . . should be dominant . . . which extend to how systems and institutions are structured to uphold this white dominance" (Saad, 2020, p. 12). Some of the authors attempt to interrogate the fiction of whiteness as a way to help readers of all races "think critically about how race functions systemically and often subconsciously to privilege people with certain perceived skin traits" (Beech, 2020, p.3). Some of the authors use culturally responsive theory and practice as a way to examine the possibility of creating radical moments and movements, however, as Gay (2018) explains, "[C]ulturally responsive teaching alone cannot solve all of the problems of improving the education of marginalized students of color. Other aspects of the educational enterprise (such as funding, administration, and policymaking) also must be reformed" (p. 1). Educational research must be part of that reformation.

The authors of these chapters come from a variety of contexts, races, classes, ethnicities, and religions, which provides the readers with multiple perspectives, unique abilities to complicate the status quo, and various ways to negotiate their locations. What started as a deeply provocative and thoughtful panel discussion has grown into the desire to combine our voices, interests, hopes, purposes, and work in order to add to the current movement for equity. By what we say and do about race, we strive to continue this work for racial equality, specifically as it relates to educational research and how it impacts K-12 education.

In chapter 1 "Curriculum and Social Movement: Combating White Supremacy in Education," doctoral student Dominique M. Brown uses critical discourse analysis to examine political rhetoric used in the 2020 executive order banning Critical Race Theory (CRT) and SB1070 in Arizona banning Ethnic Studies. She will examine white supremacist assertions as reasons for the bans on these particular curricula as well as provide supportive context for the development of CRT and Ethnic Studies curricula in education.

In chapter 2, entitled "Creating an Equitable Learning Community for Preservice Early Childhood Teachers," Angela Miller-Hargis and Helene Arbouet Harte describe their efforts to create an equitable online learning community by planning in a manner that is anti-racist, abolitionist, and universally designed. The authors provide an overview and examples of guiding strategies, reflections on their experiences, challenges faced, and suggestions for moving forward.

In chapter 3, "Toward a Pedagogy of Anti-racist Professional Discernment in Elementary Literacy Learning: Swords to Ploughshares," doctoral students Kerry Alexander and Jimmy McLean, two White literacy scholars, assess the power-laden Science of Reading (SoR) discourse surrounding elementary literacy instruction in public schools and its impact on teacher educators. In response, they propose a pedagogy of *anti-racist professional discernment*. Teachers who enact this pedagogy embrace tensions—ideological, social, and political—to make wise and just decisions, rather than hasty implementation of policies grounded in failure-rhetoric. Instead of reifying binaries, the authors suggest four qualities anti-racist literacy professionals may consider as resistance in-praxis."

In chapter 4, "Seeing Myself in the Curriculum: Engaging Black Students through Technology Usage and Culturally Responsive Teaching," authors K. Milam Brooks and Amari T. Simpson explore the existing literature on anti-Black racism, culturally relevant pedagogy and practice, and technology to examine its use as an integrated, necessary solution to transform the U.S. public school system.

In chapter 5, "Ten Years Later: Toward a Reconceptualization of the Racial Framework of Teacher Candidates," Nicole V. Williams describes how teacher candidates believe that their encounters with race and racism shape their past, present, and future experiences in teaching, learning, and interactions with others. Ten years ago, Williams (2011) proposed a reconceptualization of the racial framework of teacher candidates through her work in an educator preparation program at a large Mid-Western research university. In this chapter, Williams reflects on a systematic review of the literature within past ten years to determine if teacher candidates have reconceptualized their understanding of race and racism.

In chapter 6, entitled "The Value of Gathering Unofficially at Predominately White Institutions: Meet Me in the Third Space," professor Jennifer K. Shah discusses the potential benefits of third spaces that foster open dialogue around traditionally controversial topics and centers the voices of Black, Indigenous, People of Color (BIPOC) students. Such voluntary, heterogeneous gatherings have the potential to empower BIPOC students and shift the power dynamic at predominantly White institutions of education. An example of a third space movie club may motivate teacher educators to start conversations on their own campuses.

In chapter 7, entitled "Disrupting Institutional Racism in Higher Education: Beyond the Cultural Keeping in Curriculum," scholars Vanessa M. Rigaud and Jody Googins address the complexity of multicultural curriculum design and bring forth culturally responsive practices that navigate race, ethnicity, class, sexual identity, gender, language, nationality, learning differences, religion, and age in the classroom. Strategies, discourse, and leadership in educational practices will call all learners to the table for a global partnership in disrupting institutional racism. Educators are called to move beyond the cultural keeping of past decades and engage in culturally responsive practices, leading to a new transformation among students.

In chapter 8, "Anti-racist Research in Teacher Education: Creating Critical Online Communities," academics Lauren Angelone, Romena M. Garrett Holbert, and Joanne Baltazar-Vakil provide an overview of anti-racist teacher education and online education, sharing ways they adapted anti-racist efforts within their teaching and research settings to the online context. The chapter concludes with how their work can become far-reaching by leveraging online tools and resources to develop global interactions/ partnerships to support advocacy and foster international communities of learners.

In chapter 9, "One Man's Journey as a Black and White Educational Researcher: Self-determination through a Biracial Perspective," professor Brett Burton examines leadership structures that sanction implicit academic and racist practices among faculty, students, and influential community members. He provides current and future educational leaders with a template to address implicit racist educational systems through action and advocacy.

In chapter 10, titled "Children's Literature: Guiding Change," professors Teresa Young, Vanessa M. Rigaud, and Sara Fitzgerald describe an international research study that explored how social class, ethnicity, race, gender, and religion impact students' understanding of cultural context and the role literacy plays in different family types in Ireland and the United States.

In chapter 11, "Preservice Teachers' Understanding of Culturally Responsive Teaching and Learning: Fears of Working in a Diverse Classroom," author Winston Vaughan explores preservice teachers' perspectives of culturally responsive learning as they investigate what it means to be a culturally responsive teacher in a diverse classroom, highlighting the fears and offering strategies to help alleviate those fears.

In chapter 12, titled "Moving toward an Anti-racist Feminist Global Lens," Delane Bender-Slack addresses the tensions between culturally responsive teaching and globalizing classrooms. Specifically, she conceptually examines the intersection of culturally responsive pedagogy and global competencies through the epistemological moves of feminist standpoint theory.

In chapter 13, "When Silence Is Not an Option: Creating Space for Marginalized Voices" Francis Godwyll defines silence, identifies some of the motivating factors that produce silence as a consequence, and gives examples of societal disruptions and the complex responses that silence evokes. Additionally, societal reactions are examined, lessons learned are deduced, and possibilities for creating spaces for empowerment are examined.

In an attempt to capture the momentum of moving the journey toward equity forward, the authors also offer readers something to read, do, and/ or consider at the end of each chapter. The purpose is to provide resources and make suggestions for being or becoming a part of the radical moments and movements toward anti-racist educational research as we come together in community to do what can be done—while we dream and struggle for a better tomorrow.

As Love (2020) reminds us, freedom is a practice, rather than a possession or a state of being so that "to want freedom is to welcome struggle" (p. 9). We believe that it is important to be part of this struggle even if it may mean confronting our own complicity in policies and practices so that we can transform something oppressive into something liberatory. From moments to movements, we will continue to reflect and act with the bright light of hope for creating something better—something more equitable. "We must struggle together not only to reimagine schools but to build new schools that we are taught to believe are impossible: schools based in intersectional justice, anti-racism, love, healing, and joy" (Love, 2020, p. 10). We, the authors, believe that only working collaboratively and hopefully through the tough, tense radical moments and movements, is schooling founded in justice, anti-racism, love, healing, and joy possible.

REFERENCES

ACE, American Council on Education. (2021). *Race and ethnicity in higher education, 2020 supplement.* https://www.acenet.edu/Research-Insights/Pages/Race-and-Ethnicity-in-Higher-Education.aspx.

Beech, J. (2020). *White out.* Brill Sense.

Bender-Slack, D. (2020). *The Nicaraguan Literacy Campaign: The Power and Politics of Literacy.* Lexington Books.

Bonilla-Silva, E. and Zuberi, T. (2008). Toward a definition of white logic and white methods. In E. Bonilla-Silva & T. Zuberi (Eds.), *White logic, white methods* (pp. 3–27). Rowman & Littlefield.

Gay, G. (2018). *Culturally responsive teaching.* Teachers College Press.

Kendi, I. (2019). *How to be an antiracist.* One World.

Love, B. (2020). *We want to do more than survive: Abolitionist teaching and the pursuit of educational freedom.* Beacon Press.

Nieto, S. (2017). Identity matters: My life as a [Puerto Rican] teacher educator. In B. Picower & R. Kohli (Eds.), *Confronting racism in teacher education* (pp. 21–28). Routledge.

Nystrand, M., Gamoran, A. Kachur, R. & Prendergast, C. (1991). *Opening dialogue.* Teachers College Press.

Saad, L. (2020). *Me and white supremacy.* Sourcebooks.

Chapter 1

Curriculum and Social Movement
Combating White Supremacy in Education
Dominique M. Brown

As Gloria Anzaldúa writes:

> The answer to the problem between the white race and the colored, between males and females, lies in healing the split that originates in the very foundation of our lives, our culture, our languages, our thoughts. A massive uprooting of dualistic thinking in the individual and collective consciousness is the beginning of a long struggle, but one that could, in our best hopes, bring us to the end of rape, of violence, of war. (Anzaldúa, 1987, p. 102)

Critical scholars in K-12 and Higher Education have continuously challenged dominant curricular norms in order to center the lived experiences of marginalized, minoritized, and historically oppressed communities in the United States. This chapter uses policy analysis to examine political narratives used in Executive Order 13950 issued under 45th President Donald Trump broadly prohibiting the use of Critical Race Theory (CRT) in programs funded by the federal government (Executive Office of the President, 2020). As well as SB1070 in Arizona banning Ethnic Studies programs in public schools (Hammer, 2012). It will look at the white supremacist assertions as reasons for the bans on these particular curricula. In addition, it provides supportive context for the use of CRT and Ethnic Studies as curricular counternarratives in education.

In Deborah Stone's *Policy Paradox*, she thoughtfully articulates a robust theory of the inherent irrationality of politics and the democratic process. We are constantly negotiating and renegotiating the boundaries of what we want for ourselves, our communities, our nation, and our world. According to Stone, "Politics is a process of argument and persuasion. It entails searching for criteria and justifying choices. Equity, efficiency, welfare, liberty, security, democracy, and justice are aspirations for a community into which people read contradictory interpretations. But while the interpretations divide people, the aspirations unite us" (Stone, 2002, p. 385). The narratives we adopt as a nation guide our public discourses and ultimately the policies that are adopted that guide public life. Much of the public conversation around the history of race in the United States has been shaped by the dominant curricular narratives which have been shaped by the white lens of that history. Black educational leaders such as Anna Julia Cooper, Carter G. Woodson, Patricia Hill-Collins, among many others have long uplifted the problem with a white-centric cannon that ignores the experiences of minoritized groups. Many have worked to reshape this narrow sociocultural construction of history to center those who have been pushed to the margins. This has happened in many social spheres including education. As Stone reminds us:

> The work of imagining what a common goal means and bringing others to one's own view, join people to a common cause . . . . We may not ever see eye to eye, yet there is a huge difference between a political process in which people honestly try to see the world from different vantage points, and one in which they claim from the start that their vantage point is the right one. (Stone, 2002, p. 385)

As social movements have carved out space for broader public understanding, the pushback against those gains has intensified. Critical Race Theory or CRT is an academic framework envisioned by legal scholars Derrick Bell, Kimberlé Crenshaw, Richard Delgado, and expanded upon by education scholars like Patricia Hill Collins, as well as others. Broadly, it is an analysis of the systemic and pervasive nature of racism in U.S. law and public policy (Sawchuk, 2021). Critical scholarship has long been a target of anti-democratic political antics. Recent history leaves us with some very potent examples.

EXECUTIVE ORDER 13950

Late in the 45th Presidents' term, the administration turned its sights on what Memorandum M-20-34 called "un-American propaganda training sessions" (Executive Office of the President, 2020), specifically highlighting CRT and white privilege as examples of the types of discourse that should be excluded from any future federally funded services. That memorandum was followed up by Executive Order 13950, and subsequently Memorandum M-20-37. All of which specifically aimed at labeling a multitude of critical frameworks as "divisive" requiring all entities conducting diversity and inclusion training funded by the federal government to conduct an audit and remove "divisive" content (Executive Office of the President, 2020). The frameworks labeled as "divisive" included CRT, white privilege, intersectionality, systemic racism, positionality, racial humility, and unconscious bias (Executive Office of the President, 2020). The targeted rapid-fire nature of the executive order and accompanying memoranda created confusion in many institutions and universities about its implications. Some simply ignored them, while other institutions took the opportunity to water down existing diversity, equity, and inclusion efforts or canceling them all together (Flaherty, 2020). The outcome of the 2020 presidential election ultimately resulted in the order being rescinded; however, it is dangerous to ignore the insidious nature of attempts by a U.S. president to censor the use of critical scholarship and varying levels of institutional compliance. The hyperbolic rhetoric in these documents leans into the backdrop of American historical figures like Rev. Martin Luther King Jr. and events like the Civil War as a means of conjuring up a sense of solidarity with marginalized communities, while simultaneously deeming scholarship by, for, and about oppressed groups in the United States as anti-American.

SB1070

The narrative tactics deployed surrounding Executive Order 13950 are nothing new. Another example that looms large in recent history is the battle to protect Mexican American Studies (MAS) in Arizona. In this case, local politicians similarly misused the words of Martin Luther King in an attempt at legally prohibiting curriculum that contradicts hegemonic dominant understandings of U.S. history.

The contentious case of the MAS program in the Tuscan Unified School District (TUSD) provides an example of how this is taking shape in the city and its schools. The work of the community members who took collective action in order to develop the MAS program, protected it when challenged by hostile policymakers, and ultimately fought all the way to the Supreme Court (SCOTUS), laying out an inspirational playbook for how historically marginalized communities fight to take up space in the broader political infrastructure. My goal in framing this case through Stone's lens provides a big picture view of what has taken place in the TUSD.

Intentionally designing culturally relevant educational spaces, which honor the identities of students, might provide a path forward toward excellence, equity, and equality (Green, 1983). The TUSD ethnic studies programs provide a roadmap for how this could be accomplished, despite potential backlash from those who have historically controlled the narrative. It is central to understand *who benefits from how the story is told*? This question is at the heart of defining why cultural relevance matters for education. Culturally relevant pedagogy is influenced by multicultural educational practice. Many multicultural and ethnic studies programs have cropped up in primary, secondary, and postsecondary education across the country. However, in 2010, Arizona legislators called into question the validity of the successful MAS program, forcefully suspending the program, and sparking political opposition from students, teachers, community leaders, and activists. Ultimately, the censoring of the ethnic studies program was deemed unconstitutional by the U.S. Supreme Court.

In August of 2017, a federal judge declared the TUSD ban on ethnic studies, known as HB2281, as unconstitutional (Harris, 2017). This analysis will examine the case in Arizona, why the battle had to be fought, and how it made its way to the SCOTUS decision. This chapter explores the development of ethnic studies programs in the TUSD, couching such programs as a tool for honoring cultural heritage and maintaining cultural sustainability of communities and exploring alternative narratives outside of dominant hegemonic white culture. It will also attempt to navigate the complex political dynamics created when white citizens feel threatened by shifting dominant cultural narratives, where white stories are not centered in the curricular history.

MEXICAN AMERICAN STUDIES (MAS) IN TUSCAN

The communal make-up of Tuscan prior to the 1950s meant that the schools served a diverse student body made up of Indigenous American, Latinx, African American, and European American students. Mid-century, as white residents moved into the area at higher rates, the school system began to bifurcate into what eventually was charged a segregated school system with racially discriminatory practices (Blankenship & Locke, 2015, p. 340).

> Curriculum battles have deep historical roots in Arizona. . . . Twenty years after *Broun v. Board of Education,* Hispanic and African-American students filed a class action suit against the Tucson Unified School District for its long-standing *de jure* segregation. Four years later, in 1978, the federal court exercising jurisdiction over the case agreed with the plaintiffs and approved a desegregation plan intended to remedy decades of segregation. Like most desegregation plans implemented during the second half of the twentieth century, Tucson's plan proved sufficiently malleable to allow the White power structure to weaken and circumvent its objectives, resulting in what James E. Ryan refers to as "token compliance." (Dotts, 2015, p. 35)

Following a 1978 court ruling requiring the TUSD to take steps toward desegregation, its ethnic studies program was conceived. Programs in African

American Studies, Pan-Asian Studies, and Native American Studies were implemented in the school system. Beginning in 1997, the school district developed the MAS program (Blankenship & Locke, 2015). Prior to the development of the MAS program, TUSD had introduced courses for English language learners and in Hispanic culture, but no robust program had been developed that focused on Latinx cultural heritage similar to the other ethnic studies programs despite the fact that the Latinx population in the region made up the largest group in the school district (Jiménez-silva, 2012).

HOUSE BILL (HB) 2281

In May 2010, despite popular communal support and a nearly ten-year track record of successful implementation, resulting in higher academic success for participants, the TUSD led by then superintendent Thomas Horn passed legislation in an effort to eliminate the district's MAS program (Blankenship & Locke, 2015). The language of the bill prohibited any classes including curriculum which:

1. "Advocate ethnic solidarity."
2. Are "designed primarily for students of a particular race."
3. "Promote resentment toward a certain ethnic group."
4. "Promote the overthrow of the U.S. government."

(Jiménez-silva, 2012, p. 15)

Any educational programs that were identified as being noncompliant with the law, would lose 10 percent of annual school funding (Blankenship & Locke, 2015).

The MAS program became a political target when a local labor activist publicly declared to students in the program that Republicans were racist against the Latinx community (Harris, 2017). Ironically, the Republican leadership responded by whipping up social tensions and fears about immigrants, vowing to eliminate the MAS program and accused the program of using racist rhetoric (Hammer, 2012). This tactic, of claiming reverse racism, asserting that the very naming of oppressive experiences by historically marginalized groups as racist, might simply seem like the hyperbolic words of an overzealous politician. However, Giroux calls this "neoliberal racism" and claims it has been systematically used as a tactic in order to whip up support for neoliberal policies (Hammer, 2012, p. 67). The irony continued in the claims made from the public officials targeting the program that it was somehow "un-American" (Blankenship & Locke, 2015, p. 341) despite the fact that the

MAS curriculum is steeped in the deep history of the border region which dates the founding of Tuscan by Spanish speakers in 1775. That occurred one year before the signing of the Declaration of Independence and the creation of the country we now call the United States of America (Jiménez-silva, 2012).

In 2011, Thomas Horn's close political ally John Huppenthal succeeded him as superintendent. In efforts to find the MAS program in violation of HB2281, he proceeded to order an expensive programmatic audit from Cambium Learning. The audit report not only found the MAS program to not be in violation of the law, but it established that the program was contributing to the academic success of participating students. In response, Huppenthal commissioned his own report which made the opposite conclusion (Blankenship & Locke, 2015).

By 2012, officials determined to rid the school district of the MAS program resorted to draconian measures including the banning and removal of books used for the curriculum. Books were boxed up while crying students and teachers watched in horror, included Paulo Freire's *Pedagogy of the Oppressed* and—inadvertently—William Shakespeare's *The Tempest* (Wanberg, 2013, pp. 15–16). In all, the school district banned seven resources used in the MAS program and restricted one text for "leisure use only" (Dotts, 2015, p. 36). These actions resulted in mass communal outrage, protests, and ultimately legal challenges.

CULTURALLY CONSCIOUS AND CULTURALLY RELEVANT CURRICULUM

One cannot expect positive results from an educational or political action program which fails to respect the particular view of the world held by the people. Such a program constitutes cultural invasion, good intentions notwithstanding (Freire, as quoted by Dotts, 2015, p. 35).

Lisa Delpit's work, *Other People's Children*, provides a deeper understanding of how bias attitudes, xenophobia, and racism play out in everyday classrooms. What she terms as the "culture of power" (Delpit, 1988, p. 238) underscores how traditional curriculum created by and for dominant white cultural norms operates in the practical sense. Textbooks, standardized tests, behavioral expectations, and communication styles all cater to patterns laid out by those who hold this power (Delpit, 1988). Students from families and communities that do not have access to these cultural norms are harmed by classroom spaces operating only within these boundaries.

Delpit's work points to the need to teach students from other cultures the expectations of dominant hegemonic white societal standards, so that they might access leverage within broader social structures. This is only half the battle because it does not remedy the underlying systemic problem. This hidden curriculum (Jackson, 1990) creates an antagonistic educational environment for students whose lived experiences do not match these expectations. Their cultures should not have to be erased in favor of dominant modes of operation. This does not mean that the histories and traditional values of European American's should be discontinued in curriculum; it is possible for multiple truths to exist simultaneously. They always have. "Culturally [conscious] pedagogy seeks to perpetuate and foster—to sustain—linguistic, literate, and cultural pluralism as part of the democratic project of schooling" (Paris, 2012, p. 93). Culturally relevant pedagogies are tools for decolonizing the educational experience for marginalized groups as demonstrated through the MAS program. As one former student reflected, "These books show people that look like me, like my parents, like my grandparents. I know we went through unfair things, but it doesn't make me hate anybody, it makes me love myself" (Stockton, 2017).

As the Tuscan case demonstrates, it can be difficult to do the work of claiming space for marginalized people's voices, histories, and experiences to be represented in the curriculum, but it is crucial that students also understand the heritage of their ancestors. I would push further, by also calling for students of all backgrounds, in all communities, to be exposed to multiple cultural perspectives that complicate the historical narratives commonly told—even—and *especially*—in predominantly white communities, all of which exist on historically indigenous lands, in a country built by the labor of enslaved Africans, and all of whom come from immigrant ancestry. Ignoring these complicated and beautiful historical truths harms us all, which is what actually contributes to divisive conflicts we continue to face. The possibility of public education to engage a polis capable of the democratic process requires a critical culturally conscious curriculum.

PUBLIC POLICY AND ETHNIC STUDIES CURRICULUM

Despite the attacks by conservative politicians capitalizing on divisive identity politics in order to advance their own careers, the MAS program in Tuscan arguably represents an extremely successful educational reform. Before the implementation of HB 2281, the program enjoyed strong community support. The MAS program was born out of the community's desire to see the complex history of the Mexican American community represented in the curriculum. As of 2012, Latinx students made up 61 percent of the TUSD (Hammer, 2012). It seems like common sense that there would be extensive curricular content dedicated to the study of communities represented in the school district. However, that was not the case for the MAS program; it required concentrated thoughtful advocacy from local parents, students, and activists in order to make it a reality. This advocacy occurred despite the fact that the school district had already implemented a broader ethnic studies curriculum program developed for other cultural groups. The existence of these programs provided an opportunity for the development and adoption of the MAS program. At the time that HB 22881 was passed, the TUSD was the only district offering a fully fledged ethnic studies program for high school students (Hammer, 2012). Perhaps the success of the TUSD ethnic studies program is what made it a target for lawmakers with opposing political ideologies about how race is studied in U.S. schools.

The claim that this program represents a successful reform is made based on the definition as outlined by Cohen and Mehta (2017), which identifies at least five characteristics of successful educational reforms:

> First, some offered solutions to problems that the people who worked in or around education knew that they had and wanted to solve; they met felt needs for the people who would implement them.
> Second, some offered solutions that illuminated a real problem that educators had not been aware of or couldn't figure out how to solve, but they embraced the reform once they saw or believed that it would help; these reforms illuminated a problem of practice and offered a solution.
> Third, some reforms succeeded because they satisfied demands that arose from the political, economic, or social circumstances of schooling; these reforms worked because there was strong popular pressure on and/or in educational organizations or governments to accomplish some educational purpose.
> Fourth, in each of these cases, reforms also either offered the educational tools, materials, and practical guidance educators needed to put the reform into practice, or they helped educators to capitalize on existing tools, materials, and guidance. Less difficult reforms required less capacity building while more ambitious reforms required more.
> Fifth, in a locally controlled and democratically governed system of schooling, successful reforms have been roughly consistent with the values of the educators, parents, and students they affected, though this worked differently in system-wide than niche versions. (p. 2)

The ethnic studies programs in the TUSD meet nearly all of these criteria. This is easily demonstrated if broken down by each step.

1. In the development of the MAS program, the TUSD created a group of 34 committee members which included parents, community leaders, teachers, administrators, union leaders, university professors, and a

student representative. This committee participated in biweekly meetings for a year to develop the program prior to implementation. The committee conducted three hearings in strategically selected high schools in the district attended by 500 to 600 community participants. Overwhelmingly the community supported the creation of the MAS program. In addition, the Tuscan City Council voted 6-1 encouraging the TUSD to implement the program (Jiménez-silva, 2012).
2. The MAS program filled an obvious gap in the broader ethnic studies programming offered by the school district. The broader curriculum which ultimately included MAS had been developed in response to an Arizona desegregation law designed to bridge the [opportunity] gap between mostly white middle class students and students of color in the state. In 1974, the TUSD was found by the courts to be operating a segregated school system which harmed students. It was out of this that the district's ethnic studies program was born in 1978. In response to community pressures, nearly twenty years later in 1997, what became known as the Mexican American Studies program was developed to support the historical and cultural contributions of TUSD's largest demographic group (Blankenship & Locke, 2015).
3. The MAS program dramatically improved test scores, graduation rates, and future college attendance for some of the students who faced most challenges in the districts and might have otherwise dropped out of school. Student achievement as outlined by state guidelines saw a consistent increase over seven cohorts in Latinx student graduation rates by 90 percent, with 80 percent going on to college (Blankenship & Locke, 2015, p. 341). Reportedly student participants in the program also considerably improved skills articulated as being sought by colleges and universities, including "exceptional communication skills, both written and oral; diversity of thought and openness to multiple perspectives; and the ability to apply theoretical concepts to the analysis of every day issues" (Hammer, 2012, p. 66).
4. In developing the program in 1997, the school district employed the expertise of consultants through the Intercultural Development Research Association (IDRA) to conduct feasibility studies for the MAS program. The following year, a program director was hired to support the implementation of the MAS program. Culturally relevant curricular tools were provided to teachers and students, which focused on the contributions of the Latinx peoples in the regions (Jiménez-silva, 2012).
5. All of the previous points demonstrate that the creation of the MAS program was consistent with local community values, the democratic process, and broader national values as outlined in the U.S. Constitution.

In light of the success of the ethnic studies program in TUSD, other states and school districts should look to develop ethnic studies programs in order to increase student performance and engagement in the classroom based on the specific cultural needs of their communities. The MAS program in Tuscan is an example of the power of education to transform. Culturally relevant pedagogies should be pursued as a social good in general, but this case also points to the opportunity for them to be used as a means for elevating student achievement, even within biased assessment structures. As noted, "No other high school program has continually been vindicated by documented studies for its undeniable success in alleviating the [opportunity] gap, graduating [college-bound] students, and inspiring community engaged youth" (Dotts, 2015, p. 36).

CLOSING THOUGHTS

Echoing Stone's work, the article "Education as instrument or as empowerment—Untangling white privilege in the politics of ethnic studies: The case of the Tuscan Unified School District" sums up the reality that "schooling and public education are ubiquitously political phenomena that are indelibly messy and fraught with conflict. The fact that schooling is a public institution compels it having to endure and mediate political disputes among a number of competing interests" (Dotts, 2015, p. 35). The battles over curriculums demonstrate this reality in spades.

It is unfortunate that the passing of HB 2281 in 2010 resulted in the suspension of the MAS program and many students missed the opportunity to gain the benefits the program brought to the community's schools. The hysteria generated by politicians targeting members of the Latinx population in Arizona by placating anti-immigrant fears of Tuscan residents ultimately hurt students the most. The resilience and defiance shown by students, parents, community leaders, and activists who fought the law all the way to the Supreme Court provides hope for the continuation of ethnic studies programs in Arizona. Their example provides a guidepost for combating attacks on communities of color. While the setback for the ethnic studies program created by laws ultimately deemed unconstitutional is unfortunate, the success of the TUSD ethnic studies curriculum might provide a model to other communities seeking to develop curricula inclusive of critical and culturally relevant pedagogies which thoughtfully honor the complex peoples and histories making up what we call the United States.

We are now faced with continued attacks on CRT and other anti-racist curricular efforts at the national and rapidly spreading state level. Conservative lawmakers attempting to capitalize on the "culture wars" and advance their own political profile have taken up the baton passed down by the 45th President to make CRT a political punching bag (*The New York Times* [NYT], 2021). Thoughtful educators, parents, and community members must pick up our own baton handed to us by the example of those who fought in Arizona. It is not "anti-American" to tell the truth about U.S. history or to include the perspectives of ALL its citizens in our curriculums. This is our work in this moment of the broader movement toward anti-racist education. As we look toward a future where education is guided by this vision, we must guard against dangerous legislative attacks on ethnic studies and CRT.

Something to read, do, or consider: Please consider contacting your local and national representatives to demand they oppose this type of legislation. We must come together to protect the work of thoughtful scholars by continuing the fight for curricula that upholds the perspectives of Black, Indigenous, Latio/a/x, and Asian communities who have fought the yolk of white supremacy for centuries.

REFERENCES

Anzaldúa, G. (1987). Borderlands/la frontera: The new mestiza. *Aging*, *7*(11), 288. https://doi.org/10.1017/CBO9781107415324.004

Appiah, K. A. (2020, June 18). *The case for capitalizing the B in black*. The Atlantic. https://www.theatlantic.com/ideas/archive/2020/06/time-to-capitalize-blackand-white/613159/

Brayboy, B. M. K. J., & Castagno, A. E. (2009). Self-determination through self-education: Culturally responsive schooling for Indigenous students in the USA. *Teaching Education*, *20*(1), 31–53. https://doi.org/10.1080/10476210802681709

Cohen, D. K., & Mehta, J. D. (2017). Why reform sometimes succeeds: Understanding the conditions that produce reforms that last. *American Educational Research Journal*, *54*(4), 644–690. https://doi.org/10.3102/0002831217700078

Delpit, L. D. (1988). The silenced dialogue: Power and pedagogy in educating other people's children. *Harvard Educational Review*, *58*(3), 280–298.

Executive Office of the President. (2020, September 4). *Training in the federal government*. Whitehouse.gov. https://www.whitehouse.gov/wp-content/uploads/2020/09/M-20-34.pdf

Executive Office of the President. (2020, September 28). *Combating race and sex stereotyping*. Federalregister.gov. https://www.federalregister.gov/documents/2020/09/28/2020-21534/combating-race-and-sex-stereotyping

Executive Office of the President. (2020, September 28). *Ending employee trainings that use divisive propaganda to undermine the principle of fair and equal treatment for all*. Whitehouse.gov. https://www.whitehouse.gov/wp-content/uploads/2020/09/M-20-37.pdf

Flaherty, C. (2020, October 7). *Diversity work, interrupted.* Inside Higher Ed. https://www.insidehighered.com/news/2020/10/07/colleges-cancel-diversity-programs-response-trump-order

Green, T. F. (1983). Excellence, equity, and equality. In G. Shulman, Lee S. & Sykes (Ed.), *Handbook of teaching and policy* (pp. 318–341). Longman Inc.

Hammer, Z. (2012). Red scare in the red state: The attack on Mexican-American studies in Tuscan. *Journal of the Association of Mexican American Educators, 6*(1), 65–70.

Harris, T. (2017). Arizona ban on ethnic studies unconstitutional: U.S. judge. *Reuters.* Retrieved from https://www.reuters.com/article/us-arizona-education/arizona-ban-on-ethnic-studies-unconstitutional-u-s-judge-idUSKCN1B32DE

Jackson, P. W. (1990). *Life in classrooms.* Teachers College Press.

Paris, D. (2012). Culturally sustaining pedagogy: A needed change in stance, terminology, and practice. *Educational Researcher, 41*(3), 93–97. https://doi.org/10.3102/0013189X12441244

Sawchuk, S. (2021, May 18). *What is critical race theory, and why is it under attack? Education Week.* https://www.edweek.org/leadership/what-is-critical-race-theory-and-why-is-it-under-attack/2021/05

Stone, D. (2002). *Policy paradox: The art of political decision making.* https://doi.org/10.1017/CBO9781107415324.004

The New York Times. (2021, July 2). *The debate over critical race theory.* The Daily. https://www.nytimes.com/2021/07/02/podcasts/the-daily/critical-race-theory-debate.html

Wanberg, K. (2013). Pedagogy against the state: The ban on ethnic studies in Arizona, *4*(January 2012), 15–35. https://doi.org/10.2478/jped-2013-0002

Chapter 2

Creating an Equitable Learning Community for Preservice Early Childhood Teachers

Angela Miller-Hargis and Helene Arbouet Harte

AUTHOR POSITIONALITY

In this chapter, we will provide an overview of the frameworks that inform our teaching and our efforts to create an equitable learning community. Before we delve into our strategies and experiences, it is necessary to provide a bit of information about our backgrounds. As teacher educators in a learning community that is highly diverse, we collaborate and intentionally plan from an anti-racist, abolitionist and Universally Designed perspective. We engage in reflection and action with our students and model for them how our varied experiences and identities inform our instruction. Because our student profiles are diverse (during the 2017–2018 academic year, 60 percent of the student population identified as White, 21 percent identified as African American or Black, 3.3 percent reported as Asian, 5 percent considered themselves Hispanic or Latino, 4.4 percent indicated they were biracial, and 3.3 percent went unreported), we are deliberate in ensuring that all voices are heard in the classroom and, where possible, in the assignments. As a result, we have written this chapter with the intention of safeguarding our own voices as one Black female educator and one White female educator. We both speak throughout this chapter, we both participate in program planning, and we alternate the leadership role of program coordinator. In our examples, we are going to each speak to a particular course in our early childhood program from our particular perspectives as a White female instructor and as a Black female instructor.

DEFINING MULTICULTURAL EDUCATION

As Fermin-Gonzalez (2016) indicates, ongoing attention to "student diversity is an important part of academic discussion" (p. 148) because of the well-documented failures of university-based teacher education programs to prepare White preservice teachers for engagement with students who, unlike themselves, do not represent the dominant culture. In teacher education, the conversation surrounding diversity has historically been broad and regrettably superficial. Coursework often focuses attention on the differing experiences of individuals with an emphasis on literature, art, dance, food, clothing, ethics, religion, and less objective aspects of culture such as methods of greeting, eye contact, and verbal expressions. Often these are approached with three specific objectives in mind. According to Kehoe (1994), these include closing what has come to be known as "achievement gaps," encouraging positive subgroup interactions and attitudes, and "the development of pride in heritage."

In multicultural education coursework, the term "diversity" has been used to describe the mix of people in an organization, whether that be in terms of race, gender, education, ideologies, or beliefs. In the workplace and in individual classrooms, diversity tends to predominantly consider ethnicity, race, and gender, although these are just the most surface-level, physical forms of diversity. The failures of university-based teacher education programs in the United States regarding the preparation of White preservice teachers for engagement with students who embody marginalized racial identities in public schools are many, even though research has indicated that classroom environments are greatly enhanced when students are educated about human difference, biases, and the historical context of these within our communities (Rankin & Reason, 2005).

The concept of multicultural education, however, is often, for our purposes, inadequate, naive, and misleading. It fails to confront minority grievances and ambitions, and it neglects to provide openings for silenced voices to be heard and understood (Banks & McGee-Banks, 1989). Multicultural education ignores the institutional basis of domination and discrimination and disregards the fact that racial discrimination flows from systemic structures, resulting in a reluctance of educators and practitioners to challenge the larger organizational and hierarchical structures of those institutions (Lynch, 1987). For teacher educators, this creates a significant gap in what preservice teachers need to understand about education in order to be effective in their future classrooms. As a result, we choose to utilize anti-racist pedagogical approaches in our planning for preservice teacher training to intentionally highlight the systemic nature of racism and emphasize the roles and responsibilities these future teachers will have once they enter the classroom.

DEFINING ANTI-RACIST EDUCATION

For our purposes, anti-racist education helps to focus the conversation more fully on the educational systems that perpetuate inequalities. Kendi (2019), for example, notes that racial inequity is an issue of policy rather than people. In order to address racial inequity, then, one must identify and eliminate racist policies. By using anti-racist objectives and concepts for the purpose of informing praxis, the active process of course design may allow teacher educators and the preservice educators they engage with to create and reflect upon course policies, assignments, and materials in order to move toward equity.

Because racial inequity is an issue of policy rather than people, the substance of addressing racial inequity must identify and work toward the elimination of racist policies in every area of education from curricular decision-making to institutional policy making. Specifically, the movement toward equitable design requires an active collaboration between teacher educators and preservice teachers in not only the overall course design of individual classes, but also in the development of activities that scrutinize course policies, common assignments, standard pedagogical processes, and traditional materials that are often taken-for-granted aspects of many curricular choices. Vague statements like "all students are welcome" may give us license to think that statement is enough without actually making students feel welcome (Siliman & Maynell, 2019). It is intentional actions—not empty gestures—that lead to equitable outcomes.

The actions we take as teacher educators should create a space where students are free to build on their strengths. One way to do this is to engage in abolitionist teaching. According to Love (2020), "Abolitionist teaching is built on the creativity, imagination, boldness, ingenuity and rebellious spirit and methods of abolitionists to demand and fight for an educational system where all students are thriving, not simply surviving" (p. 695). In order to go beyond simply surviving, it is important to be sure students know the rules and have the tools to meet expectations. Consequently, to provide an equitable environment, educators ought to be transparent in all areas, especially in their pedagogical attempts to make connections among concepts. Transparency is not just a good idea in general, but a specific support for marginalized students (Winkelmes et al., 2016) in that it allows them to understand the objectives for instructional methodology and make connections to their prior knowledge and understanding. Transparency removes the assumption that we are all starting from the same place, providing background knowledge, purpose and relevance for assignments and experiences.

Abolitionist teaching addresses racism directly. It emphasizes not only a discussion of past and present racism, but also speaks to stereotyping and discrimination in society by focusing on the economic, structural, and historical roots of inequality (McGregor, 1993). This is done so that teacher educators and preservice teachers are able to recognize and confront institutional racism that exists at the very core of the educational system. It is our belief that unless preservice teacher candidates understand the nature and characteristics of these discriminatory barriers, the prevailing distribution of resources and rewards will remain intact—both within the context of school boundaries and outside of them.

MULTICULTURAL AND ANTI-RACIST DESIGNS IN TEACHER EDUCATION

Because of the ongoing debate of the relative meaning and merits of both multicultural education and anti-racist education, we have utilized both for our purposes. On the one hand, we use multicultural education strategies that are directed at changing individual attitudes and behaviors; on the other, we utilize anti-racist education to suggest that social structures preexist in our society. Indeed, one might even go so far as to state that the individual racist need not exist for institutional racism to persist pervasively and permanently in dominant culture (Ladson-Billings, 1998; McIntosh, 1998). In the courses we design for our preservice teachers, we utilize both multicultural and anti-racist education, and meld them both within the Universal Design for Learning (UDL). UDL involves the way of thinking about teaching and learning that provides all students an equal opportunity to succeed. It is intentionally flexible in the way students access material, engage with it, and then show what they know. Using the principles of representation, action and expression, and engagement, we, as the teacher educators, try to ensure that information can be accessed, understood, and used to the greatest extent possible by all people regardless of their age, gender, background, ability or disability (CAST, 2018). Planning with UDL in mind, instructors present materials in a variety of ways and students have a range of ways to show what they know and students are engaged in different ways (CAST, 2018). Fritzgerald (2020) aligns UDL and anti-racist teaching highlighting that UDL is intentional and anti-racist teaching is an active process. UDL is about removing barriers and racist systems are barriers. She also notes that honor is imperative to both. Teachers honor students by creating a welcoming environment in which students have agency and the teacher is not the sole expert in the classroom. Students are empowered as decision-makers (Fritzgerald, 2020).

EQUITY IN ONLINE EDUCATION

It is important to note that as more education courses are being taught online and programs shifted to a virtual education orientation, we are intentional in our integration of multicultural and anti-racist pedagogy in online courses. As a result, it is necessary to specify and describe some concepts on which inclusive virtual education (IVE) is based. We begin with the principles that govern educational designs that aim to address the diversity of the student body, seen as the core of inclusive education. In addition, we will provide a conceptual explanation of some terms that we will use regularly, such as diversity and differences. This will allow us to contextualize our view of inclusive education and will make our perspective clear.

Consideration of cultural diversity needs to be part of online course design from the onset. Ignoring cultural differences can further marginalize students (Darby & Lang, 2019). Part of building a sense of belonging and community is acknowledging differences, as well as recognizing that how students engage and interact online does not happen in isolation from their cultural contexts. Review examples, materials, images, and videos and identify whose voices are present and whose are absent. Even the names and pronouns used in case studies can send a message of inclusion or exclusion.

Online teaching requires particular attention to being explicit about the purpose behind various activities and assessments (Darby & Lang, 2019). Use transparent teaching as a way to avoid privileging those with prior knowledge of the rules, culture, and "right" way of being and knowing online. Make the rules explicit and known to everyone. Pull back the curtain, avoid assumptions, and make the expectations clear as a way to level the playing field. When assignments are transparent and problem-centered, students report feeling more confident in their academics as well as an increased sense of belonging (Winkelmes, et al., 2016).

Use of Multicultural Educational Design: Experiences and Examples

In introductory education and methods courses, for example, it is not uncommon to see teacher educators providing instruction about the importance of teaching English as a second language; embracing student backgrounds in order to instruct students in a manner consistent with their culture; promoting sensitivity to variances in psycholinguistics or cognitive style; and ensuring that the families and communities of their students are invited to participate in school activities, events, and culture. In addition, instructors in these courses tend to develop instructional plans that help preservice educators uncover their own implicit biases, work toward developing empathy, explore pedagogies that teach critical thinking skills, and discover information about and encourage exploration of other cultures that may be represented in diverse classrooms. It is important that preservice educators do not remain insulated from the realities of racism or shielded from opportunities to reflect upon and confront their own biases and prejudices. These provide the impetus to change both their attitudes and their behaviors.

The Foundations of Early Childhood course is one of the first classes that early childhood preservice teacher candidates take as they begin their studies in the teacher education program. This survey course is designed to introduce preservice teacher candidates to the historical, philosophical, and social foundations of contemporary early childhood programs. The course is required for all early childhood education majors; as a result, the course usually comprises mostly female students, primarily between the ages of eighteen and thirty. The course has no more than twenty-five students in a section, with a typical section including less than five students of color. The course incorporates three state teaching standards into its design: an overview of human learning and development as it relates pedagogy; an emphasis on developing respect for the diversity of the students they teach; and a synopsis of the methods and means of developing responsibility for professional growth.

The diversity unit in this course generally begins with a lecture about classroom issues related to diversity and inclusion. Statistics and terms related to the topic of racism are introduced, and a classroom discussion emerges from this lecture. During this time, we also use a small group activity to develop a working definition of the words prejudice, stereotype, and racism after which they are provided with course definitions as follows:

- Prejudice: a preconceived notion of others not based on logical reasoning or actual experience (the word literally means to "prejudge" someone—to make a decision about someone before you know them as a person.) All people have the potential to carry prejudice.
- Stereotype: a widely held but fixed and oversimplified or overgeneralized perception of a group of people that is often applied to individuals within that group. All people have the potential to stereotype groups of people.
- Racism: the *systemic* oppression of a nondominant group by a dominant group that is based on race. People who are NOT in the dominant group cannot be racist as they do not have systemic power. Dominant does not mean "majority," it means the race that holds the power in a society. In the United States, the dominant group is white Americans.

While this activity usually creates a robust dialogue, some students struggle to adopt (or accept) the definitions created for the course which evolved over time during the instructor's own journey as both an individual and a teacher educator. Using readings, classroom trial-and-error, and student input, these definitions have been determined to be effective in challenging student thinking and framing concepts. Despite some resistance, the objective of the lecture is to highlight important considerations for prospective educators. We discuss the fact that educators who do not develop cultural competence and responsiveness may overgeneralize their understanding of minorities and assume they understand family needs, priorities, and values when they do not. For example, some teachers may presuppose that children of color who live below the poverty level are from homes with only one parent or that children who arrive without completed homework do so because the parents are disengaged. We talk about the possibility that teachers who do not take the time to become culturally aware or do not engage in reflection and self-analysis may hold misconceptions in stereotypes that bias them against individual children or family members or whole groups of people. A case in point is when some teachers believe that children from Asian backgrounds ought to excel in mathematics or science and fail to provide the necessary scaffolds for a specific child who may be struggling. As a result of these issues, as educators they may one day avoid interactions with children and families who differ significantly from their own background, or, on a smaller scale, may lack confidence in their ability to say or do the "right" things in difficult, uncomfortable, or unfamiliar situations.

As a white female instructor for this particular course, it is important that I am intentional and honest in sharing my own struggles as an entry year teacher, especially when developing cultural competence. I share anecdotes about my first teaching assignment in a parochial, inner-city school where 100 percent of my students were children of color and 100 percent of the families were living below the poverty line. Sharing narratives from my own experiences and ongoing anti-racist journey helps preservice teachers understand that confronting our own fears, biases, and insecurities requires effort, hard work, and lifelong learning. Furthermore, it provides an opening to engage in conversations about the importance of building a rapport with other educators who can provide us with other perspectives, engage in dialogue, and encourage our professional growth and development.

As a follow-up to this, the preservice educators are then required to explore the Project Implicit website and take at least one of the social attitude tests available (https://www.projectimplicit.net/). Although they are not required to report the results of those assessments to the class, they are asked to write a reflection paper explaining their thinking and feelings about the results that are submitted directly to the instructor. In addition, they are asked to make a public discussion board post that requires them to think about racism as it has been experienced in their own life. Specifically, they are required to "share a narrative about a time when you either experienced racism in your own life (you were a victim) OR found yourself in a position of having to check your own privilege (you had to think about whether you were victimizing someone else, either in word, deed, or thought). The latter may include a time when you were with people who were doing things that appeared racist to you, whether you decided to go along or not."

This multicultural educational strategy exemplified in this introductory course is clearly aimed at providing opportunities for preservice educators to reflect upon their own understanding of racism and is directed at changing individual attitudes and behaviors. By providing occasions, both personal and shared, to explore these ideas, we move one step closer to encouraging positive subgroup interactions and attitudes that we hope will encourage preservice educators in their own practice in future classrooms.

Use of Anti-racist Educational Design: Experiences and Examples

While this is an important aspect of diversity and inclusion training, the fact is that students of color in teacher education programs (in predominantly White institutions) continue to remain at the margins. They are often the only Black or Brown person in the room and may find themselves in positions where they are both obliged to speak out against racist narratives and impacted by racist policies (Faison & McArthur, 2020). Anti-racist strategies are directed at highlighting the social structures that exist in a society that is frequently based on race. These include the individual classroom, which is a microcosm of society at large. Our efforts are, then, directed at not only changing racist attitudes but also changing the social realities that racism appears to explain.

In the Foundations of Early Childhood course from the section above, the unit extends its emphasis on developing respect for the diversity of the students they teach using a multicultural education lens to understanding the systemic nature of racism outside individual classrooms and one-on-one interactions using anti-racist education. After preservice teachers complete their personal reflection and public discussion board post, they are required to look beyond classroom walls and school boundaries to consider how racism is perpetuated elsewhere. Preservice educators are shown several video clips of what it means to be Black in America and analyze why the reporters in one of the videos indicate that even though racism is "mainly a Black issue," it is primarily "a white problem." These videos include a BBC report called *Inside the mind of White America* and a TED Talk by Clint Smith called "How to raise a Black son in America."

Students in this class discuss many examples in the news about (mostly White) individuals questioning the behaviors of others (non-Whites) in public spaces. Some of these might include individuals challenging people of color who are barbequing in parks, ranting about race in restaurants against patrons, co-workers, and employees, and even teachers creating a scene against a Black parent in a parking lot. The preservice educators are required to secure a video link or article link that directs the reader to the incident in focus, and then to discuss one of these in a paper of at least one page. For their write up, preservice educators are expected to respond, at a minimum, to the following questions:

- What words are being used during the event or in the article that are indicators of bias, prejudice, stereotyping, unreasonable assumptions, etc.?
- What issues of prejudice and privilege are at play here? This is an analysis which will definitely require more than a sentence or two.
- What are your personal thoughts and feelings about the particular situation? Why did you choose this article or video? What can you learn from the exchange? What do you want others to learn from the exchange? Do you have ideas about how the situation could have been avoided or de-escalated?

The anti-racist strategy typified here is designed to draw attention to larger contexts and provide opportunities for preservice educators to consider how racism is systemic and institutionalized. By providing occasions to explore the ways in which we can view the pervasive and permanent aspects of racism "out there," we move closer to helping preservice educators reflect upon their role in eliminating discrimination and prejudice in their own classrooms.

As a Black first-generation American, I am going to share perspectives on another course in our program through my personal lens. It is informed by and builds on the previous required course described above. This course, Families, Communities and Schools, occurs in the second year of the early childhood program. This is also an introductory survey course; it is primarily an exploration of home, school and community partnerships, and authentic family engagement. The course outcomes address family characteristics, access to resources, advocacy, and involving families in student learning. There is an emphasis on relationship-building and doing things with families rather than to them (Ferlazzo, 2011; Halgunseth et al., 2009). This is important because it recognizes that families are partners with strengths, who have something to contribute. For example, one of the course outcomes is to "describe the importance of building rapport with families in respectful, culturally responsive ways, when solving classroom problems, supporting learning, and including families in the assessment of their child's development and learning" (Ohio Department of Education, 2016).

This course outcome necessitates going beyond one's personal experiences with family involvement and what it looks like. Students may need to shift from a model of family involvement that centers whiteness and decenter themselves as white preservice educators. They are encouraged to center families and remember that how families are perceived matters when building rapport, interacting with families, and responding in culturally responsive ways. Preservice teachers need to identify the strengths of their students and recognize funds of knowledge that their students may possess, including cultural knowledge, resources, and skills (Moll et al., 1992). This involves reframing and reconceptualizing families with a focus on strengths and includes what Love (2019) refers to as "Black Joy."

In this course, we engage in discussions about the importance of family engagement and unpack and analyze the narrative that some families don't show up because they don't care. In perpetuating this narrative, we problematize families and question the rather narrow definition of "showing up" that is often embraced by educators, such as the notion that in some districts or neighborhoods families don't attend parent-teacher conferences because they don't care. We discuss the varied ways in which families from marginalized groups do "show up" and consider how these ways are often ignored, rather than being highlighted and celebrated. Moreover, it is important that we contemplate the reasons why families are not present at school and consider various perspectives about "why" that don't involve the need to blame or fix families.

We consider the possibility that we may be retraumatizing families for whom entering a school building entails reliving their own racist school experiences. "Nice White Parents" is the model for family involvement with which most preservice teachers are familiar. When asked how families are involved or should be involved in schools, our students often share examples of the room mother who comes to the classroom during the school day to plan parties and activities. Joffe-Walt and Snyder (2020) refer to "Nice White Parents" as the most powerful force in public schools. Those are the families whose voices are heard. Their needs and norms remain at the center. Rather than let white fragility guide us as teacher educators and shield preservice teachers, we need to push everyone out of their comfort zones. This begins with difficult conversations about inequity in schools not just for PreK-12 students, but also for families. Creating an equitable learning community for our students requires getting comfortable with being uncomfortable together, rather than only those at the margins experiencing discomfort.

As a Black woman teaching this course, I combat stereotypes students may have using my personal counternarrative. In my personal presentation, I am professional, including how I dress and ask students to address me as "doctor." Having had to prove myself to peers in higher education, I go above and beyond with students to attempt to leave little room to question my credentials, qualifications, or organization; however, that does not mean it does not occur. One challenge is being viewed as the exception. I share personal stories of microaggressions and racism, and I navigate explicitly teaching about systemic racism and culturally responsive practice without it being perceived as my personal opinion with which students can just disagree. Part of this is helping students move away from either/or thinking. I make myself vulnerable sharing stories of missteps and assumptions I made as an educator and parent in interacting with families due to biases. My identity does not make me exempt from bias, nor does it mean I did not need to learn knowledge and skills related to culturally responsive teaching. Helping students to see intersectionality is important. Intersectionality is about both/and thinking. It recognizes the interconnectedness of systems of power such as race, class, and gender. Those power relations overlap resulting "interdependent social inequalities of race, class, gender, sexuality, nationality, ethnicity, ability and age (p. 43)." Where we are located socially as individuals and as group members influences our worldview and our experiences (Collins, 2019). I am informed by my lived experiences, and I am a lifelong learner developing knowledge, skills, and dispositions over time to be an effective educator. I am both in a position of power as an instructor and impacted by issues of race and systemic racism. Families can care about their children but also not attend school events.

We require preservice educators to begin with families. What are their strengths? How do you know? The goal of teachers should be to learn from families and their experiences (Moll, 2015). In this context and with guidance and consideration, students can interview families in programs where they work. Students view films, TED Talks, and materials that center families from diverse backgrounds. Using these resources, students are tasked with identifying strengths and funds of knowledge. The goal of this assignment is to create a counternarrative to stereotypes (their own or those of others). Having a range of materials to access, students should also be afforded multiple ways to respond. This is part of UDL which we intentionally use as a guiding principle to our teacher education course planning. UDL models how we do not have to privilege one way of knowing and showing what you know. For example, focusing on writing essays or papers showcases a particularly more traditional way to demonstrate knowledge. The method by which we assess students may confound the actual learning outcome. If writing an essay is integral to the learning outcome, that is one thing, but explanation, comparison, analysis, synthesis of information, and application of concepts can happen in a variety of ways. The education debt or lack of opportunity produced in our school systems (Ladson-Billings, 2006) may be perpetuated if we focus on narrow assignments without choice. In the assignments for the course Families, Communities, and Schools, students will not only look for strengths but also be able to respond in a way that showcases their own strengths, giving a voice to all. These ways of responding may include, but are not limited to, a written reflection, a podcast, artwork, poem, or a playlist. In each of these formats, students will need to justify and provide evidence for the ideas presented because those connections allow them to both use their strengths and show mastery of the content. Citing evidence demonstrates a depth of knowledge.

CHALLENGES FACED

Despite our intentional planning and the use of UDL, multicultural, and anti-racist strategies, it remains a challenge to create an equitable learning community in our teacher education program. Cognitive dissonance is difficult and uncomfortable, yet it is a critical aspect of the cognitive growth required for ongoing professional development. Helping all of our students move outside of their own background, personal encounters, and long-held biases to fully perceive the struggles of marginalized groups requires, in essence, a suspension of disbelief. It means that we must convince students, in a meaningful and profound way, that they must temporarily accept as believable the very events and situations that they would ordinarily see as incredible, impossible, or implausible. It means that we must show them that the world they have perceived and experiences they have had have been discerned through a screen, a lens, if you will, that filters out difficult ideas that they might not want to see or have been preconditioned not to see. We recognize that if students feel attacked, they may push back on anti-racist content which emerges as white fragility and creates a barrier to and silences dialogue about race, and yet we realize that accepting the necessity of embracing cognitive disequilibrium is at the core of what we propose here.

Before even delving into course content, barriers exist. Recognizing and grappling with those challenges is part of the work of anti-racist and abolitionist teaching. This brings us back to the notion mentioned earlier in the chapter, additional challenges exist for faculty of color in predominantly White institutions who may be perceived as promoting personal agendas or have their credibility attacked (Evans-Winters & Hines, 2020). We come back to this because authentically addressing this issue means we have to talk about it with each other and students. The societal stereotype of the angry Black woman looms large over a Black female teacher educator whose students are predominantly White, as are the majority of preservice teachers heading into teach schools which are increasingly diverse. It is not uncommon for us to hear from White students that it is the first time they have had a Black teacher. When coupled with difficult conversations about race, while navigating White guilt, fragility, and emotionality, responses can range from microaggressions to refusal to participate in class discussions to passive aggressive complaints to department chairs (Evans-Winters & Hines, 2020).

WHERE DO WE GO FROM HERE?

The anti-racist educational design of individual assignments and courses can only be a first step toward truly creating an equitable learning community. If outside of our classrooms, whether face to face or virtual, there is a return to the status quo, this is insufficient to address systems of inequity in which our preservice teachers exist and operate. The goal is to engage students with the knowledge, skills, and dispositions to be anti-racist reflective practitioners. In any setting they should not only be designing anti-racist activities for their students but also seeking social justice in their schools, thus creating the actual freedom for the students in PreK-12 settings to thrive. Where we go from here is for both teacher educators and our students to recognize and labor as if there is no magical moment of enlightenment or end point in this journey. It is an ongoing pedagogical practice that requires consistent accountability and constant reflexivity.

We also need to examine our institutions of higher education including the use of language and actions, or lack of action. Stewart (2017) suggests a shift from diversity and inclusion to equity and justice and from talk to actual change. Stewart (2017) points out that in universities, diversity can mean focusing on numbers and remaining content with adding one or two people at the table without actual engagement in transformative dialogue or impactful change. Inclusion can focus broadly on everyone belonging, but justice requires the intentional interrogation of policies and practices; true equity aims to reduce harm. Similarly, Gorski (2019) cautions against equity detours that are often deficit-based and center the interests of those who are not really interested in progress, change, or transformation. One example is the use of scripted reading programs in schools with underserved populations. Rather than focus on overhauling the literacy curriculum to meet the long-term needs of readers that highlight and utilize the cultural and academic capital these children bring to school tasks, there is a focus on short-term "solutions" that produce the quantitative data (test scores) that appear to indicate progress but do not create lifelong, engaged, and critical readers.

Love and Muhammad (2020) remind us that racism persists because it serves the self-interest of White people both in and out of our education system. In the end analysis, we agree with them that we have nothing to lose in creating a new system focused on love and social justice that decenters White people. Focusing on injustice is a key component of equity literacy. Equity literacy involves identifying racial inequity in your school, asking how to redistribute opportunities and access by centering students of color, committing to understanding the dynamics of racism and focusing on abolishing racist conditions rather than "fixing" students (Gorski, 2019).

Simmons (2019), in particular, provides guidance on being anti-racist educators. The five recommended actions include: (1) ongoing self-reflection and examination, (2) acknowledging racism, (3) learning and teaching history in a representative manner, (4) engaging in dialogue about race with students, and (5) having the courage to act when you see racism at any level. Becoming anti-racist as an educator is an active process that includes all of these suggestions. "An anti-racist educator actively works to dismantle the structures, policies, institutions and systems that create barriers and perpetuate race-based inequities for people of color" (Simmons, 2019, p. 3).

Moving forward, we recognize that one resource we have in the creation of an equitable learning community among students is ourselves. To begin by designing an equitable learning community among diverse faculty is a critical first step. If we cannot have uncomfortable conversations as faculty, how can we expect our students to do so? Rather than working in isolation in our individual courses, we must engage in meaningful dialogue and work in solidarity with one another not only to create comprehensive and transformative postsecondary curricula but also to model culturally competent behavior. "Solidarity is not the same as support. To experience solidarity, we must have a community of interests, shared beliefs and goals around which to unite, to build Sisterhood. Support can be occasional. It can be given and just as easily withdrawn. Solidarity requires sustained, ongoing commitment" (hooks, 1984, p. 67).

We intentionally endeavor in courses to follow each of Simmons (2019) five recommended actions mentioned above. Where we go from here is beyond the courses. Where we go from here is forward—with the work at all levels.

SOMETHING TO DO AND SOMETHING TO CONSIDER

Something to do: Engage in intentional dialogue with your colleagues. Aim to work in solidarity as "co-conspirators" (Love, 2019).

Something to consider: Consider Simmons' (2019) five recommended actions for becoming an anti-racist educator. How can they be applied at the course level, department level, college level, and university level?

REFERENCES

Banks, J. A. & McGee-Banks, C. A. (1989). *Multicultural education.* Allyn & Bacon.

BBC report called *Inside the mind of White America* (https://www.bbc.com/news/av/world-us-canada-36551938)

CAST. (2018). *Universal design for learning guidelines version 2.2.* Retrieved from http://udlguidelines.cast.org

Collins, P. H. (2019). *Intersectionality as critical social theory.* Duke University Press.

Darby, F. & Lang, J. M. (2019). *Small teaching online: Applying learning sciences in online classes.* Jossey-Bass.

Evans-Winters, V. E. & Hines, D. E. (2020). Unmasking white fragility: How whiteness and white student resistance impacts anti-racist education. *Whiteness & Education, 5*(1), 1–16. https://doi-org.proxy.libraries.uc.edu/10.1080/23793406.2019.1675182

Faison, M. Z. & McArthur, S. A. (2020). Building black worlds: Revisioning cultural justice For Black teacher education students at PWIs. *International Journal of Qualitative Studies in Education (QSE), 33*(7), 745–758. https://doi-org.proxy.libraries.uc.edu/10.1080/09518398.2020.1754489

Ferlazzo, L. (2011, May). Involvement or engagement? *Educational Leadership, 68*(8), 10–14.

Fermin-Gonzalez, M. (2016). Research on virtual education, inclusion, and diversity: A systematic review of scientific publications (2007–2017). *International Review of Research in Open and Distributed Learning, 20*(5), 146–167.

Fritzgerald, A. (2020). *Antiracism and universal design for learning: Building expressways to success.* CAST, Inc.

Gorski, P. (2019, April). Avoiding racial equity detours. *Educational Leadership, 76*(7), 56–61.

Halgunseth, L., Peterson, A., Stark, D. R. & Moodie, S. (2009). *Family engagement, diverse families, and early childhood education programs: An integrated review of the literature.* NAEYC and Pre-K Now.

hooks, b. (1984). *Feminist theory from margin to center.* South End Press.

Joffe-Walt, C. & Snyder, J. (producers). (2020). *Nice white parents* [Audio podcast]. Serial Productions, A New York Times Company. https://www.nytimes.com/2020/07/23/podcasts/nice-white-parents-serial.html

Kehoe, J. W. (1994). Multicultural education vs. anti-racist education: The debate in Canada. *Social Education, 58*(6), 354–358.

Kendi, I. X. (2019). *How to be an antiracist.* One World.

Ladson-Billings, G. (1998). Just what is critical race theory and what's it doing in a nice field like education? *International Journal of Qualitative Studies in Education, 11*(1), 7–24. DOI: 10.1080/095183998236863

Ladson-Billings, G. (2006). From the achievement gap to the education debt: Understanding achievement in U.S. Schools. *Educational Researcher, 35*(7), 3–12. https://doi.org/10.3102/0013189X035007003

Love, B. L. (2019). *We want to do more than survive: Abolitionist teaching and the pursuit of educational freedom.* Beacon Press.

Love, B. L. & Muhammad, G. E. (2020). What do we have to lose: Toward disruption, agitation, and abolition in Black education. *International Journal of Qualitative*

Studies in Education (QSE), 33(7), 695–697. https://doiorg.proxy.libraries.uc.edu/10.1080/09518398.2020.1753257

Lynch, J. (1987) *Prejudice reduction and the schools.* Cassells.

McIntosh, P. (1998). *White privilege: Unpacking the invisible knapsack.* In M. McGoldrick (Ed.), *Re-visioning family therapy: Race, culture, and gender in clinical practice* (pp. 147–152). The Guilford Press.

Moll, L. C. (2015). Tapping into the "hidden" home and community resources of students. *Kappa Delta Pi Record, 51*(3), 114–117.

Moll, L. C., Amanti, C., Neff, D. & Gonzalez, N. (1992). Funds of knowledge for teaching: Using a qualitative approach to connect homes and classrooms. *Theory Into Practice, 31*(2), 132. https://doi-org.proxy.libraries.uc.edu/10.1080/00405849209543534

Ohio Department of Higher Education. (2016, April 1). *Families, Communities and Schools TAG course.* https://www.ohiohighered.org/sites/ohiohighered.org/files/uploads/transfer/documents/TAG/Finalized%20Endorsed%20Families%2C%20Communities%2C%20and%20Schools%20TAG%20Course%20-%204-1-2016.pdf

Rankin, S. R. & Reason, R. D. (2005). Differing perceptions: How students of color and white students perceive campus climate for underrepresented groups. *Journal of College Student Development, 46*, 43–61.

Siliman, S. & Maynell, L. (2019, November) *Foundations of inclusive teaching.* Drake Institute for Teaching and Learning. https://www.youtube.com/watch?v=awXKY2mjJvw&feature=youtu.be

Simmons, D. (2019, October). How to be an antiracist educator. *ACSD Education Update, 61*(10). http://www.ascd.org/publications/newsletters/education-update/oct19/vol61/num10/How-to-Be-an-Antiracist-Educator.aspx?fbclid=IwAR1tsIowEXR1-D6K64ZU3ej8bBcGT0OuRJFr4yENJu8A0kwbAMwGhsbtJec

Stewart, D. L. (2017, March 30). *Language of appeasement.* Inside Higher Ed. https://www.insidehighered.com/views/2017/03/30/colleges-need-language-shift-not-one-you-think-essay

TED Talk by Clint Smith called How to raise a Black son in America (https://www.ted.com/talks/clint_smith_how_to_raise_a_black_son_in_america?referrer=playlist-talks_to_help_you_understand_r%20(Links%20to%20an%20external%20site.).

Winkelmes, M.-A., Bernacki, M., Butler, J., Zochowski, M., Golanics, J. & Weavil, K. H. (2016). a teaching intervention that increases underserved college students' success. *Peer Review, 18*(1/2), 31–36.

Chapter 3

Toward a Pedagogy of Anti-racist Professional Discernment in Elementary Literacy Learning

Swords to Ploughshares

Kerry Alexander and Jimmy McLean

Ten years and 1,100 miles apart, we (the authors) came to our callings as literacy educators in university-affiliated teacher education programs, nurtured by literacy scholars and teacher educators whose critical orientations to teaching and passions for social justice nurtured in us the same. We embarked on careers as leaders of classrooms filled with children who brought a wealth of knowledge, experiences, and ideas to the literacy experiences we shared with them at school. Having exited the role of classroom teacher, we now find ourselves as graduate students walking alongside preservice and in-service teachers in their teaching praxis. Recently, our teaching and research have taken on new dimensions in response to the political resurgence of the Science of Reading (SoR) in state legislatures, spurred by media reports that play on the fears of the public and ignore the professional knowledge of literacy professionals.

Literacy teachers, teacher educators, and researchers are familiar with the so-called reading wars (Gill, 2005; Pearson, 2004). The "reading wars" are theoretical debates about what reading is (decoding words or meaning-making), what evidence "counts" in research on reading (qualitative or quantitative data), and how children learn to read (through authentic experience and immersion or through systematic instruction). The debate was given a national stage when in 1998 the United States Congress directed the National Institute of Child Health and Human Development to convene the National Reading Panel in order "to assess the status of research-based knowledge, including the effectiveness of various approaches to teaching children to read" (National Institute of Child Health and Human Development, 2000, p. 1). Shortly after the publication of the panel's report, Panel member Joanne Yatvin published an insider's perspective on the Panel's proceedings that raised serious concerns about the makeup of the committee as well as the team's process and decisions (Yatvin, 2002). Nevertheless, the Panel's skewed findings, which were never intended to be prescriptive, were taken as gospel. Not long after, the Bush administration's No Child Left Behind legislation similarly privileged scientific and empirical research studies in its crusade to improve learning. As a result, knowledge about reading and literacy instruction that was emic and borne out of the experience and practice of teachers themselves was delegitimized and subordinated (Hoffman et al., 2020). These consequential events at the federal level have bolstered a "scientific" (experimental, psychological) theory of reading that threatens the vibrant literacy scholarship and literacy teacher professional knowledge that focus on the sociocultural processes of making meaning. Such scientific studies that focus primarily on decoding, fluency, and systematic instruction comprise the core of SoR. SoR has maintained an axiomatic status in the field of literacy, as evidenced by the recent issue of *Reading Research Quarterly* devoted entirely to the topic.

What we have to contribute to this particular volume on anti-racist educational research is grounded in our experiences as anti-racist coconspirators (Love, 2019; McLean & Alexander, 2020) and literacy teacher educators who, like today's classroom teachers, wrestle with the authoritative rhetoric and policy stronghold of SoR and the humanizing pedagogies that are still often discounted. These experiences have led us to a shared set of priorities regarding literacy learning in the elementary school that follow the lead of Scholars of Color and community stakeholders. Considering the contradictory and power-laden SoR discourse around elementary literacy instruction in public schools and its impact on us as teacher educators, we favor *a pedagogy of anti-racist professional discernment*. Teachers who enact this pedagogy embrace tensions—ideological, social, and political tensions—in order to make wise and just decisions, rather than hastily implement policies grounded in failure-rhetoric. The "reading wars" lead policymakers, the general public, and sometimes even teachers themselves to believe that there is one right way to teach and one desired outcome (Duffy & Hoffman, 1999), reinforcing the idea that teachers are merely cogs in the wheel whose work is only valuable in relation to the quantitative outcomes they produce. Anti-racist professional discernment asserts that teachers are intellectual beings who have a responsibility to consider more than just diagnostic assessment data when planning for instruction. By choosing one "side" of the war, we effectively deny space for the other, thereby maintaining binaries, reifying hierarchical thinking, and gatekeeping the diversity of relational practices.

To reject one or the other approach outright is irresponsible, but not to take a stand against stronghold systems of oppression—like SoR—is, too, a form of epistemic exceptionalism that continues to oppress and marginalize children and communities.

Therefore, in this chapter we stake out a more peaceful, but still vigilant, position. We take a step sideways from the "reading wars" to consider the means of educational justice in literacy instruction. By that we mean examining methods and practices for teaching young readers and writers that take as their starting point the material realities of their lives. First, we make clear our ethical and moral commitments, critiquing the SoR discourse, especially in our own political context. Next, we advocate for humanizing, anti-racist, and transformative approaches to literacy instruction that are overlooked by some of the damaging pedagogies connected to the SoR. Then, we articulate some possible characteristics of a *pedagogy of anti-racist professional discernment*, particularly for elementary literacy teachers. We end with suggestions for literacy teachers, teacher educators, and researchers who share our desire to refigure the tools of war into pedagogies that lead to transformative practice.

EXPOSING THE SCIENCE OF READING DISCOURSE

Among the many critiques leveled against the campaign for the SoR is the idea that, despite assurances that systematic phonics instruction reduces racial inequity, it actually upholds it (Willis, 2019). Characteristics of White[1] supremacy culture manifest in systematic discourse patterning (Jones & Okun, 2001) that demand perfection without deviation, urgency in regard to "loss" or "gaps," worship of standardization over sociocultural variation, paternalism that determines who is qualified to teach, and championing individualism through isolated rote learning over shared discourse. SoR state legislation(s) in this manner follow a long tradition of Eurocentric patterning that determines the measures and modes of success in schooling (Hursh, 2007; MacLeod, 1995; Mills, 1997; Selden, 2000). Advocacy for schooling reform like the SoR mimics normalization practices disguised into White-palpable, neoliberal programming by offering silver-bullet solutions (Duffy & Hoffman, 1999; Thomas, 2020). Consider how No Child Left Behind and standardizing "science" words such as *objective, honest,* and *observant* resonate from a place of capitalist power—fervent in gaining trust (and therefore, purchase and use).

History also reminds us that use language like "what is best" for "at-risk" children tend to exclude community voice and input, reify saviorisms, and distort authentic learning efforts through heavy assessment culture in classrooms and communities (Hursh, 2007). Similarly, use of aggregated talk around success for "all" in many cases clearly ignores discussing clear racial patterning and insists the fix be thrust back upon the children, families, and teachers, rather than attending to the systems that perpetuate them (Pollock, 2004). Science, or "science," in this case, is a stuffed duck; a foie gras façade.

Popular SoR sites and initiatives, such as The Science of Reading Coalition, post language such as, "If [SoR] is not used correctly by all stakeholders, our education system will continue to fail our children," and insist on a "worldwide commitment" that feels akin to propaganda or fear mongering. Authoritative discourses of who holds the knowledge(s) and who is qualified to "correctly" administer the interventions also fuel expensive training by private enterprises and foster educator anxiety about which programs and books pass muster with fidelity.[2] Gatekeeping of acceptable resources and language soliciting "worldwide commitment" is power-laden and colonizing. In addition, surveillance over university syllabi and district scope and sequence plans, despite seemingly benign intentions toward "best practices," impede intellectual rigor and ignore the rich, speculative nature of transformative literacy research.

Researchers recognize this discourse as denying a full conceptualization of the field of literacy development beyond the SoR framework in anti-oppressive ways (Hoffman et al., 2020; Wetzel et al., 2020). In Texas, for example, House Bill 3 introduced "sweeping" education finance changes in 2019 that, per the Texas Education Agency: "(1) Requires districts and charters to provide a phonics curriculum using systematic direct instruction in grades K-3, and (2) Requires each teacher and principal in grades K-3 to attend reading academies by 2020-2021" (TEA, 2019). Wetzel et al., who participated in Texas's House Bill 3 (HB 3) required LETRS training noted: "When participants pushed back on the use of direct instruction and deficit views of language and culture and sought to discuss the content of the program, the trainers cited research *as a way of discounting alternative perspectives*" (Wetzel et al., 2020, p. 2, italics added). For critical educators, alternative perspectives and models of practice are imperative to researcher's anti-racist efforts toward educational equity. To acknowledge researcher partiality and endeavor to widen studies in relation to the living people who experience these initiatives must remain the academy's north star. Authoritarian and political discourses of urgency and one-right-way, often cater to a White upper-class sector of influential parents and policymakers, further polarizing any intentional collective growth. By effectively undermining the wishes, stories, and rights of communities, for example, the political usage of "science" and predetermined practices communicates assumptions that students may interpret as mechanical, demoralizing, and/or alienating. Such actions reify the very binaries and inequities of personhood that contemporary scholarship should venture to redress:

> Specifically, we conclude that viewing science as an accumulation of quantifiable empirical data and unqualified inductive generalizations embeds a number of problems that undermine any claims from that perspective to having exclusive authority in understanding reading and guiding reading instruction. These include the issues that the SOR, as we suggested in the introduction, relies on a limited conception of science, ignores relevant environmental factors, and uncritically accepts experimentation as the only valid approach to social science inquiry in literacy. (Yaden, Reinking, & Smagorinsky, 2021)

Key to this quote are decisions to "ignore" and "uncritically accept" behaviors which align with oppressive practice writ large. Teacher education programs, too, are then required to privilege particular knowledge, like the SoR, over the community- and identity-based pedagogies of connection that our campuses and students deserve (Brayboy, 2005; Carter-Andrews et al., 2021; Sealy-Ruiz, 2020; Tatum, 2017). Early identification initiatives, mandatory teacher trainings, and hierarchical "ownership" of knowledges distort what could be construed as deep concern for our nation's children. How this translates into university courses can, in turn, manifest into absolutes and reify binaries that engender racialized, cultural, and linguistic harm. Our work as anti-racist professionally discerning instructors and researchers demands that we seek nuance and turn our questions into how to exist inside acerbic binaries by continually returning to the children and our relationships with literacy as grounded in historical, cultural, and situated meaning-making. Doing so requires a historical and contextually situated understanding of both race and literacy, which we provide in the next section.

Historical Perspectives on Race and Literacy

From early common schools and continuing through the 1900s, a colonial narrative of citizenship and merit began to form around what it meant (and means) to be an American with full personhood (Gonzáles, 1999; Lomawaima, 1993; Rice, 1893; Selden, 2000). White leaders wanted to create a system that effectively unified the hearts, minds, and bodies of the nation's children around this collective ideology. Believing that it was most civilized, most intellectual, and most advanced to be this one-way, non-White students and families endured culturally and physically violent means of assimilation and subjugation (Mills, 1997). In fact, the visible and manifested effects of this, or what we call *normalization*, continue to propagate in schools today: high-stakes standardized measures and English-only policies, denial and/or rejection of ethnic and cultural studies, rote memorization, evaluative transaction, and physical comportments of time and activity. Patterns of cultural subtraction (Valenzuela, 1999) and denigration engender specific lived, continuous, and material consequences on Black, Mexican, Indigenous, and immigrant families.

Literacy education and research, specifically, is far from exempt from this racializing history of power over knowledge (Willis, 2002). Neither is it exempt from constraints of colonization (Anderotti, n.d.), notions of property (Buras, 2005; Ladson-Billings & Tate, 1995), and ownership around how language is used, measured, and controlled for "quality." Because language and languaging are not neutral vehicles, urgent demands for "worldwide commitment" to the English-based SoR evokes a distinctly racist epistemic superiority. Not only this, but the labor thus required of the human bodies involved in this commitment to institutional knowledge requires continuous iterations of diagnosing deficits in praxis. In Texas, for example, universal testing is now mandatory for children in Texas Kindergarten classrooms. TEA writes: "In fall 2021, all Texas districts must use Texas Kindergarten Entry Assessment (TXKEA) by CLI Engage or mCLASS Texas Edition by Amplify Education as the BOY literacy instrument per Texas Education Code, §28.006." Alongside the state-wide shift to virtual learning during the 2020–2021 school year, the education department is quick to follow: "Diagnosing reading development and comprehension of kindergarten students is vital, in whatever form it may take" (Texas Education Agency, 2021).

Urgent discourses of "learning loss" or "gaps" as stated above often partner with prescriptive and time-consuming initiatives that control teacher agency, script teacher voice, and ignore community input and reciprocity. If teaching through a socially just lens, tenets such as these are nonnegotiable. Mandated progress monitoring can also, per one in-service teacher we interviewed, demand nearly an hour of teaching time with each child (consider this × 20), whereas more relational and age-appropriate assessments can inform instruction immediately (field notes, 2021). Per this in-service teacher, it is not *whether* to engage in the SoR standards, but rather, *how* they are engaged, *when* they are engaged, and most importantly, *what is denied* in the demands for the systematic, transactional, and teacher-(rather than child-)centered programming.

In our teacher education program, we insist on centering the sociocultural knowledges of our students, their communities, and the political contexts in which we practice. To do anything otherwise (cultural non-recognition) in efforts to strengthen literacy instruction could be considered epistemic racism, asserting knowledge-as-property (Leonardo, 2009), where certain knowledge-beliefs become parcels of schooling-territory, embedded with exclusive rights and privileges. Practices of exceptionalism in this manner perpetuate cultural subtraction rather than deep respect and (re)generation (Valenzuela, 1999). Instead, we draw on a wide spectrum of instructional and pedagogical theories, and we reject narratives targeting teacher preparedness, student or community deficits, and/or lump-sum rhetoric that denies the complexity and locality of reading development (Milner, 2020, Wetzel et al., 2020). We follow in the footsteps of scholars who seek radical, transformative pedagogies grounded in critical love (Sealy-Ruiz, 2020) and deep intellectual study (Muhammad, 2020). We provide time and space for our teachers to wrestle with the nuances of phonological awareness, phonemic awareness, phonics instruction, fluency, vocabulary, and comprehension (NICHD, 2000), but we do so alongside living children in-community. We do so with humility, recognizing all that we do not yet know about our students, about their brilliance, and all the rich ways they use language to make meaning individually and collectively (Sealy-Ruiz, 2020; Muhammad, 2020). In this effort, we also recognize our partiality and our duty to remain cognizant of how power, especially whiteness-at-work (Yoon, 2012), manifests in our daily interactions through discursive strategies. As white scholars and teacher educators, our responsibility to examine how skills and concepts of language are taught are just as imperative as examining the curriculum itself. Pedagogy, too, is steeped in Whiteness.

"Whiteness-at-work" (Yoon, 2010, p. 596) includes ideologies and patterns of talk and behavior that are collectively assembled in institutions to maintain the White status quo. It keeps scholarly work in silos; it prefers transactions over relation. It tricks us into believing competition along a normed measure will raise everyone up, when we know it means most certainly divide, marginalize, and oppress. We have a tremendous hope that "cultivating agentive reading lives" (Wetzel et al., 2020, p. 9), not only for our students, but for ourselves in the academy, will encourage more learning from each other, and sharing in the knowledges of all people for the sake of the children. But we also need more. We need community voice and resistance to systems that uphold harmful (and outdated) absolutism.

The SoR, too, in this context, at this time, as we've seen above, is *not* a new idea. It is simply a current iteration of functional dominance that, again, *demeans* and *delays* our collective way forward (Bennet & LeCompte, 1990). We have community commitments as literacy educators. We have commitments to that which is still unknown to the academy, and though we value what contributions are made, we reject standing still upon them. We reject undiscerning patterns of research and evaluation that take us farther from the community relevance we serve. So we're in this conundrum, and in our roles as new scholars, and as people who are bringing folks onboard to be transformative teachers, we have to make decisions about how we write the syllabus, how we engage power/knowledge discourses in class, and how we break out of academic silos to honor research and community broadly. Holding this tension, for as long as we serve, is critical because it demands that we continuously seek epistemic equity.

SOCIOCULTURAL PERSPECTIVES ON LITERACY AND HUMANIZING LITERACY PEDAGOGIES

Clearly, rejecting the authoritarian language of SoR and the absolutist positions represented in the media does not mean embracing relativism or simply suggesting that teachers should use whatever methods work for them. As critical educators, we maintain moral and ethical commitments to transformative justice. Herein lies the paradox of our work as teacher-researchers and instructors: teaching someone to read is an intricate negotiation among identities, society's expectations, and the ethical facilitation between the two. Such a delicate endeavor can be haunted by predetermined pacing guides, scripted lessons, and prescriptive diagnostics. We object to *systematic* phonics instruction advocated by SoR for the same reasons we object to spelling-test pedagogy and leveled reading programs. These systems and structures are top-down, one-size-fits-all pedagogies that divorce literacy learning from meaningful contexts. Instead, we believe decisions about literacy instruction—for instance, teaching letter-sound patterns of a language—must always attend to sociocultural knowledges and must consider the potential for liberation. We follow a long tradition of literacy educators and researchers who have advocated for such literacy pedagogies, and their contributions influence how we think about anti-racist professional discernment.

Sociocultural Perspectives on Literacy

Much of the scholarship rejected out-of-hand by the National Reading Panel and subsequent federal and state policies stems from traditions that understand literacy as social and cultural rather than just individual and psychological. Influential to this way of thinking are the seminal works of Shirley Brice Heath (1983) and Brian Street (1984). Heath's ethnography compares two working-class communities in the Piedmont region of the Southern United States, one Black and one White. In her comparison, she found that young children's literacy learning was inextricably tied to their community's social and cultural ways of being. Street's work asserts that literacy is ideological, and that the field has suffered from a West-centric, colonizing approach to understanding how "other" communities communicate. He articulates that literacy is "a social process, in which particular socially constructed technologies are used within particular institutional frameworks for specific purposes" (p. 97). Both scholars, still often cited today, solidified a space in the literacy research community for continued inquiry into social and cultural meaning-making practices from insider perspectives.

Also borne out of this sociocultural tradition, the New London Group (1996) broadened the definition of literacy, the concept of a text, and, consequently, the scope of inquiry for the field. The Group's widening of the epistemological circle explicitly emphasized sociocultural knowledges, multiculturalism, and the plurality of ways that we create meaning including and beyond the written word. This can be read as an expansive moment in literacy research, despite some critiques that it continues to promote logocentrism (Leander & Boldt, 2013; Skerrett, 2016). Still, their Pedagogy of Multiliteracies has provided teachers and researchers alike with the theory to see the meaningful literacies of diverse youth populations and the tools to meaningfully participate in their own semiotic environments (Kim, 2016; Park et al., 2017).

Contemporarily, we agree with Winn (2018) that, when it comes to transformative justice literacy instruction, "history matters, race matters, justice matters, and language matters" (p. 219). In their anti-racist professional discernment, teachers must recognize who they are as racialized beings, the historical context of the communities they serve and/or live in, and how they interplay in the context of practice. A sociocultural perspective on literacy urges teachers to see far beyond the bounds of standardized assessments and scripted curricula. Instead, a sociocultural perspective on literacy bolsters the anti-racist professional discernment of literacy teachers because it values linguistic and community cultural resources equally (Canagarajah, 2013; Flores, 2019; Zapata, 2014; Zapata & Laman, 2016). A sociocultural perspective also clearly sees the role of ideology and power in literacy, for example illuminating the ways that White supremacy is reinforced and upheld in school literacy learning experiences (Dernikos, 2018; Thomas & Dyches, 2019). In stark contrast to the paradigm under which SoR operates, sociocultural perspectives allow teachers and researchers to identify, value, celebrate, and leverage the multiplicity of semiotic, cultural, and linguistic resources children already possess. Additionally, sociocultural perspectives allow teachers to attend to systemic barriers and historically oppressive processes that keep them in place. These are key to anti-racist literacy instruction.

Humanizing Literacies: Literacy for Liberation and Abolition

Not only is literacy deeply social and cultural, but also it can be the foundation of one's liberation (Freire, 1993). The pedagogical polaris for this *critical literacy* is Brazilian educator Paolo Freire, whose work with working-class communities to raise consciousness and sociopolitical awareness through literacy skills contributed to liberation-oriented political projects, ultimately leading to his exile from the country for a time. Freire's dialogic pedagogical work in Brazil inspired similar literacy projects in Nicaragua (Bender-Slack, 2018, 2020) and Appalachian communities in the United States (Horton & Freire, 1990). These ideas applied in literacy more broadly comprise a subfield in the area of literacy research that interrogates oppression and power known as *critical literacy* (Comber, 2015; Lewison et al., 2008; Luke, 2012). United States history also contains a plethora of examples of marginalized communities responding to their oppression using literacy (nineteenth-century Black literary societies as described by Muhammad (2020) and the lives of women like Jovita Idár and Ida B. Wells come to mind). That literacy has revolutionary consequences is made obvious by the clear opposition to the uses of literacies toward liberatory ends.

A major critique suggests that a whole-language or process approach to literacy instruction does not explicitly teach children language skills, and despite this misconception, we can agree with its concern: any instructional approach that does not offer support or guidance to children in their development of the tools for self-actualization or self-/community liberation has little potential for liberation. What cannot be overlooked in the work of revolutionaries like Freire is that they taught particular literacy skills in service of critical conscious-raising and transformation. As Muhammad (2020) writes, historically, literacy for Black people in the nineteenth-century United States "was not just for self-enjoyment or fulfillment, it was tied to action and efforts to shape the sociopolitical landscape of a country that was founded on oppression" (p. 22). As a result of her historical inquiry, "skill development" is one of the four layers of Muhammad's framework for "culturally and historically responsive literacy." Notably, Lisa Delpit (2006) raises similar concerns about pedagogies that emphasize voice and fluency over skills, noting that specific literacy skills are a requisite for survival. Delpit argues, and we agree, that "Students need technical skills to open doors, but they need to be able to think critically and creatively to participate in meaningful and potentially liberating work inside those doors" (p. 19). In order to be anti-racist, then, a sociocultural perspective cannot eschew instruction in fundamental elements of literacy. In this area we find the most agreement with the SoR: teachers have a responsibility to equip children with the literacy skills and tools that will give them access to the "codes or rules for participating in power" (Delpit, 2006, p. 25) that will set them up for a fulfilling life for themselves and their communities.

When literacy teachers lift their heads from their pacing guides and diagnostic assessments, they see children who are entangled in a spider web of discursive, ideological, social, cultural, and political power. While it may seem like teaching phonics in the scientifically proven, systematic way will level the playing field, such instruction does not get close enough to the skills to help them navigate the real worlds they inhabit. In fact, it may inhibit such navigation. Meaningful, context-dependent (but still explicit) literacy instruction can both nurture and sustain cultures and identities while liberating and humanizing.

FROM SWORDS TO PLOUGHSHARES: A PEDAGOGY OF ANTI-RACIST PROFESSIONAL DISCERNMENT

While we don't find ourselves attached to the Biblical origins of the phrase, we find the concept of turning swords into ploughshares useful in our quest to think beyond the reading "wars." We are drawn to it because it implies that the same raw materials that make up the swords used in the reading wars (the theories, logics, and morals) can, in fact, be repurposed into ploughshares that till and cultivate responsibility toward an anti-racist discernment. In our scholarship and teaching, we seek to abandon the rhetoric and tactics of "war" in favor of principles and practices that contribute to collective liberation and abolition. It would be foolish to suggest that children should never know or learn about letter-sound relationships, phonology, or morphology. What we take issue with, however, is the fervor with which the SoR has gained status as unquestionable dogma in literacy instruction. SoR as popularly represented shuts down conversations about the plurality of pedagogical perspectives and approaches to literacy learning, particularly approaches that are anti-racist, anti-oppressive, liberatory, culturally sustaining, and humanizing. It's not that we don't find the robust debates about the nature of literacy and learning necessary and healthy, but rather that we don't see how platitudes and fear mongering contribute directly to liberation and humanization of marginalized communities. We aren't dismissing the morals and ethics that underpin the "reading wars" in favor of a relativistic position; in the previous two sections, we have outlined just where we stand. Instead, we argue that these personal and intellectual commitments (to anti-racism, to humanizing pedagogies) can be bent toward justice in actual teaching practice instead of simply reverberating in the halls of the academy.

We're arguing that teachers and researchers have a professional responsibility, a moral mandate, and a sometimes-overlooked ability to make decisions about what kind of literacy experiences go on in their classrooms. As Gill (2005) argues, teachers are more than just "technician(s), trying every new method that comes along," adding that such a view discounts the critical intellectual role that teachers play in society (p. 219). Our work with preservice and in-service teachers and our own experiences as teachers remind us that even in the most highly regulated schools, the ultimate decision-maker about the enacted pedagogies and curriculum is the classroom teacher. So, while standards and pacing guides and even state legislatures are granted the authority to prescribe and direct, we suggest that teachers retain a great deal of agency and that a pedagogy of anti-racist professional discernment can be a stance that empowers.

Characteristics of a Pedagogy of Anti-racist Professional Discernment

What do we mean by a *pedagogy of anti-racist professional discernment*? We believe the pedagogy needed in our present moment is one that recognizes anti-racist teachers and their intellectual work as instrumental in movements for racial justice. Informed by the work of a constellation of students, teachers, scholars, writers, as well as our own experiences in these capacities, we suggest four possible qualities of this pedagogy: reject absolutist curricula and instructional methods, embody radical responsiveness, favor transformative over transactional pedagogies, and honor the wisdom and intuition of classroom teachers.

Reject Absolutist Curricula and Instructional Methods

One way that the "reading wars" detract from the march toward racial justice is in the ways that they distance us from the lives of students and distract us from the struggle for liberation. Rather than adopting one or the other *method* of teaching reading, we believe teachers who enact anti-racist professional discernment should adopt a *theoretical stance* on children and literacy against which they weigh their instructional decisions. In our literacy courses, for example, we teach broadly the sociocultural and critical stances necessary to humanize the learning experiences. Not only is this more intellectually rigorous, it demands adaptation, flexibility, and sensitivity to the nuances and fullness of reading the word and the world (Freire, 1983). A theoretical stance—such as a commitment to dismantling white supremacy, a firm belief in children's agency, and a valuing of children's literac*ies* (plural)—is a more flexible way of thinking. Such a stance does help a teacher recognize the material consequences connected to Black and Brown children acquiring the tools to decode words quickly and fluently, but rejects the systematic instruction demanded by SoR. In sum, theoretical absolutes like the ones proffered by SoR do little to contribute either to projects of liberation or abolition.

Embody Radical Responsiveness

What do we mean by *embody radical responsiveness?* According to Carruthers (2019), the Black radical tradition is "a collection of cultural, intellectual, action-oriented labor aimed at disrupting social, political, economic, and cultural norms originating in anticolonial and antislavery efforts" (Carruthers, 2019, Author's Note, X). As white scholars intent on anti-racist discernment, it is imperative that we first listen, but then also *act*, under the wisdom and guidance of BIPOC leaders, mentors, and friends. To *listen*, for many White people, is radical in and of itself, but it is not nearly enough. We must learn to listen to the languaging of our students, our students' families, and colleagues of color, their lived and living experiences with the space, tools, histories, and people around us, *radically*: deep, fully immersed, vigilant listening; we need to take note, reflect, and remain in dialogue with community members and trusted educators. We cannot be radically responsive if we isolate our understanding of reading behind quantitative studies (Milner, 2020), entrepreneurial programming, or our own White gaze and white imagination (Morrison, 1992).

Many scholars have attended carefully to notions of "responsiveness" and relevance with great care (Ladson-Billings, 1995), each speaking to how students are positioned through curriculum, instruction, and pedagogy and how students' "funds of knowledge" (Gonzalez, Amanti, & Moll, 2005) are respected, nurtured, sustained (Paris, 2012), cultivated alongside history (Muhammad, 2020), in-context, and with critical love (Sealy-Ruiz, 2020). *Responsiveness*, from our stance as teacher educators, then, must include critical lenses on how research and policy are taken up into our coursework, implemented in field experiences, and alongside and in-conversation with communities. We keep a careful eye on our own pedagogies because we recognize our embodiment of "best practices" are experienced and *felt* acts of learning itself. We know, for example, teaching someone to read is an intricate negotiation that *does indeed* include decoding, but without ethical, anti-racist facilitation of that process, patterns and characteristics of whiteness prevail (Milner, 2020). The teacher is *never* the only teacher in the room. Distancing the teacher's relational practice from the children, from the child's reading by way of normed, transactional assessments *demeans* and *delays* the professional development of responsive teaching.

Favor Transformative over Transactional Pedagogies

In a recent class, guest scholar, Dr. Sealy-Ruiz (2021), asked: "How could life-stories be part of our research? How can we *unapologetically* center ours and our students' lives in the classroom?" These questions demand educators' vulnerability, radical listening, and "like a balm," offer our students the gifts of presence, observation, and relation to the sensory world—often unexplored under demand of rote transaction, or the "banking method" (Freire, 1993). The current iterations of phonics instruction, for example, follow this tradition and assume the students as incapable of wrestling these complex ideas in a more relational manner. Because the methods of determining explicit phonetic patterning were achieved through isolated, quantitative means does not mean the implementation in classrooms should remain this way. Educators can be explicit with phonetic meta-language, understand the trajectory and importance of syllabication and vowel blends (for example), and *also* recognize the way they engage a child has profoundly rich science behind it, too. To conceive transformative pedagogies, educators must first recognize their own histories, emotions, identities, and experiences as valuable, relational, and sedimented with context and history, or they run the risk of becoming human worksheets. We recognize it is our duty to engage complexity *with* relation, and that how we negotiate history, race, justice, and language matters tremendously in service to these goals (Winn, 2018). Learning is constructed, not demanded.

Honor the Wisdom and Intuition of Classroom Teachers, Communities, and Families

The alarmist discourse about SoR in the media pits teachers against students and families by regularly suggesting that we are teaching reading the "wrong" way. However, we would like to believe that literacy teachers who embody a pedagogy of anti-racist discernment can never teach the "wrong" way. Rather than making literacy pedagogies confrontational and black-and-white, a pedagogy of anti-racist discernment requires teachers to draw on the deep knowledge of their students. As curious learners themselves, teachers learn about the children in their care at all times: on the playground, in the hallway on the way to music class, out and about in the community, and more. A method for teaching children that pretends to know more about who the children are and what they need than the classroom teacher or their community cannot succeed in transformative, liberating education. No matter how "scientific" a method claims to be, it can never know more than the public intellectuals, communities, and families who devote their lives to walking alongside children as they grow and learn and make meaning.

CONCLUSION

At the end of the day, the real questions will be: Are these teachers ready to go into communities (many that will not look 80 percent White like themselves) to learn with them? To learn from them? To recognize and welcome their needs and desires for their children's education? Are they ready to see the child in front of them as a whole person? From this standpoint, it's clear that the systematic vision of teaching and learning proffered by proponents of the SoR (as an authoritative, one-size-fits-all pedagogy for early literacy) will not be the means toward anti-racist, liberatory ends. We also acknowledge that moving forward requires the same relational, anti-racist discernment in our research as it does in our classes and in the communities in which we work: cross-pollination and abolition of academic silos, rejection of outdated and harmful methods, radical listening, and humility.

We recognize that a pedagogy of anti-racist professional discernment is not abolition (Love, 2019). It does not meaningfully divest from the structures that construct Black and Brown children as "at-risk" in the first place (Brown, 2016). What it can do is interrupt the dehumanizing allegiance to linguistic code embedded in the rhetoric of SoR and slow down, hold still, and recognize that many knowledges speak wider truths. A pedagogy of anti-racist professional discernment returns the paradox and struggle—the plowshares—to practicing teachers, which is exactly where we believe the research belongs. By joining inquiry with and alongside living children in-community, teachers and researchers can come out from behind their data and meet the faces of real readers, hear their voices, stories, and dreams, and recognize human vitality depends on a chorus of difference. It doesn't assume to know the "right" way or that teachers and students can't pursue the discourse(s) of linguistic complexity without direct knowledge-guidance. Instead, it holds up teaching and learning as a fertile, unfinished field and delights in the brilliance of innovation. Our commitment to the health and well-being of our nation's youngest readers and writers reminds us that "wars" do not nourish and that fields stripped of diversity cannot sustain growth. Literacy pedagogies, we argue, are practices wielded alongside the spirits of our students and cannot be divorced from sociocultural nuance or a vigilant communion of ideas. Here is where we, especially as white educators and researchers, listen. Here is where we grow.

SOMETHING TO READ, DO, OR CONSIDER

Locate, read, and suggest revisions to your school or organization's policies about reading, reading development, and reading achievement. Where do you see the workings of White supremacy? How is literacy defined? Where is the word "science" used and how?

ACKNOWLEDGMENTS

To our literacy teacher educator mentors who sow seeds of change: Kathy Batchelor, Laney Bender-Slack, Denise Dávila, Tracey Flores, Jim Hoffman, Grace MyHyun Kim, Allison Skerrett, Melissa Wetzel, and Jo Worthy.

NOTES

1. The choice to use the uppercase "W" in the word "White" when used to refer to a group of people is strictly in adherence to APA guidelines.
2. Similar to conversations of dyslexia (Worthy et al., 2018) authoritarian discourses on who holds the "knowledge" to teach reading "correctly" is not new. (For more, see: Worthy et al., 2018; Worthy, et al., 2018.)

REFERENCES

Andreotti, V. (n.d.). *Engaging the (geo)political economy of knowledge construction (working paper)*. Available: https://ubc.academia.edu/VanessadeOliveiraAndreotti

Bender-Slack, D. (2018). ¡Puño en alto! The Nicaraguan literacy campaign and what it means for literacy today. *Educational Studies, 54*(3), 271–284.

Bender-Slack, D. (2020). *The Nicaraguan literacy campaign: The power and politics of literacy*. Lexington Books.

Bennett, K. P. & LeCompte, M. D. (1990). Theoretical and historical overview of the purposes of schooling. In *The way schools work: A sociological analysis of education* (pp. 1–34). Longman.

Brayboy, B. M. J. (2005). Transformational resistance and social justice: American Indians in ivy league universities. *Anthropology and Education Quarterly, 36*(3), 193–211.

Brown, K. D. (2016). *After the at-risk label: Reorienting educational policy and practice*. Teachers College Press.

Buras, K. (2011). Race, charter Schools, and conscious capitalism: On the spatial politics of whiteness as property (and the unconscionable assault on Black New Orleans). *Harvard Educational Review, 81*(2), 296–331.

Canagarajah, A. S. (2013). Negotiating translingual literacy: An enactment. *Research in the Teaching of English, 48*(1), 40–67.

Carruthers, C. (2019). *Unapologetic: A black, queer, and feminist mandate for radical movements*. Beacon Press.

Carter Andrews, D. J., Richmond, G. & Marciano, J. E. (2021). The teacher support imperative: Teacher education and the pedagogy of connection. *Journal of Teacher Education, 72*(3), 267–270.

Comber, B. (2015). Critical literacy and social justice. *Journal of Adolescent & Adult Literacy, 58*(5), 362–367.

Delpit, L. D. (2006). *Other people's children: Cultural conflict in the classroom.* Distributed by W.W. Norton.

Dernikos, B. P. (2018). 'It's like you don't want to read it again': Exploring affects, trauma and 'willful' literacies. *Journal of Early Childhood Literacy*, 1–32 (Epub ahead of print 8 March 2018).

Duffy, G. & Hoffman, J. (1999). In pursuit of an illusion: The flawed search for a perfect method. *The Reading Teacher*, *53*(1), 10–16.

Flores, T. T. (2019). The family writing workshop: Latinx families cultivando comunidad through stories. *Language Arts*, *97*(2), 59–71.

Freire, P. (1993). *Pedagogy of the oppressed* (New rev. 20th-Anniversary ed). Continuum.

Freire, P. & Slover, L. (1983). The importance of the act of reading. *The Journal of Education*, *165*(1), 5–11.

Gill, S. R. (2005). Are disagreements about theories of reading instruction a destructive force or are they essential to moving forward as a field? *Language Arts*, *82*(3), 214–221.

Gonzáles, G. G. (1999). Segregation and the education of Mexican children, 1900-1940. In J. F. Moreno (Ed.), *The elusive quest for equality: 150 years of Chicano/Chicana*. Harvard Educational Review.

Gonzalez, N., Amanti, C. & Moll, L.C. (2005). *Funds of knowledge: Theorizing practices in households, communities and classrooms.* Erlbaum.

Heath, S. B. (1983). *Ways with words: Language, life, and work in communities and classrooms.* Cambridge University Press.

Hoffman, J. V., Hikida, M. & Sailors, M. (2020). Contesting science that silences: Amplifying equity, agency, and design research in literacy teacher preparation. *Reading Research Quarterly*, *55*(S1), S255–S266.

Horton, M. & Freire, P. (1990). *We make the road by walking: Conversations on education and social change* (B. Bell, J. Gaventa & J. M. Peters, Eds.). Temple University Press.

Hursh, D. (2007). Assessing "no child left behind" and the rise of neoliberal education policies. *American Educational Research Journal*, *44*(3), 493–518.

Jones, K. & Okun, T. (2001). *DRWORKSBOOK. Dismantling racism: A workbook for social change groups.* http://www.dismantlingracism.org/

Kim, G. M. (2016). Transcultural digital literacies: Cross-border connections and self-representations in an online forum. *Reading Research Quarterly*, *51*(2), 199–219.

Ladson-Billings, G. (1995). But that's just good teaching! The case for culturally relevant pedagogy." *Theory into Practice*, *34*(3), 159–165.

Ladson-Billings, G. & Tate, W. F. IV (1995). Toward a critical race theory of education. *Teachers College Record*, *97*(1), 47–68.

Leander, K. & Boldt, G. (2013). Rereading "a pedagogy of multiliteracies": Bodies, texts, and emergence. *Journal of Literacy Research*, *45*(1), 22–46.

Leonardo, Z. (2009). *Race, whiteness, and education.* New York: Routledge.

Lewison, M., Leland, C. & Harste, J. C. (2008). *Creating critical classrooms: K-8 reading and writing with an edge.* L. Erlbaum Associates.

Lomawaima, K. T. (1993). Domesticity in the federal Indian schools: The power of authority over mind and body. *American Ethnologist*, *20*(2), 227–240.

Love, B. L. (2019). *We want to do more than survive: Abolitionist teaching and the pursuit of educational freedom.* Beacon Press.

Luke, A. (2012). Critical literacy: Foundational notes. *Theory into Practice, 51*(1), 4–11.

MacLeod, J. (1995). Social reproduction in theoretical perspective. In *Ain't no makin' it: Aspirations & attainment in a low-income neighborhood* (pp. 11–24). Westview Press.

McLean, J. & Alexander, K. (2020). Disrupting White teacher education. *Texas Education Review, 8*(2), 71–78.

Mills, C. (1997). *The racial contract.* Cornell University Press.

Milner, H. R. (2020). Disrupting racism and whiteness in researching a science of reading. *Reading Research Quarterly, 55*(S1), S249–S253.

Morrison, T. (1992). *Playing in the dark: Whiteness and the literary imagination.* Harvard University Press.

Muhammad, G. (2020). *Cultivating genius: An equity framework for culturally and historically responsive literacy.* Scholastic.

National Institute of Child Health and Human Development. (2000). *Report of the National Reading Panel. Teaching children to read: An evidence--based assessment of the scientific research literature on reading and its implications for reading instruction* (NIH Publication No. 00-4769). Washington, DC: U.S. Government Printing Office.

New London Group. (1996). A pedagogy of multiliteracies: Designing social futures. *Harvard Educational Review, 66*(1), 60–92.

Paris, D. (2012). Culturally sustaining pedagogy: A needed change in stance, terminology, and practice. *Educational Researcher, 41*(3), 93–97.

Park, J. Y., Michaels, S., Arancibia, E., Dimanche, S. C., Lembert, D. D., Moon, A. & Sanchez, K. (2017). Multiliteracies and multilingualism in action: An intergenerational inquiry through a poetry translation program. In *Remixing multiliteracies: Theory and practice from New London to new times.* Teachers College Press.

Pearson, P. D. (2004). The reading wars. *Educational Policy, 18*(1), 216–252.

Pollock, M. (2004). *Colormute: Race talk dilemmas in an American school.* Princeton University Press.

Rice, J. M. (1893). *The public-school system of the United States.* Forum publishing company. http://archive.org/details/publicschoolsys00riceuoft

Sealy-Ruiz, Y. (2020). *Love from the vortex & other poems.* Kaleidoscope Vibrations, LLC.

Sealy-Ruiz, Y. (2021). *Arch of Self.* Yolanda Sealy-Ruiz. https://www.yolandasealey-ruiz.com/

Selden, S. (2000). Eugenics and the social construction of merit, race and disability. *Journal of Curriculum Studies, 32*(2), 235–252.

Skerrett, A. (2016). Attending to pleasure and purpose in multiliteracies instructional practices: Insights from transnational youths. *Journal of Adolescent & Adult Literacy, 60*(2), 115–120.

Street, B. V. (1984). *Literacy in theory and practice.* Cambridge University Press.

Tatum, B. (2017). *Why are all the black kids sitting together in the cafeteria?: And other conversations about race.* 3rd edition. Basic Books.

Texas Education Agency. (2021). Approved kindergarten instruments. https://tea.texas.gov/

Thomas, D. & Dyches, J. (2019). The hidden curriculum of reading intervention: A critical content analysis of Fountas & Pinnell's leveled literacy intervention. *Journal of Curriculum Studies, 51*(5), 601–618.

Thomas, P. (2020). "Science of reading" advocacy stumbles, falls. *Medium.* https://plthomasedd.medium.com/science-of-reading-advocacy-stumbles-falls-1740979ba27a

Valenzuela, A. (1999). *Subtractive schooling: U.S.-Mexican youth and the politics of caring.* State University of New York Press.

Wetzel, M. M., Skerrett, A., Maloch, B., Flores, T. T., Infante-Sheridan, M., Murdter-Atkinson, J., Godfrey, V. C. & Duffy, A. (2020). Resisting positionings of struggle in "science of teaching reading" discourse: Counterstories of teachers and teacher educators in Texas. *Reading Research Quarterly, 55*(S1), S319–S330.

Willis, A. I. (2002). Literacy at calhoun colored school 1892-1945. *Reading Research Quarterly, 37*(1), 8–44.

Willis, A.I. (2019). Race, response to intervention, and reading research. *Journal of Literacy Research, 51*(4), 394–419.

Winn, M. T. (2018). A transformative justice approach to literacy education. *Journal of Adolescent & Adult Literacy, 62*(2), 219–221.

Worthy, J., Long, S. L., Salmerón, C., Lammert, C. & Godfrey, V. (2018). "What if we were committed to giving every individual the services and opportunities they need?" Teacher educators' understandings, perspectives, and practices surrounding dyslexia. *Research in the Teaching of English, 53*(2), 125–148.

Worthy, J., Salmerón, C., Long, S. L., Lammert, C. & Godfrey, V. (2018). "Wrestling with the politics and ideology": Teacher educators' responses to dyslexia discourse and legislation. *Literacy Research: Theory, Method, and Practice, XX*, 1–17.

Worthy, J., Svrcek, N., Daly-Lesch, A. & Tily, S., (2018). "We know for a fact": Dyslexia Interventionists and the power of authoritative discourse. *Journal of Literacy Research, 50*(3), 359–382.

Yaden, D. B., Reinking, D. & Smagorinsky, P. (2021). The trouble with binaries: A perspective on the Science of Reading. *Reading Research Quarterly, 56*(S1), S119–S129.

Yatvin, J. (2002). Babes in the woods: The wanderings of the National Reading Panel. *Phi Delta Kappan, 83*(5), 364–369.

Yoon, I. H. (2012). The paradoxical nature of whiteness-at-work in the daily life of schools and teacher communities. *Race Ethnicity and Education, 15*(5), 587–613.

Zapata, A. (2014). Examining the multimodal and multilingual composition resources of young Latino picturebook makers. In L. B. Dunston, S. K. Gambrell, V. R. Fullerton, K. Gillis, K. Headley & P. M. Stecker (Eds.), *62nd Yearbook of the Literacy Research Association* (pp. 104–121). Literacy Research Association.

Zapata, A. & Laman, T. T. (2016). "I write to show how beautiful my languages are": Translingual writing instruction in English-dominant classrooms. *Language Arts, 93*(5), 366–378.

Chapter 4

Seeing Myself in the Curriculum

Engaging Black Students through Technology-Usage and Culturally Responsive Teaching

K. Milam Brooks and Amari T. Simpson

The legacy of racism continues to impact the lived experiences of Black students navigating the U.S. education pipeline. Critical race scholars have illuminated the inequality present in the U.S. education system from ideologies, policies, and practices, all of which steeped in deficit thinking (Valencia, 2012). In 2015, the Center for Intersectionality and Social Policy Studies and the African American Policy Forum collaboratively published *Black Girls Matter: Pushed Out, Overpoliced, and Underprotected*, highlighting the connections between disproportionate discipline of Black girls and the school-to-prison pipeline. During the same year, the Schott Foundation published *Black Lives Matter: The Schott 50 State Report on Public Education and Black Males* to bring much-needed attention to Black males' dire state in the public education system. One striking finding in the report was that only 13 percent of Black male eighth-graders could read proficiently, compared with 21 percent of Latino males and 45 percent of white males. The report also found that Black students, in general, are not provided with support, including access to high-quality teachers, quality time in school, and mentoring. Both reports highlighted the shortcomings of the educational system when it comes to Black students. Scholars have also pointed out the lack of diversity among educators. The most recent data collected by the National Center for Education Statistics (NCES) (2018) on teacher demographics during the 2015–2016 school year states that 80 percent of teachers identified as White, while the percentage of teachers who identified as Black, Hispanic, and two or more races were 7 percent, 9 percent, and 1 percent, respectively. NCES (2019) also reports that the student body composition of public schools in fall 2015 was White (49 percent), Black (15 percent), Hispanic (26 percent), Asian/Pacific Islander (5 percent), American Indian (1 percent), and two or more races (3 percent). Little has been done to balance these racial composition differences between teachers and students regarding strategically recruiting Black teachers and other teachers of color, while retaining those who are already working in the school system. In addition to the racial composition differences, schools have not been environments that recognize, support, and honor the culture and identity of its diverse student population. One way to address this is through culturally responsive teaching (CRT) and technology use.

By connecting instruction to students' culture and identity, CRT uses students' cultural experiences and knowledge to advance learning. CRT also provides students with multiple opportunities to demonstrate what they learn, incorporate different perspectives, and empowers student sociopolitical consciousness (Gay, 2010; Ladson-Billings, 2014; Nieto, 1992; Paris, 2012; Villegas & Lucas, 2002). To support these efforts, technology can create an environment that fosters student learning and self-esteem while empowering educators to embrace existing pedagogical choices and instructional strategies, such as differentiated, student-centered instruction. However, as technology has emerged and evolved, teachers have struggled to utilize it to aid in content and curricular goals appropriately. A large body of research explores the digital divide (or concern for differences in literacy and skills among young people because of access and income) (boyd, 2014; Pew Research Center, 2020), and how public schools may mitigate these divides. Teachers can design and implement innovative pedagogical strategies and practices that facilitate students' preparation for life beyond the classroom and their school setting (Becker, 2000; boyd, 2014; Warschauer et al., 2004, 2010).

In this chapter, we examine the body of literature on culturally relevant pedagogy (CRP), CRT, and technology use in schools/classroom and illustrate the possibility of integrated instructional practices that can serve as a bridge between teachers' and students' current and future need in understanding, appreciating, and valuing what a diverse student population offer to the school/society. We use Ladson-Billings' definition of CRP, where the curriculum promotes the development of learners through explicit connection to their cultural and social identities, and CRT constitutes the manifestation of CRP via teacher instructional practices and choices. For this chapter, we use CRP and CRT interchangeably. Given the continued growth of a diverse student population within K-12 education, oppression of Black people in the United States, and the prominence of technology as essential for learning and instruction due to the COVID-19 pandemic, we must raise fundamental questions, such as (1) What are the characteristics of a culturally responsive teacher? (2) How can technology be leveraged to support CRP? and (3) What is the role of technology in these practices?

LITERATURE REVIEW

Contextualizing the Realities of Students

Structural and cultural representations of race are the consequences of how messages, interpretations (of said messages), and strategies (based on interpretations) organize and distribute resources along racial lines (Omi & Winant, 1993). This process occurs through historically situated "projects" that link interpretation to action, and hence, structure to process individuals' lives and livelihoods (Omi & Winant, 1993). In other words, both past and current treatment of people based on their race continues to structure inequality between and among racial groups. Due to such a racialized context, literature supports that Black parents attempt to prepare their children to survive and thrive by helping them develop a positive racial identity and by teaching them strategies for coping with racism and discrimination (Hughes & Chen, 1997). In school settings, the existence of microaggressions by way of zero-tolerance policies, academic tracking policies, and Eurocentric curriculum is harmful to Black and Latino students. For these reasons, the racial socialization practices of the Black parents are essential and can be exacerbated when families are economically challenged. The relationship between particular spaces and their accompanying resources (i.e., material, human, and social capital) intersects to create additional challenges. Schools are spaces where Black students feel unwelcome, unwanted, undervalued, and unable to perform academically or meaningfully engage with their school due to the sociohistorical legacy of race and racism in the United States and absence of representation in state- and national-based curriculum (Allen et al., 2013).

Researchers should focus on the racist, sexist, and social inequalities that are part of the students' lived reality and students' positions, rights, and responsibilities within larger sociopolitical contexts (Astuto & Ruck, 2010; Diemer et al., 2006). The United Nations Convention on the Rights of the Child encourages nations to foster children's understanding of their political, social, economic, civic, and cultural rights (Astuto & Ruck, 2010). It also states that children have a right to play (which enhances their cognitive and social development) and take an active role in decisions regarding their own lives (or self-determination). Youth should be allowed to exercise these rights in a way that protects them and addresses their best interests and developing capacities. This suggests that even young children should be taught in a way that best fits their understanding and developmental abilities (Astuto & Ruck,

2010). One way schools can support youth is through a curriculum that is socially engaging and relevant.

A socially engaged and relevant curriculum aims to facilitate academic achievement by allowing youth to explore and critically examine their experiences, while empowering them to utilize their voice and establish a learning environment that supports their academic journeys (Cammarota, 2007). Because of an emphasis on students' lived experiences and how knowledge can be used to address real community problems, students, regardless of race, can become more connected with the educational process and see how education can be used to solve real issues, challenges, and concerns that they have (Fox et al., 2010; Hart & Gullan, 2010). This can result in increased motivation for academic achievement and persistence so that students can ultimately *give back* to their communities and families (Cammaroto, 2007). Indeed, a supportive school environment can improve student learning outcomes as demonstrated in factors like relationships between teachers and students, opportunities for student participation and responsibility, and curricular and student support structures for teachers (Bond et al., 2001). In addition, in positive and supportive environments, students are more likely to stay in school longer, develop a love of learning, and utilize the institution to their advantage (Wang & Holcombe, 2010). This type of supportive learning environment can negate the harm caused by microaggressions. Therefore, a positive, supportive school environment can make a critical contribution to the academic achievements of its students and their overall sense of well-being (Patrick et al., 2007).

Understanding the Need for Culturally Relevant Pedagogy

Anti-Black racism, as a mechanism of discrimination, is an important topic across all fields because it explores how structures of white supremacist culture within the United States have and continue to marginalize Black people. Such structures are pervasive and systematic and include mechanisms of oppression such as slavery, segregation laws, and lynchings (Grant et al., 2015), to name a few. Anti-Black racism also speaks to the specific ways Black people are seen, targeted, dehumanized, and killed, which is often very different than any other racial/ethnic group in the United States. Such categorization, along with historical silence around anti-Black racism, can have devastating effects, including stifling interventions and resistance, which is needed (Mosely et al., 2020). Indeed, anti-Black racism is endemic to the foundation of America (Dumas, 2016).

In schools, anti-Black racism is attributed to Black students feeling unwelcome, unwanted, undervalued, and unable to perform academically or meaningfully engage with their school (Bottiani et al., 2017). Consequently,

Black students report a lack of Black teachers, curricula in which Blackness is absent or minimized, and being treated differently from their non-Black peers (Bottiani et al., 2017). Educational institutions must challenge anti-Black racism if students are to achieve their full potential. As part of professional teaching standards, educators must think systematically about their practice and learn from experience (see National Board for Professional Teaching Standards). In this way, research insists that anti-Black racism should be a fundamental component of teaching practice and education (Lopez & Jean-Marie, 2021). Dumas (2016) explains it is important for educators to acknowledge that anti-blackness can infect their work and serve as a form of violence against Black children and their families (p. 17). Thus, it is important to examine ways to incorporate effective strategies for combating anti-Black racism in school settings. One strategy to combat anti-Black racism in schools is through the application of CRP and CRT in practice.

Culturally Relevant and Culturally Responsive Frameworks Defined

According to Ladson-Billings (1995), CRP has been described as "a pedagogy that empowers students intellectually, socially, emotionally, and politically by using cultural referents to impart knowledge, skills, and attitudes" (p. 382). Gay (2010) defines CRT "as using cultural knowledge, prior experiences, frames of references, and performance styles of ethnically diverse students to make learning encounters more relevant to and effective for them" (p. 31). What this means for teachers is that they create a bridge between students' home and school lives while still meeting the expectations of the students to inform the teacher's lessons and methodology (Ladson-Billings, 1995). Many Black and other non-white students in the United States perceive school as a place where they cannot be themselves because their culture is not valued. Ladson-Billings contends that "culturally relevant teachers utilize students' culture as a vehicle for learning." Teachers who focus on developing cultural competence encourage students to learn to maintain their "cultural integrity" (Ladson-Billings, 1995). Teachers, using CRP, also provide students with a curriculum that builds on their prior knowledge and cultural experiences (Ladson-Billings, 2009). Culturally relevant teachers "engage in the world and others critically," and to do this, "students must develop a broader sociopolitical consciousness that allows them to critique the cultural norms, values, morals, and institutions that produce and maintain social inequities" (Ladson-Billings, 1995, p. 17). Teachers have been shown to increase students' efficacy, motivation, and academic achievement when they successfully incorporate texts and pedagogical strategies that are culturally and linguistically responsive (Ladson-Billings, 1995; Lee, 2004; 2006).

Impact of Culturally Relevant and Responsive Frameworks on Academic Outcomes

According to Ladson-Billings (1995), CRP has been described as "a pedagogy that empowers students intellectually, socially, emotionally, and politically by using cultural referents to impart knowledge, skills, and attitudes" (p. 382). Gay (2010) defines CRT "as using cultural knowledge, prior experiences, frames of references, and performance styles of ethnically diverse students to make learning encounters more relevant to and effective for them" (p. 31). Carol Lee (1993, 2004, 2006, 2007) has written extensively on CRT. She writes that there are several principles that teachers should follow to be engaged in CRT. Principle 1: learning is optimized when students can make connections between what they know and what they are expected to learn. Principle 2: the meaning or significance that learners impose on experience shapes how and whether knowledge is stored in long-term memory. Principle 3: learners can demonstrate competence in nontraditional ways. Principle 4: ability is not static or finite; as human beings, we build our owner's engagement with experience. In short, students must experience academic success; students must develop and/or maintain cultural competence; students must develop critical consciousness through which they challenge the status quo of the current social order. Learning style research reports that cultural/ethnic groups have distinct ways of processing information, interacting, communicating, and learning (O'Neil, 1990), and there are positive outcomes linked to CRT, including students taking ownership in and becoming a part of the learning process.

Many Black and other non-white students in the United States perceive school as a place where they cannot be themselves because their culture is not valued. Ladson-Billings (1994) contends that culturally relevant teaching utilize students' culture as a vehicle for learning, and in doing so, students are intellectually, socially, emotionally, and politically empowered. Cultural competence, or an awareness of student's cultural and ethnic background, can be tool in creating a positive learning environment. When teachers successfully incorporate texts and pedagogical strategies that are culturally and linguistically responsive, teachers have been shown to increase students' efficacy, motivation, and academic achievement (Ladson-Billing, 1995). What this means for teachers is that they create a bridge between students' home and school lives, while meeting the expectations of other stakeholders (Ladson-Billings, 1995). Indeed, students process new information best when it is linked to what they already know. Embedded within CRP is a strong emphasis on providing opportunities for students to think critically about inequities in their own or their peers' experience. Student's success is not just meaningful engagement in ones' citizenship; instead, Ladson-Billings suggests that providing opportunities for students to critique society may encourage them to change oppressive structures, while maintaining their cultural integrity. Recent studies on the effectiveness of CRP suggests a link to several positive outcomes for students, including increased academic achievement and persistence, improved attendance, and increased school connectedness (Ladson-Billings, 1995; Lee, 2004, 2006).

Culturally Relevant Teaching and Positive Identity Development

In addition to the positive academic and personal outcomes from culturally relevant teaching, researchers have discussed how CRP contributes to healthy identity development. For example, Winkler (2012) found that youth experience a pro-cultural orientation, or positive racial socialization, when blackness is normalized, as was the case of the youth in Detroit. However, since most cities are not majority Black like Detroit, the task of healthy racial identity development may be challenging, especially for Black youth navigating and negotiating anti-Blackness in the cities they reside in and through messaging from mainstream media. Through teachers and administrators, schools can play a significant role in their students' healthy and positive identity development through their practices. Indeed, when youth receive culturally affirming messages in school, positive racial/ethnic identity is promoted, and students feel more connected to the school and others (Byrd, 2016).

Another principal aim of a culturally relevant curriculum is to foster an understanding of the social context where the students reside, including their own social identities and how they are structured in relation to societal power and privilege (Cammarota, 2007). Again, attention to pedagogy is essential here. Freire (1970) criticized the traditional methods of education, where students passively receive information from teachers as experts, and the students' needs, context, and life experiences are entirely ignored. In contrast, the ideal conditions for an empowered education integrate the student's understanding and perspective into the educational and learning process (Freire, 1970). Thus, to enhance this process, students become knowledgeable about and affirm their own cultural and sociopolitical identity, which can, in turn, liberate their understanding of self and challenge the oppressive elements of dominant culture (Freire, 1970; Watts et al., 2003).

Technology Use in Schools

Although educators have used technology to teach beginning in the 1920s with film and radio, and other devices (e.g., overhead projector, B.F. Skinner'

Teaching Machine, whiteboards), computers were not widely utilized until the 1980s and 1990s (Cuban, 1993; Russell, 2006). When Common Core Standards were established and called for schools to build critical thinking skills that will help students perform well in colleges and universities or make them competitive in the workforce, educators incorporated technological tools into their curriculum (Delgado et al., 2015; National Governors Association, 2010). The COVID pandemic forced traditional schools to integrate technology quickly and in ways that many were ill-prepared. However, a recent survey conducted by EducationWeek found teachers' opinions about technology are improving, along with their ability to use it (Bushweller, 2020). We presume that this shift is likely due to the need for remote instruction, increased available funding for student technology resources and supports, increased professional development opportunities focused on technology use, and additional administrative support for schools.

Organizations like Digital Promise have taken the lead on identifying specific ways in which technology can not only create an equitable learning environment but also assist in that mission. Digital Promise posits that technology provides students with the ability to access learning materials outside of the classroom/school; technology provides students and educators with more tools to create a learning environment that fosters personalized learning, and technology provides educators and district leaders with data that can be used to make informed decisions (Pape & Vander Ark, 2018). But, of course, technology alone won't solve the issue of anti-blackness in schools. Creating an environment where all students feel welcome, wanted, valued, and able to perform academically requires a commitment from schools to increase access to learning tools for students and their families, equipping teachers with the knowledge and skills to use tech powerfully, and using student data effectively to make informed decisions about improving their learning experiences (Angevine et al., 2019).

Technology and Young People

According to the Pew Research Center (2018), over 95 percent of teens of United States have smartphone access, and 45 percent also shared that they are "almost constantly online." Breaking down this access, White, Black, and Hispanic teens have access to desktop/laptop computers at 90, 89, and 82 percent, respectively, and access to smartphones at 94, 94, and 95 percent, respectively. Despite high levels of engagement, young people have mixed interpretations of the benefits of social media and technology in their lives. Young people report mostly positive, neutral, and mostly adverse effects of social media at 31, 45, and 24 percent, respectively. In addition, there is still a range of technological access concerns for low-income and first-generation students (Pew Research Center, 2018, 2020). However, the constant technological engagement demanded of young people has led to complicated, yet difficult conversations related to young people's identity, privacy, and safety (boyd, 2014; Carr, 2010). Young people have not received consistent messaging on appropriately interfacing with—or best practices for—using technology as an online tool. The main challenge of researching youth's technology use include conducting research on continually shifting and evolving technologies used by young people and the difference these technological tools are used according to one's demographic background and technological expectations from peers, families, educators, and other constituents (Livingstone & Helsper, 2010; Pew Research Center, 2013).

Some schools have attempted to face challenges of navigating technology use by incorporating technology into the classroom and curriculum or banning it entirely from school premises (Klein, 2019). Schools have gone as far as to justify their technology ban by showing students how frequent cell phone notifications occur and distract students' learning (THV11, 2019). Despite this, technology remains an essential resource for the foreseeable future that continues to evolve and change over time. Therefore, schools must negotiate, develop, and challenge young people's habits, attitudes, and behaviors to engage with and use technology beyond students' K-12 school setting.

Applying Culturally Relevant and Culturally Responsive Frameworks through Technology Use

Digital technology plays a central role in affecting student engagement and is recognized for its' potential to increase the self-efficacy and self-regulation of students (Clark & Luckin, 2013; Diemer et al., 2012). In addition, digital literacy is often cited as a means to integrate learning and technological innovation (boyd, 2014). In the edited book, *The Digital Youth Network: Cultivating Digital Media Citizenship in Urban Communities*, the authors explore the reality of diverse forms of learning that are taking place as a result of new digital tools and networks. To this end, youth are finding new ways to express their identity, independence, and creativity, as well as their ability to learn, exercise judgment, and think systematically (Barron et al., 2014). Indeed, today's young scholars crave content related to their interests, but more times than not, public school systems fail to deliver relevant content.

Culturally responsive computer-related technology first appeared in education in 1999 with the Hispanic Math Project funded by the National Science Foundation (Kinard & Bitter, 1997) and the work of Nicole Pinkard (2001), which found that students gained in word recognition skills and were motivated as a result of the culturally relevant interface. Similarly, Eglash and colleagues (2013) found that a culturally responsive framework effectively engaged Black, Latino, and Indigenous students in STEM.

At a crossroads where education can satisfy students' interests and teach technical skills, an integrated instructional approach and strategy that utilizes CRP, CRT, and technology can provide Black students the capacity to discover their cultural and familial history and experiences. These pedagogical practices and choices are important because they center students and their lived experiences within curriculum, instruction, and learning and provide agency for students to address personal, real-world challenges and concerns. Teachers of all content specialization areas can cultivate healthy identity development of their Black students, non-Black students, families, and educators alike would appreciate the value of incorporating an integrated instructional approach into the curriculum (Snoeyink & Ertmer, 2001). An integrated instructional approach can allow Black students to engage in cultural topics and document their experiences and knowledge while satisfying national and state-based content standards (National Governors Association, 2010).

A CRP, CRT, and technology-integrated instructional approach is vital for several reasons:

1. It brings technology into the classroom, where teachers can offer content-rich, positive messaging and alternate instructional practices to engage in learning.
2. It allows students to compile a wealth of information about their cultural and familial backgrounds that can be used to create and sustain meaningful relationships and connections.
3. It can aid teachers in supporting and contributing to the development of their students.

An integrated instructional approach can provide Black students an opportunity to discover their culture and family stories while engaging in technology use for educational purposes. For example, in Howard's (2001) research on Black students' perceptions of CRT, students reported that when teachers incorporate CRT practices, school "feels like home" (p. 146). Indeed, when students feel connected to their schools, there is a direct correlation to academic success (Ladson-Billing, 1994).

A democratic education needs to be geared toward helping every human being reach the full measure of their humanity (Ayers et al., 2009). However, this is possible only when educators understand the lived experiences of their students (Freire, 1998). Once understood, both parties can work together to create the condition by which they can collectively develop their knowledge. Education can therefore be a liberating experience, not only for the student, but for the teacher as well. Freire reminds us that whoever possesses and controls our textual world possess a significant part of the hegemonic landscape. We are all creators of language and can therefore create and control the text of our world and can expand the very sense of the text. This act of transformation, Freire argues, can reorganize our society and transform it into something new—a more equal and just society (Freire, 1970). A key assumption of this curriculum is that even young children can meaningfully participate in these democratic processes and play an important role in the transformation of their communities.

CONCLUSION

Today there exists new racism, one that is more covert and hidden than the racism of the past. A democratic education needs to be geared toward helping every human being reach the full measure of their humanity (Ayers et al., 2009). Unfortunately, Black youth continue to fall through the existing gaps within the education pipeline of the United States. Since the education attainment gap exists between Black people and their white counterparts (NCES, 2018), we need to explore pedagogical alternatives that can positively impact Black students' academic retention and persistence outcomes in K-12 settings.

When we consider the outdated, paradigmatic legacy of Eurocentric history and values in the U.S. education system, schools need to consider novel strategies to support the development of diverse learners, especially Black students. Inviting today's young people to engage critically in cultural identities and experiences with the use of technology should be the norm and standard. Therefore, developing and implementing integrated instructional strategies and practices that center students and their lived experience are an empowering, liberating, and conscious-raising learning experience that also supports the social and emotional needs of Black students. In turn, we would expect to find gains in students' cultural knowledge and identity development due to utilizing the various features of the integrated approach of CRP, CRT, and technology into learning, which may manifest in increased student attendance, increased student achievement, and increased student retention.

Students and teachers can build strong, respectful relationships founded on an appreciation of similarities and differences, learn to examine root causes of inequity critically, and develop collaborative solutions to communal and societal problems (Diemer et al., 2006). This is possible only when educators understand the lived experiences of their students (Freire, 1998). These alternatives must appropriately use relevant, relatable tools to promote Black students' (and their peers') development in a manner that aids students in school and beyond (Ladson-Billings, 2014). Future research should examine the effects of this integrated approach on learning, as well as other novel pedagogical alternatives that work to improve the educational outcomes of K-12 Black students. Instead of forcing Black students to disconnect from their cultural identities, educators should instead plug into the culture of their students, and technology provides a path for engagement.

SOMETHING TO READ, DO, OR CONSIDER

Read

- Ladson-Billings, G. (2009). *The dreamkeepers: Successful teachers of African American children*. John Wiley & Sons.
- YOUmedia Toolkit and Community of Practice https://youmedia.org/tools/

Do

- Implement a lesson or curriculum that incorporate student's cultural and personal experiences based on your reading of *Dreamkeepers* and this edited volume.
- Implement co-working time that supports teachers developing lessons that incorporate student's cultural and personal experiences either as professional development or teacher preparation course experience.

Consider

- Revising a previous lesson or curriculum to incorporate technology, as well as student's cultural and personal experiences.
- Reviewing the professional development opportunities or teacher preparation programs to consider how your teacher educators can better incorporate technology, as well as student's cultural and personal experiences into their curriculum and instructional practices.

REFERENCES

Allen, A., Scott, L. M., & Lewis, C. W. (2013). Racial microaggressions and African American and Hispanic students in urban schools: A call for culturally affirming education. *Interdisciplinary Journal of Teaching and Learning, 3*(2), 117–129.

Angevine, C., Cator, K., Liberman, B., Smith, K., & Young, V. (2019). *Designing a process for inclusive innovation: A radical commitment to equity*. Digital Promise

Astuto, J., & Ruck, M. D. (2010). Early childhood as a foundation for civic engagement. *Handbook of research on civic engagement in youth*, 249–276.

Ayers, W., Quinn, T., & Stovall, D. (2009). Editors' conclusion. In Ayers, W., Quinn, T., & Stovall, D. (eds.), *Handbook of Social Justice in Education* (pp. 725–728). Routledge.

Barron, B., Gomez, K., Pinkard, N., & Martin, C. K. (2014). *The digital youth network: Cultivating digital media citizenship in urban communities*. MIT Press.

Bottiani, J. H., Bradshaw, C. P., & Mendelson, T. (2017). A multilevel examination of racial disparities in high school discipline: Black and white adolescents' perceived equity, school belonging, and adjustment problems. *Journal of Educational Psychology*, *109*(4), 532.

boyd, d. (2014). *It's complicated: The social lives of networked teens*. Yale University Press.

Bushweller, K. (2020). How COVID-19 is shaping tech use. What that means when schools reopen. *Education Week*.

Byrd, C. M. (2016). Does culturally relevant teaching work? An examination from student perspectives. *Sage Open*, *6*(3). DOI: 2158244016660744.

Cammarota, J. (2007). A social justice approach to achievement: Guiding Latina/o students toward educational attainment with a challenging, socially relevant curriculum. *Equity & Excellence in Education*, *40*(1), 87–96.

Carr, N. G. (2011). *The shallows: What the internet is doing to our brains* (Norton pbk. [ed.]). W.W. Norton.

Crenshaw, K., Ocen, P., & Nanda, J. (2015). *Black Girls Matter: Pushed Out, Overpoliced, and Underprotected*. African American Policy Forum.

Clark, W., & Luckin, R. (2013). *What the research says: iPads in the classroom*. London Knowledge Lab Report. Retrieved from http://digitallearningteam.org/

Cuban, L. (1993). *How teachers taught: Constancy and change in American classrooms, 1890-1990*. Teachers College Press.

Delgado, A. J., Wardlow, L., McKnight, K., & O'Malley, K. (2015). Educational technology: A review of the integration, resources, and effectiveness of technology in K-12 classrooms. *Journal of Information Technology Education*, *14*, 397–416.

Diemer, M. A., Kauffman, A., Koenig, N., Trahan, E., & Hsieh, C. A. (2006). Challenging racism, sexism, and social injustice: Support for urban adolescents' critical consciousness development. *Cultural Diversity and Ethnic Minority Psychology*, *12*(3), 444–460. doi: 10.1037/1099-9809.12.3.444.

Diemer, T. T., Fernandez, E., & Streepey, J. W. (2012). Student perceptions of classroom engagement and learning using iPads. *Journal of Teaching and Learning with Technology*, *1*(2), 13–25.

Dumas, M. J. (2016). Against the dark: Anti-blackness in education policy and discourse. *Theory into Practice*, *55*(1), 11–19.

Eglash, R., Gilbert, J. E., & Foster, E. (2013). Toward culturally responsive computing education. *Communications of the ACM*, *56*(7), 33–36.

Fox, M., Mediratta, K., Ruglis, J., Stoudt, B., Shah, S., & Fine, M. (2010). Critical youth engagement: Participatory action research and organizing. In L. R. Sherrod, J. Torney-Purta & C. A. Flanagan (Eds.), *Handbook of Research on Civic Engagement in Youth* (pp. 621–649). John Wiley & Sons, Inc.

Freire, P. (1970). *Pedagogy of the oppressed*. Routledge.
Freire, P. (1998). *Pedagogy of freedom: ethics, democracy, and civic courage*. Rowman & Littlefield Publishers, Inc.
Gay, G. (2010). Acting on beliefs in teacher education for cultural diversity. *Journal of Teacher Education, 61*(1–2), 143–152.
Gay, G. (2018). *Culturally responsive teaching: Theory, research, and practice*. Teachers College Press.
Grant, C. A., Brown, K. D., & Brown, A. L. (2015). *Black intellectual thought in education: the missing traditions of Anna Julia Cooper, Carter G. Woodson, and Alain Leroy Locke*. Routledge.
Hart, D., & Gullan, R. L. (2010). The sources of adolescent activism: Historical and contemporary findings. In L. R. Sherrod, J. Torney-Purta & C. A. Flanagan (Eds.), *Handbook of research on civic engagement in youth* (pp. 67–90). John Wiley & Sons, Inc.
Howard, T. C. (2001). Telling their side of the story: African-American students' perceptions of culturally relevant teaching. *The Urban Review, 33*(2), 131–149.
Kinard, B., & Bitter, G. (1997). Multicultural mathematics and technology: The Hispanic math project. *Computers in the Schools, 13*(1–2), 77–88. https://doi.org/10.1300/J025v13n01_09
Klein, A. (2019, September 7). Schools say no to cellphones in class. But is it a smart move? *Education Week*. https://www.edweek.org/technology/schools-say-no-to-cellphones-in-class-but-is-it-a-smart-move/2019/09
Ladson-Billings, G. (1995). Toward a theory of culturally relevant pedagogy. *American Educational Research Journal, 32*(3), 465–491. Retrieved January 4, 2021, from http://www.jstor.org/stable/1163320
Ladson-Billings, G. (2009). *The dreamkeepers: Successful teachers of African American children*. John Wiley & Sons.
Ladson-Billings, G. (2014). Culturally relevant pedagogy 2.0: aka the remix. *Harvard Educational Review, 84*(1), 74–84.
Lee, C. D. (1993). *Signifying as a scaffold for literary interpretation: The pedagogical implications of an African American discourse genre*. National Council of Teachers of English, Urbana, IL.
Lee, C. D. (2004). Bridging home and school literacies: Models for culturally responsive teaching, a case for African American English. In J. Flood, S. B. Heath & D. Lapp (Eds.), *Handbook of research on teaching literacy through the communicative and visual arts* (pp. 335–345). Routledge.
Lee, C. D. (2006). 'Every good-bye ain't gone': Analyzing the cultural underpinnings of classroom talk. *International Journal of Qualitative Studies in Education, 19*(3), 305–327.
Lee, C. D. (2007). *Culture, literacy, & learning: Taking bloom in the midst of the whirlwind*. Teachers College Press.
Livingstone, S., & Helsper, E. (2010). Balancing opportunities and risks in teenagers' use of the internet: The role of online skills and internet self-efficacy. *New Media & Society, 12*(2), 309–329. https://doi.org/10.1177/1461444809342697

Lopez, A. E., & Jean-Marie, G. (2021). Challenging anti-Black racism in everyday teaching, learning, and leading: From theory to practice. *Journal of School Leadership, 31*(1–2), 50–65.

National Board for Professional Teaching Standards. (2016). *What teachers should know and be able to do*. Retrieved from https://www.nbpts.org/standards-five-core-propositions/

National Center for Educational Statistics. (2018). The condition of education 2018 (Report No. NCES 2018-144). Retrieved from: https://nces.ed.gov/pubs2018/2018144.pdf

National Center for Education Statistics. (2019). *Indicator 6: Elementary and secondary enrollment*. Retrieved from https://nces.ed.gov/programs/raceindicators/indicator_rbb.asp

National Governors Association. (2010). *Common core state standards*. Washington, DC.

O'Neil, J. (1990). Making sense of style. *Educational Leadership, 48*(2), 4–9.

Omi, M., & Winant, H. (1993). On the theoretical status of the concept of race. In C. McCarthy & W. Crichlow (Eds.), *Race, Identity and Representation in Education* (pp. 3–10). Routledge.

Pape, B., & Vander Ark, T. (2018). *Policies and practices that meet learners where they are*. Digital Promise.

Patrick, H., Ryan, A. M., & Kaplan, A. (2007). Early adolescents' perceptions of the classroom social environment, motivational beliefs, and engagement. *Journal of Educational Psychology, 99*(1), 83.

Pew Research Center. (2013). Instagram, Vine, and the evolution of social media. *Pew Research Center*. Retrieved June 1, 2021, from https://www.pewresearch.org/fact-tank/2013/06/20/instagram-vine-and-the-evolution-of-social-media/

Pew Research Center. (2018). Teens, social media & technology 2018. *Pew Research Center*. https://www.pewresearch.org/internet/2018/05/31/teens-social-media-technology-2018/

Pew Research Center. (2020). As schools close due to the coronavirus, some U.S. students face a digital 'homework gap.' *Pew Research Center*. https://www.pewresearch.org/fact-tank/2020/03/16/as-schools-close-due-to-the-coronavirus-some-u-s-students-face-a-digital-homework-gap/

Pinkard, N. (2001). Rappin' reader and say say oh playmate: Using children's childhood songs as literacy scaffolds in computer-based learning environments. *Journal of Educational Computing Research, 25*(1), 17–34.

Russell, M. (2006). *Technology and Assessment: The Tale of Two Interpretations*. Information Age Publishing, 137–152.

Schott Foundation. (2015). *Black lives matter: The Schott 50 state report on public education and Black males*. New York: Beaudry, A.

Snoeyink, R., & Ertmer, P. A. (2001). Thrust into technology: How veteran teachers respond. *Journal of Educational Technology Systems, 30*(1), 85–111.

THV11. (2019, March 14). *Teacher explains ban on cell phones in class*. https://www.youtube.com/watch?v=QRX0dqICAvU&ab_channel=THV11

Valencia, R. R. (Ed.). (2012) *The evolution of deficit thinking: Educational thought and practice*. New York, NY: Routledge.

Villegas, A. M., & Lucas, T. (2002). Preparing culturally responsive teachers: Rethinking the curriculum. *Journal of Teacher Education, 53*(1), 20–32.

Wang, M. T., & Holcombe, R. (2010). Adolescents' perceptions of school environment, engagement, and academic achievement in middle school. *American Educational Research Journal, 47*(3), 633–662.

Warschauer, M., & Matuchniak, T. (2010). New technology and digital worlds: Analyzing evidence of equity in access, use, and outcomes. *Review of Research in Education, 34*(1), 179–225.

Watts, R. J., Williams, N. C., & Jagers, R. J. (2003). Sociopolitical development. *American Journal of Community Psychology, 31*(1/2), 185–194. doi: 10.1023/A:1023091024140.

Winkler, E., 2012. *Learning race, learning place: Shaping racial identities and ideas in African American childhoods*. Rutgers University Press.

Chapter 5

Ten Years Later

Toward a Reconceptualization of the Racial Framework of Teacher Candidates

Nicole V. Williams

Ten years ago, I conducted my dissertation study on how teacher candidates believe their encounters with race and racism shape their past, present, and future experiences in teaching, learning, and interactions with others (Williams, 2011). I used Critical Race Theory (CRT) as a framework to "theorize, examine and challenge the ways race and racism implicitly and explicitly affect social structures, practices, and discourses" (Yosso, 2006, p. 168). The fundamental CRT argument was (and still is) that race and racism are "normal, not aberrant, in American society . . . [racism] is an ingrained feature of our landscape, it looks ordinary and natural to persons in the culture" (Delgado & Stefancic, 2000, p. xvi.). CRT posits that racism is pervasive and endemic to American norms and institutions and therefore rejects dominant claims of meritocracy, neutrality, objectivity, and color-blindness. Instead, it argues interest convergence serves those in power even in instances in which they claim beneficial advantages to marginalized peoples. It demands recognition of both the experiential knowledge and critical consciousness of people of color in understanding law and society, which includes an interdisciplinary claim that the intersections of race and law overrun disciplinary boundaries. CRT works toward the liberation of people of color as it embraces the larger project of liberating all oppressed people (Mutua, 2006).

In my study, I interviewed eleven teacher candidates in their third of five quarters in the Middle Childhood Education (MCE) Master of Education program at a large mid-Western university. The mission of the MCE program was the preparation of professionals who possess the knowledge, skills, and dispositions to interpret and construct learning environments in ways that are critical, engaging, culturally responsive, and anti-oppressive.

More specifically, the program was committed to building relationships and improving conditions for teaching and learning in urban schools. The interviews followed a predetermined instrument which included questions that asked:

- What leads you to call this situation racism?
- What ideas, thoughts, or confusions did you have?
- What feelings or emotions did you experience, and looking back at this encounter with racism, do you think it impacted or will impact your teaching, learning, and interactions with others?

Gee's (2005) introduction and interpretation of discourse analysis was employed as the data analysis framework for this study. Gee argued that discourse analysis provides the researcher with the opportunity to look for "patterns and links within and across utterances in order to form hypotheses about how meaning is being constructed and organized" (p. 118). Each interview was analyzed independent of the others. The interviews were first coded for themes based on Gee's seven themes of significance, activities, relationships, politics, connections, sign systems, and knowledge.

From the synthesis of the seven themes, a framework emerged in respect to the teacher candidates' definition of racism and how they believe racism influences the social, emotional, and political position of those involved. The teacher candidates defined racism as an *overt* behavior committed by an individual or group of individuals. The person or persons who committed the racism was referenced by the participants as "racist." The behaviors were also termed "racist," and these behaviors impacted the social, emotional, and political positions of the people involved. The participants in this study were only cognizant of the influences of racism on the institution and failed to see the influences of the institution on racism. Therefore, they did not see themselves as part of institutions who are racist or commit racist acts, and they were unable to identify how race and racism will impact their future teaching, learning, and interactions with others.

In my study, I argued for a reconceptualization of how teacher candidates needed to be challenged to view race and racism and its influence on the social, emotional, and political as situated *within* these institutions to more wholly recognize the "larger historical patterns, institutionalized process, and everyday practices" of racism (Lewis, 2000, p. 625) The initial step is in an understanding of racism that eradicates the individual and the overt actions of the individual as the primary operatives and to focus more purposefully on the institutions through which the social, emotional, and political constructs of racism may be further deconstructed. In other words, racism through this framework is understood as located *within*, not separate of institutions. If the teacher candidates were able to reconceptualize the concepts of race and racism as occurring within institutions and social interactions as an element within racism in an institution, they would be less inclined to view themselves as simply an individual outside of institutions, racism, and/or social interactions. Similarly, they could then view their own emotional reactions to their encounters with racism, anger, guilt, and shame of their Whiteness as normal and to be expected in the transition through racial understanding and reconciliation as opposed to emotions to be battled and utilized to distract racial discourse from its purpose. Finally, they would recognize the need as future teachers to "expose white lies, maneuvers, and pathologies that contribute to the avoidance of a critical understanding of race and racism" (Leonardo, 2009, P. 265).

METHODS

The purpose of the current chapter is to determine if teacher candidates have transitioned toward this reconceptualized racial framework within the past 10 years. The research questions that guided this discussion included: (1) How do teacher candidates conceptualize race and racism and what are the implications for their future students? And (2) How do educator preparation providers perceive they can best prepare teacher candidates to reconceptualize race and racism in respect to curriculum, pedagogy, courses, field experiences, and other programmatic features? To answer these research questions, I collected and analyzed peer-reviewed journal articles published in English between 2011 and 2021 with a focus on teacher candidates' conceptualization of race and racism and the impact on P-12 students. I used Academic Search Complete and chose the following databases: Academic Search Complete, APA PsycInfo, Education Full Text (H.W. Wilson), Education Research Complete, and Education Source. Academic Search Complete is perhaps the most extensive database with more than 7,300 full-text peer-reviewed journals. Although much smaller, APA PsycInfo is the American Psychological Association's (APA) database that includes the largest resource dedicated to peer-reviewed literature in the behavioral sciences and mental health. Unlike Academic Search Complete and APA PsycInfo, Education Full Text (H.W. Wilson), Education Research Complete, and Education Source focus solely on topics within education. Education Source is the largest in that it provides more than 1,800 journals followed by Education Research Complete with 1,200 journals and Education Full Text (H.W. Wilson) with 350 journals.

The PRISMA (Preferred Reporting Items for Systematic Reviews and Meta-Analysis) (Moher et al., 2015) was used as a foundation for this review. The search terms included teacher candidates and preservice teachers and race. Initially, 356 records were identified through the databases; however, 227 records were automatically removed for duplication. Therefore, 129 records were screened with an abstract screening tool that included yes/no questions on the study characteristics (teacher candidate participants, educator preparation provider setting, research study design, race-centered scope) and report characteristics (publication data between 2011 and 2021, English language, peer-reviewed). The researcher screened the 129 records over a 1-month period and 95 records were eventually excluded primarily due to scope and participants. Thirty-four full-text articles were then read for eligibility. One full-text article was excluded as a duplicate and one article was excluded for scope. Therefore, 32 studies were included in the qualitative analysis.

FINDINGS AND DISCUSSION

The first section of the findings and discussion examines how the 32 reviewed studies address the first research question: How do teacher candidates conceptualize race and racism and what are the implications for their future students? The section is organized around the two themes of teacher candidate conceptualization of race and racism and the classroom implications. The second section of the findings and discussion examines the second research question: How do educator preparation providers perceive they can best prepare teacher candidates to reconceptualize race and racism in respect to curriculum, pedagogy, courses, field experiences, and other programmatic features? This section is organized around the two themes of curriculum and pedagogy and field experiences which inherently includes the significance of this study and the implications for educator preparation programs.

Conceptualization of Race and Racism

Wilson and Kumar (2017) employed CRT and Critical Content Analysis to examine teacher candidate definitions of racism at the beginning and end of their educator preparation program. The teacher candidates defined racism within three main themes: overt actions with a reason, overt or covert actions with no reason, and thinking and/or feeling superior. Much like the teacher candidates in my study 10 years ago, these teacher candidates identified racism as an individual phenomenon rather than an institutional or structural phenomenon and therefore they could remove themselves or their own experiences, thoughts, or feelings from racism. And the teacher candidates could not make any connections between their construction of racism and their positionality as future teachers (Wilson & Kumar, 2017).

In their study of teacher candidates, Matias and Zembylas (2014) interrogated White teacher candidate experiences, thoughts, feelings, and particularly emotions and found below the surface may be "hidden expressions of disgust for the Other" (p. 319). More specifically, interpretative analysis from an ongoing political action research project, the researchers used CRT, Whiteness studies, and Critical Emotion studies to illuminate how false professions of care, sympathy, and love by White teacher candidates need to be critically examined and sensitively unpacked. In another study by Matias et al. (2014), the researchers interviewed 16 teacher candidates on what they learned about race and racism in their educator preparation program and how they believe it impacted their development as new teachers. They discovered four themes: (1) teacher candidates were emotionally (dis)invested in racial justice; (2) students recognized that they are White, but did not push themselves beyond that acknowledgment; (3) students resonated in "white guilt"; and (4) there was an overall engagement and endorsement of hegemonic whiteness (p. 293). More explicitly, as in my own study, the White teachers' nonchalant claims that they never experienced racism further reinforced the dominant racist ideologies as did their simple acknowledgments that they are White. In a similar study, Smith and Crowley (2015) investigated how White elementary teacher candidates made sense of issues of race and education through a case study of multiple participants that transformed into a more in-depth look at a single participant. The researchers found what they called a "not race" paradigm in that the participants argued against the salience of race which "took the form of both overt, explicit denials of racism and race privilege, as well as subtler forms of resistance to naming race, such as through an implication that other factors may supersede race as a determining consideration" (p. 22). As in my own study, this is problematic in that the teacher candidates may then remove themselves as racialized beings.

Oftentimes, this "not a race" paradigm that silently endorses hegemonic whiteness will cause White teacher candidates to resist challenges to their deeply entrenched views. For example, Buchanan (2015) reported teacher candidates frequently refer to race discussions as controversial, problematic, uncomfortable, and even offensive to them. House-Niamke and Sato (2019) explored the diversity coursework (weekly reading reflections, an identity paper, and a service-learning reflection paper) of teacher candidates to discover instances of resistance to the existence of systemic oppression in K-12 schools. Much like Matias et al. (2014) and Smith and Crowley (2015), Niamke and Sato (2019) found:

> White people and people of color are susceptible to be inculcated into these grand narratives that work to mask systemic oppression. Thus, when faced

with new evidence that challenged their views, the students responded with resistance. (p. 175)

However, Ohito (2016) found that a pedagogy of discomfort was able to puncture this White supremacist resistance. More specifically, the researcher, a Black teacher educator, and the predominately White teacher candidates collectively made meaning out of racial oppression through an intentional focus on the interactions between their bodies and emotions. Initially, the White teacher candidates reported feelings of racialized anger and fear and yet the discomfort provided an opportunity for them to critically examine their reactions in an effort to "be(come) more vigilant at perceiving and disordering White supremacy" (p. 463). Puchner et al. (2012) also discovered courses with an intentional focus on readings and activities centered on race, racism, and critical White studies could move teacher candidates away from a racist identity as characterized by Helms' obliviousness to racial issues (Contact), confusion about racial issues (Disintegration), or belief in White supremacy (Reintegration). In other words, "the positive change in scores indicates that the race-related courses may have been successful in the short-term at making white students aware of their race and of the need to focus on whites to combat racism" (p. 407).

Similarly, Bryant et al. (2012) found it was possible for teacher candidates to become aware of their racial dispositions and biases and how they impact teaching and learning through an open dialogue of critical reflections on the three-film series *Race: The Power of an Illusion*. The authors analyzed the teacher candidates' narratives through the lens of CRT and uncovered evidence of three of the six tenets: (1) endemic racism, (2) interest convergence/materialist determinism, and (3) race as a social construction. Analogous to my own study, the researchers learned that teacher candidates could not conceptualize race or racism as institutionalized or the inherent privilege experienced in social, political, or economic circumstances. Wender (2017) explored teacher candidate reflections to Jacqueline Woodson's *Hush* in a young adult literature course and found they were either color-blind, acknowledged racial differences but not a White racial identity, directly discussed racism and its harmful effects, or understood racial difference as an external force and an internal awareness.

However, Gachago et al. (2018) analyzed the collective digital storytelling narratives of nine South African teacher candidates in which themes of social segregation, White privilege, internal oppression, and hegemonic standards prevailed. Although the Black teacher candidates attempted to point out injustices and help their peers understand their lived experiences, White teacher candidates were uncomfortable with discussions on race, reacted defensively and refused to take responsibility for past injustices, and displayed anger and frustration in their failure to acknowledge systemic oppression and their position of privilege within in it. In a study of six teacher candidates born outside of the country of their educator preparation program, Farahnaz (2012) found that race was the most significant factor that hindered the "non-White" teacher candidates from asserting their status as native speakers. The White teacher candidates displayed privilege, White superiority, and native speaker status and that they could take advantage of their whiteness to avoid racism. Whereas "non-White" teacher candidates expressed concerns about racism, and they felt their honesty and sincerity were questioned.

However, Kreamelmeyer et al. (2016) observed a statistically significant "shift" in teacher candidate pre- and postintervention preference *toward* color-blindness. The purpose of their study was to examine the impact of a diversity course on teacher candidate acknowledgment of their students' race as it relates to teaching and learning. A sample of 85 teacher candidates enrolled in the diversity course were asked to complete the Common Beliefs Survey created by The Teaching Diverse Students Initiative (TDSI) which identifies beliefs teacher candidates might have about instruction and learning that could have negative consequences on students of diverse races. The researchers found teacher candidates were conscious of their racial bias toward students. However, they attempted to prevent their racial bias from impacting their students by veiling the visible racial difference to ensure equal treatment. In other words, to these teacher candidates

> actively "not seeing color" is equated with "not seeing the bad that I believe about people of that race"—in fact—"not seeing color" in this category, is more synonymous with "seeing children as if they are White" to ensure equitable treatment. (p. 146)

In their study of five teacher candidates of color and one White professor, Bower-Phipps et al. (2013) met biweekly for a year to construct meaning from participants' teacher education program experiences. The researchers found teacher candidates faced significant challenges in respect to their race due to their resistance to discussions of race in the curriculum, isolation, tokenism, and silencing. More specifically, the teacher candidates of color acknowledged their complex racial identities that are beyond the White versus non-White binary:

> [The] members struggled with self-definition. They wanted to authentically represent themselves, yet they acknowledge their sense of "identity crisis." This challenge of self-definition was intensified as teacher candidates of color were asked to be spokespeople for their races during class discussions. Teacher

educators must avoid the practice of tokenism, for it only heightens some teacher candidates' sense of isolation. (p. 8)

Relatedly, Kondo (2019) studied six Black teacher candidates who were enrolled in a diversity course and encountered "front streeting" or the "vulnerability teachers of color experience when their minoritized identities are fetishized in diversity classrooms, through an expectation of confirmed lived experiences or expert knowledge of their demographic groups" (p. 145). The teacher candidates of color were racialized based on assumptions specific to their cultural competencies and experiences such as literacies, specific aesthetic preferences, and/or knowledge of cultural referents. Kraehe (2015) also studied Black teacher candidates and their racialized experiences in their educator preparation program. Through case studies based on interviews from an ethnographic investigation of teacher identity, the researcher found that "in an environment defined by racial silence, making sense of race and racism becomes an integral—but often hidden—part of negotiating an art teacher identity" (p. 204). I believe the researcher argues this is integral to creating radical change movements whereas it may also be seen as an obstacle.

Viesca et al. (2014) determined to conduct their study when they learned teacher candidates of color faced racialized issues in their program focused on social justice and equity. So, they conducted 14 semi-structured interviews with both teacher candidates of color and White teacher candidates. Through a CRT lens, the researchers located a clear pattern that exposed the power of "majoritarian stories of a 'racism without racists' (Bonilla-Silva, 2006) or 'there is no story about race' (Mitchell, 2013)" that were only minimally disrupted through the educator preparation program. Although the teacher candidates of color did attempt to counter these majoritarian stories, the White teacher candidates still expressed White guilt, could not identify their White identity, and were unable to identify issues of race in schools.

Classroom Implications

In her study of the dilemmas and constraints that teacher candidates faced in the final field experience, Pearce (2012) explored their responses to unexamined White norms and priorities in the instructional materials. The researcher found:

> Their ability to recognise, criticise and at times challenge dominate white norms in the schools they served offers support for Ladson-Billings' optimism that new teacher can provide more socially just approaches in the classroom, and can at time challenge more established colleagues' assumptions and practices. (p. 469)

However, VanDuesen (2021) investigated White teacher candidates' discourse about their experiences and interactions with students of color in an immersion field experience. The teacher candidates verbalized *they* were the racial minority in these field experiences and reported feelings of discomfort, distress, fear, and anger reflective of White fragility (DiAngelo, 2011) and White emotionality (Matias, 2016). They also centralized their whiteness as "normal" and privileged themselves with the ability to use their racial identity which again becomes problematic for their future P-12 students who do not possess normalized whiteness.

In an interpretive case study, Martell (2017) used CRT as a framework to analyze how eight elementary teacher candidates teach race in social studies. The researcher discovered two teacher candidates viewed their role as tolerance oriented. They focused on helping their elementary students "tolerate" people who were different than them. Much like the findings in my own study, the teacher candidates in Martell's study portrayed racism as "primarily a result of individual prejudice [and] it sent a message to students that racism is not a normal part of American life, but rather something perpetrated by a small number of individuals" (p. 81). These teacher candidates did not understand the need to teach race and racism as organized within a larger systemic and as a structural social problem. However, in a hopeful indicator of forward progress from my own findings, six of the teacher candidates in Martell's study were more equity-oriented and taught race as part of a larger social structure in which racism is a normal, endemic part of American life. They helped their elementary students understand how race is situated historically and in current events and tied it to the elementary students' sense of fairness. However, Demoiny (2017) also studied teacher candidates' beliefs about race and social studies and how well they believe they are prepared to discuss race with their students. Through interviews with teacher candidates, the researcher learned teacher candidates' family and school background impacted their need to include race in the social studies curriculum. However, even when the teacher candidates wanted to teach race and identified specific strategies, they did not know how to respond to potential controversy. They also couldn't provide specific examples of when they were taught how to discuss race in their educator preparation program.

Campbell and Valauri (2019) examined how teacher candidates situate race within larger social systems through the use of video-cued ethnography (VCE) to facilitate conversations about race between parents of color and teacher candidates. The researchers specifically wanted to learn if the lived experiences of parents of color would "shift" or a change the way teacher candidates conversed about race. They located two key shifts in the teacher candidates as a result of the parents' shared narratives: the necessity to participate in racial conversations to end racial oppression and the importance of recognizing and challenging structural and institutional inequities. For example, the parental "cues" such as those around problematic curriculum and materials pushed the teacher candidates to "think about the need to acknowledge race and racism with young children as part of their future curriculum (Yosso, 2002) regardless of the potential backlash from school officials" (p. 337).

Curriculum and Pedagogy

Bower-Phipps et al. (2013) argued teacher educators need to support teachers of color by understanding their identities, vision, and racialized challenges through intentional discussions about race that do not permit isolation, tokenism, and silencing. Kraehe (2015) also advocated for educator preparation programs to "become attentive and responsive to emergent counter-narratives" (p. 209). As Kondo (2019) explained, "Faculty need to explore how traditionally marginalized students are framed and the relationships required to unpack their funds of knowledge while maintaining their student status" (p. 147). Faez (2012) specifically recommended teacher educators and educator preparation programs:

> Need to problematize the white racial ideology of native-speakerism and deconstruct racial assumptions about who qualifies as a good teacher. In a globalized world where English is recognized as a global language, it is vital to recognize that its speakers or native-speakers need to be positioned globally. Teacher education and TESL program should include content that draws on critical race theory to challenge the inequities that dominate society generally and the teaching profession specifically. (p. 138)

In addition, teacher educators of color, who facilitate these courses should form communities that discuss approaches to manage and address student resistance due to the difficult challenges that may occur (House-Niamke & Sato, 2019). As the researchers argue in this study, these communities provide a necessary and safe space for teacher educators of color to unpack student resistance and approach change movements collectively.

Martell (2017) and Demoiny (2017) called specifically for social studies methods courses that build a framework for how teacher candidates will address race in their future classrooms. In my own study, I argued for a reconceptualization of how prospective teachers need to be challenged to view race and racism and its influence on the social, emotional, and political as situated within these institutions to more wholly recognize the "larger historical patterns, institutionalized process, and everyday practices" of racism (Lewis, 2000, p. 625). This was evident in Martell's division between tolerance-oriented and equity-oriented teacher candidates. Kreamelmeyer et al. (2016) further emphasized "for White educators, to achieve meaningful transformation of color-blindness this intentional discourse cannot occur in sporadic or isolated experiences during preservice or inservice teacher training" (p. 150) and Ohito (2016) advocated for the necessity of a pedagogy of discomfort to detangle the meaning of these intentionally White supremacist discourses that go beyond simply one course. Anti-racist pedagogy should be central to the curriculum of mainstream educator preparation programs (Ohito, 2016). However, educator preparation providers must follow up to determine if potential changes in racialized beliefs result in changes in educational practices with P-12 students (Puchner et al., 2012).

Bryant et al. (2012) identified the curricular and pedagogical value of films as a means to document the construction and sources of race, racial domination, and oppression as well as how racism is maintained through policies and procedures that intentionally marginalize race-based groups. Matias and Zembylas (2014) also recommended video and argued for a more visually representative approach to teacher candidate responses to readings, discussions, and other course activities. More specifically, digital storytelling could be used as a medium for self-reflexivity in understanding the emotional journey of how White teacher candidates understand their racialized experiences as well as counter-stories. Wenger (2021) advocated for the use of young adult literature as:

> A space where we teach attentive listening to other voices . . . . A space where we offer students' diverse versions of the world through well-crafted texts and in discourse with each other; a space where we push students to encounter unknown realities . . . a space where we teach students how to construct meaning and identity. (p. 13)

Gachago et al. (2018) suggested a "world-traveling" space as posited by Lugones (1987) in which teacher candidates could engage across differences beyond the binaries of White fragility and Black pain and beyond independence and indifference to rediscover entanglements and interconnectedness by traveling to each other's' worlds. In other words, we need to experience "somebody else's world, not in her place, but with or next to her" (p. 201). Demoiny (2017) also recommended cross-rail experiences with structured reflections. Viesca et al. (2014) posited "the field of Critical Whiteness Studies (CWS) offers valuable perspectives and models for White teacher candidates to critically examine their positionality, racialization, as well as the distribution of power and privilege across their life experiences" (p. 15).

Field Experiences

In addition, educator preparation providers must create opportunities for teacher candidates to teach in urban settings. This is particularly important for teacher candidates of color so they may serve as role models who value diversity and challenge cultural norms and race-related experiences (Bower-Phipps et al., 2013). Campbell and Valuri (2019) suggested these urban teaching settings also provide an opportunity for White teacher candidates to learn from the racialized lived experiences of parents of color to "shift" how they will address race in their future classrooms. Martell (2017) argued for urban experiences and courses for all teacher candidates, as well.

However, Matias et al. (2019) suggested instead of "field trips" in "Black communities," teacher candidates "should also deconstruct how White communities are normalized as good communities . . . [and] to deconstruct the sense of community and pride there" (p. 302). Smith and Crowley (2015) explained how White teacher candidates often inhabit spaces that do not require even an acknowledgment let alone an interrogation of the implications of their White identity and how they espouse meritocratic views of society while also knowing how race affects the life experiences of people. They argued:

> Rather than struggling with a different mode of lesson design or an alternative instructional methodology, white preservice teachers must grapple with issues of ontology and epistemology. They must rethink their personal histories, the merit of their life accomplishments, and how their place in the world comes at the expense of others. (p. 26)

Buchanan (2015) further advocated for a reoccurrence of opportunities across semesters in which teacher candidates engage in meaningful discourse and activities in multiple courses. A more blended approach between courses and field experiences is needed to create radical change.

The purpose of this chapter was to determine if teacher candidates have transitioned toward this reconceptualized racial framework within the last ten years. Although the studies reviewed demonstrate teacher candidates of all races have not reconceptualized race and racism and implications for their future students within the last ten years, there are still spaces of hope in teacher educators have "shifted" teacher candidates' racial frameworks. In addition, in many of the studies, educator preparation providers perceive they can and will prepare teacher candidates to reconceptualize race and racism in respect to curriculum, pedagogy, courses, field experiences, and other programmatic features. Future research should investigate how these "shifts" in teacher candidate racial frameworks transferred into their P-12 classrooms as well as the immediate and long-term effectiveness of these shifts as well as the recommended curriculum, pedagogy, and field experiences. In the next ten years, we need a change movement that requires teacher candidates and teacher educators alike to not only name their racialized identity but investigate and dismantle the impact on their students.

REFERENCES

Bower-Phipps, L., Watanabe Tate, R., Mehta, S., & Satire, A. (2013). Everyone has a story: A collaborative inquiry project by five teacher candidates of color and one white professor. *Current Issues in Education, 16*(1), 1–14.

Bryant, L. C., Moss, G., & Boudreau, A. Z. (2015). Race dialogues in teacher preparation: Beginning the conversation. *International Journal of Critical Pedagogy, 6*(2), 43–59.

Buchanan, L. B. (2015). "We make it controversial Elementary preservice teachers' beliefs about race. *Teacher Education Quarterly*, Winter, 2015, 3–26.

Campbell, K. H., & Valauri, A. (2019). Our voices matter: Using video-cued ethnography to facilitate a conversation about race between parents of color and preservice teachers. *Anthropology & Education Quarterly, 50*(3), 333–339.

Delgado, R., & Stefancic, J. (2000). *Critical race theory: The cutting edge.* Temple University Press.

Demoiny, S. B. (2017). Are you ready? Elementary pre-service teachers' perceptions about discussing race in social studies. *Multicultural Education*, 15–33.

DiAngelo, R. J. (2011). White fragility. *International Journal of Critical Pedagogy, 3*, 54–70.

Faez, F. (2012). Linguistic identities and experiences of generation 1.5 teacher candidates: race matters. *TESL Canada Journal, 29*(6), 124–141.

Gachago, D., Bozalek, V., & Ng'ambi, D. (2018). Travelling into the other's world: South African pre-service teacher education students' construction of difference, belonging and identity. *South African Journal of Higher Education, 32*(3), 189–208.

Gee, J. P. (2009). *An introduction to discourse analysis: Theory and method* (2nd Ed.). Taylor and Francis, Inc.

House-Niamke, S., & Sato, T. (2019). Resistance to systemic oppression by students of color in a diversity course for preservice teachers. *Educational Studies, 55*(2), 160–179.

Kondo, C. S. (2019). Front streeting: Teacher candidates of color and the pedagogical challenges of cultural relevancy. *Anthropology & Education Quarterly, 50*(2), 135–150.

Kraehe, A. M. (2015). Sounds of silence: Race and emergent counter-narratives of art teacher identity. *Studies in Art Education: A Journal of Issues and Research, 56*(3), 199–213.

Kreamelmeyer, K., Kline, A., Zygmunt, & Clark, P. (2016). To see or not to see: Preservice teacher attitudes toward color blindness. *The Teacher Educator, 51*, 136–152.

Lewis, B. F., Collins, A., & Pitts, V. (2000). *An investigation of preservice teachers' perceptions of African American students' ability to achieve in mathematics and science.* Paper presented at the Annual Meeting of the American Educational Research Association, New Orleans, LA.

Martell, C. C. (2017). Approaches to teaching race in elementary social studies: A case study of preservice teachers. *The Journal of Social Studies Research, 41,* 75–87.

Matias, C. E., & Zembylas, M. (2014). When saying you care is not really caring': Emotions of disgust, whiteness ideology, and teacher education. *Critical Studies in Education, 3,* 319–337.

Matias, C. E. (2016). *Feeling white: Whiteness, emotionality, and education.* Sense Publishers.

Matias, C. E., Viesca, K. M., Garrison-Wade, D. F., Tandon, M., & Galindo, R. (2014). "What is critical whiteness doing in OUR nice field like critical race theory?" Applying CRT and CWS to understand the white imaginations of white teacher candidates. *Equity & Excellence in Education, 47*(3), 289–304.

Moher, D., Shamseer, L., Clarke, M., Ghersi, D., Liberati, A., Petticrew, M. Shekelle, P., & Stewart, L. A. (2015). Preferred reporting items for systematic reviews and meta-analysis protocols (PRISMA-P) 2015 statement. *Systematic Reviews, 4*(1), 1–9.

Mutua, A. D. (2006). The rise, development and future directions of critical race theory and related scholarship. *Denver University Law Review, 84*(2), 329–394.

Ohito, E. O. (2016). Making the emperor's new clothes visible in anti-racist teacher education: Enacting a pedagogy of discomfort with white preservice teachers. *Equity & Excellence in Education, 49*(4), 454–467.

Pearce, S. (2012). Confronting dominant whiteness in the primary classroom: Progressive student teachers' dilemmas and constraints. *Oxford Review of Education, 38*(4), 455–472.

Puchner, L., Szabo, Z., & Roseboro, D. L. (2012). The short-term effect of a race-related course on racial identity of white students. *Teaching in Higher Education, 17*(4), 399–410.

Smith, W. I., & Crowley, R. M. (2015). Pushback and possibility: Using a threshold concept of race in social studies teacher education. *The Journal of Social Studies Research, 39,* 17–28.

VanDeusen, A. (2021). Revealing whiteness in preservice music teacher preparation. *Action, Criticism, and Theory for Music Education, 20*(1), 121–141.

Viesca, K. M., Matias, C. E., Garrison-Wade, D., Tandon, M., & Galindo, R. (2014). "Push it real good." The challenge of disrupting dominant discourses regarding race in teacher education. *Critical Education, 5*(11), 1–24.

Wender, E. (2021). Developing conceptions of racial difference: Pre-service teachers in a swing state read Hush during the fall 2016 presidential election. *Ohio Journal of English Language Arts, 57*(1), 7–13.

Williams, N. V. (2011). Anti-racist teacher education curriculum: Toward a reconceptualization of the racial framework of prospective teachers. *Surveying Borders, Boundaries, and Contested Spaces in Curriculum and Pedagogy,* 209–224.

Wilson, M. B., & Kumar, T. (2017). Long ago and far away: Preservice teachers' (mis)conceptions surrounding racism. *International Journal of Multicultural Education, 19*(2), 182–198.

Yosso, T. J. (2006). Whose culture has capital? A critical race theory discussion of community cultural wealth. In A. D. Dixson & C. K. Rousseau (Eds.), *Critical race theory in education: All God's children got a song* (pp. 191–212). Taylor & Francis.

Chapter 6

The Value of Gathering Unofficially at Predominately White Institutions

Meet Me in the Third Space

Jennifer K. Shah

Destiny was one of the only Latina students in my introductory-level education class at a small liberal arts college in the Midwest. She never spoke in class and told me she hated group work. Having my own lived experiences as one of few if any BIPOC (Black, Indigenous, and/or People of Color) students in my own teacher preparation program, I understood how she felt. I invited Destiny to join me at a conference on our campus that focused on equity and social justice where she took on a leadership role and vocalized much of what she had learned in my class as well as her own lived experiences. As the year went on, we developed a close-knit relationship. One day I asked Destiny why her demeanor in class drastically differed from her leadership at the conference, which she then attended year after year. Her response was simply, "It's just different." In further conversations with Destiny, I learned about the value of third spaces at predominantly white institutions, particularly for BIPOC students. This chapter will elaborate on the concept of third spaces by telling the story of what happened next and how this moment created a movement for our campus community.

Third spaces, such as the social justice-oriented conference mentioned earlier, are already present on our campuses (Soja, 2004) and serve as a middle ground between classrooms and personal spaces. Third spaces are often hosted by Academic Affairs departments (e.g., Office of Multicultural Affairs), though sometimes academic departments also initiate them. What makes third spaces unique is that they take a reciprocal approach to knowledge creation (Hallman, 2012) and aim to bring students' individual lived experiences to the forefront (Kirkland, 2010). In third spaces, "binaries are challenged and new possibilities and spaces for meaning-making are created" (Hallman, 2012, p. 244). These intentionally created spaces allow for BIPOC students to share and build on each other's experiences and focus on peer learning (Cochran-Smith & Villegas, 2015; Zeichner, 2010). I contend that third spaces are valuable for all who participate voluntarily, despite race or other social identities. While affinity groups certainly occur in the third space, not all third spaces are characterized as affinity groups.

MOVIE CLUBS AS THIRD SPACES

Destiny was not the only one who saw value in third spaces at our institution. The following semester, Margarita, Sofia, and Suzanna (pseudonyms chosen by participants) approached me about hosting a movie club for education majors. That month, ten teacher candidates and I watched the first episode of *America to me*, a documentary series by Kartemquin Films about the racial inequities at Oak Park River Forest High School. The conversation after the viewing lasted well into the night. The following morning, the same three teacher candidates were waiting outside my office. They wanted to talk, share, and understand more about why they felt so energized. A participatory action research study resulted in some major findings including the importance of differentiated social justice curriculum through nontraditional uses of text and that female teachers of color felt more seen and heard in third spaces on campus which varied from their traditional classroom experience, because it disrupted power dynamics (see Shah & Apantenco, 2020).

What was very clear was that the classroom, even mine, was in fact different from other purposefully created, social justice–oriented spaces on campus. Margarita explained to me that the biggest threat to authentically speaking her mind in the classroom was fear of white fragility. In our focus group, she stated,

> In the classroom, you have to be careful with what you say more or less, because whatever happened, the students sometimes . . . do not want to be part of that conversation. Then for you to say something . . . puts this sort of tension between you guys later. And so you have to be careful not to offend anybody even though sometimes you feel like you should push back.

On the other hand, Margarita explained that the voluntary participation in third spaces outside of the classroom allowed her to be her authentic self without worrying. Peers who opted into these conversations were more willing to be open during discussions about race, specifically. She elaborated,

Whereas with the book and movie club, I can say what I want because these people want to be here. These people are interested in talking about this and having a lot of them can at least relate to one thing that was going on in the movie. And even if they don't relate, they're having that empathy and they're willing to put in the work to have that empathy. Whereas in the classroom, you can't really do that.

Similar to Margarita, Susana described the advantage of the third space as "purposeful without the pressure." It is clear that Margarita and Susana felt more comfortable sharing their perspectives during movie clubs rather than in class, even those they took with me. Creating third spaces for students, with students, and by students made space for female teacher candidates of color to be themselves and state their point of view based on their lived experiences.

Fast forward one year, and I began to see the value of third spaces for all students, not just teacher candidates in our department. After receiving a portion of the campus-wide Ashoka Changemaker grant, I moved forward with the creation of campus-wide movie clubs. This undertaking was much bigger than anything I had done before. I was only in my second year as an assistant professor at the time and had barely made campus-wide connections, but that was all about to change.

With my mission and vision explicitly articulated, I began to recruit students, faculty, and staff who were similarly interested in third space movie clubs on our campus. We assembled into three teams: a design team, an implementation team, and a research team. The design team was composed of undergraduate and graduate students from various departments including education, staff from the Office of Multicultural Affairs and the Center for Social Impact, and me. Our task was to create a format for the campus-wide movie clubs, which included agreements for participation (Appendix A) and a flow of events. The intention was to tweak the format based on feedback from the other two teams.

The implementation team was the most interesting aspect of this research. This team consisted of only undergraduate students with me as a bystander. Half the team were teacher candidates who were also members of a student-led organization focused on equity and social justice known as Project LEAD (Leaders in Education Advocating for Diversity), of which I was the faculty sponsor. The other half of the implementation team was composed of student leaders of other student-led organizations such as the Black Student Association (BSA), the Latinx Student Association (LSA), or the Muslim Student Association (MSA). Typically around ten to twelve students would meet at a designated time to discuss the movie/documentary which all of them had previously independently screened. Their goal during this time was to agree on three discussion questions that would integrate into the movie club dialogue. Topics such as illegal immigration, the prison industrial complex, and domestic terrorism led to heated discussions as multiple viewpoints and lived experiences emerged. Though there were disagreements, there was also empathy. As time went on, the voices who's lived experiences in the movie/documentary mirrored their own got louder in a way that reminded me of Destiny's positive experience the year before. Ultimately, all implementation teams came up with questions for each of the movie club dialogues (Appendix B). All team members were also dialogue facilitators at the movie club events and offered anecdotal feedback afterward.

Finally, the research team in the initial year of the movie clubs consisted of another BIPOC female junior faculty member and me. While we asked students if they would like to research this topic, all declined our request. The reason is currently unknown to me, but I would like to venture that perhaps the workload seemed daunting or that they were content with participating on the other two teams. The research team analyzed survey data collected after each of the movie clubs. Our responsibility was to analyze the findings and report back to the design team so that changes could be made toward growth.

The movie club hosted two events in the 2019–2020 academic year: one in collaboration with BSA and another with the LSA. Just before Halloween, over fifty students, faculty, and staff gathered at our newly renovated Student Activities Center to watch and discuss Eva Duvarney's Netflix original documentary, *13th*, which focuses on the industrial prison complex in the United States and how it disproportionately affects African Americans. We ate deep-dish pizza for dinner and all were encouraged to sit at tables with other students, faculty, and staff that they did not know. Participants at these tables also introduced themselves only by first names. When most were finished with their dinner, we viewed the documentary as a community in the same space. After the viewing, facilitators from the implementation team at each table led a discussion based on issues brought up by what they saw and heard. All participants were also encouraged to ask their own questions.

It was well beyond the 9:00 p.m. stop time, and some groups were still intently discussing issues related to the 13th Amendment. I walked over to a table and found one of the heads of our African American Alumni Association surrounded by many of our mainly African American students. They were asking him all kinds of questions and eagerly awaiting his response. After the conversation ended, I had a chance to discuss what took place with our representative from the Alumni Association. He told me that over the years he had several opportunities to speak to students in the classroom, but that this somehow, "just feels different." His words reminded me of Destiny's comments yet again. Was this space in fact different? If so, what was it that made this space so different? A few things came to mind. First, all participants were there voluntarily and wanted to dig into the topic through discussion. As often happens in college, I had thought that many were there for the free food too, but the survey results proved me wrong.

Of the 50 participants, twenty-nine filled out a Qualtrics survey after attending the movie club. Of those, 58.62 percent identified as White, 24.14 percent identified as Black, 6.9 percent as Latinx, 6.9 percent as Asian, and 3.45 percent as other. As far as gender, 48.28 percent identified as female while 44.83 percent identified as male with 6.90 percent identifying as non-binary. An overwhelming 86.2 percent of participants identified as students while 6.90 percent identified as faculty, 3.45 percent as staff, and 3.45 percent as community members.

When asked for all the reasons why they chose to attend the event that day, zero percent of participants identified that they came for the dinner. On the contrary, data shows that 58.62 percent of participants were interested in the topic of race relations and 31.03 percent wanted to dialogue with others on the topic (see table 6.1).

When it came to questions regarding safety, feeling heard, and listening to other perspectives, participant reactions were motivating. One hundred percent of survey participants felt very safe or somewhat safe in the movie club space while 72.41 percent indicated that they felt they were heard to a great extent. No survey participants indicated that they felt that they had not been heard. Finally, 96.55 percent of survey participants said that they heard what others had to say to a great extent. Even more encouraging, 100 percent of participants said that they gained new insights due to this experience (see table 6.2).

When asked about the main takeaways of this experience through an open-ended qualitative response, the answers varied but were overwhelmingly centered on raising awareness about the histories and varied lived experiences of marginalized communities. One participant also wrote about their voice being heard while another indicated that more dialogues such as these were needed on campus (see table 6.3).

Overall, the findings from the first movie club survey demonstrated that the third space created was in fact different from the classroom experience. Of

Table 6.1 Reasons that Students, Faculty, and Staff Chose to Attend the Movie Club

Answer	Percentage	Number of responses
Interest in the topic of race relations	58.62	17
Free food	0	0
Interested in dialogue across the campus	31.03	9
Friends were going	3.45	1
Other	6.90	2

Table 6.2 Feelings of Safety

Answer	Percentage	Number of responses
Very safe	75.86	22
Somewhat safe	24.14	7
Somewhat unsafe	0.00	0
Very unsafe	0.00	0
Total	100	29

the open-ended answers, one stood out to me: a BIPOC student in this space explicitly indicated that they felt heard. I wondered if this event had been a unique, one-time experience in general that perhaps could not be replicated. It turns out that it was not.

In February of the same academic year, the movie club with LSA watched a PBS documentary, *Beyond Borders: Undocumented Mexican Americans*. Before this took place, the research team relayed information from the first survey to the design team. The design team then made appropriate changes such as having the event in a larger space and choosing a shorter movie but having a lengthier discussion time. What I remember most from that time, though, was the implementation team meeting. Two weeks before the event, a team of five Project LEAD ambassadors and five members of the LSA Executive Board sat in a room for over two hours discussing and deciding on the questions for the movie club. Students shared personal stories, shed tears, and ultimately forged a connection between insiders and outsiders to this topic, perhaps due to their own personal or familial histories or the current political climate. I urged for some consensus regarding the discussion questions and one Latinx student offered to write our ideas on the board. Ideas included DACA, being referred to as an illegal alien, how the political

Table 6.3 Participant Takeaways after the First Movie Club (Open-Ended and Optional)

Question: What was your biggest takeaway from the movie club experience?
Student openness to this film.
We need systemic change in this country. It left me with the question of how can I help change that?
Things are usually worse than we think.
We look back and think it's an atrocity to have slaves or have segregation but the time of treating people differently because of their skin.
Inequality and racism are systemic and until we fix our institutions, it will never go away.
That I felt like my voice was heard.
Racial injustices are loud, they are prevalent, and they are relevant.
Every student at the College should see this film.
More dialogues needed. People need to be aware of bigger problems. Depth of racial issues.

climate dehumanized undocumented persons, and the cost of the American Dream. I was jazzed for this conversation to take place with the larger campus community.

On a rather chilly early March evening, we hosted the second movie club experience on our campus. It was energizing to see that BSA members from the last movie club were present in support of their LSA peers. Sixteen participants completed the post-viewing survey, and results were very similar to the first movie club.

This time around, 16 out of the 35 movie club participants completed the post viewing survey. Of those, 43.75 percent identified as White and 12.5 percent as Black, 12.5 percent as Latinx, 6.25 percent as Middle Eastern or North African, 6.25 percent as biracial, and 18.75 percent as multiracial (with some of these categories being created as a result of feedback). Similar to the first movie club, 50 percent of participants identified as female and 43.75 percent as male with one participant identifying as nonbinary. At this movie club, 8.57 percent gave food as a reason for attending the event while 40 percent of participants listed interest in the topic of race relations and other issues such as immigration and another 40 percent came due to their interest in dialogue across campus.

In the area of safety, 88 percent of participants stated that they were very comfortable or somewhat comfortable with the dialogue at the movie club. An overwhelming 94 percent of survey participants felt safe to express their views in this space, and 93.75 percent agreed to a great extent that they heard what others had to say. Yet again, 100 percent of survey participants agreed that they gained new insights based on this experience. When asked about their biggest takeaway in an optional open-ended question, answers varied from learning about differences to building compassion (see table 6.4).

Empathy begins with building awareness. Anecdotal evidence from the LSA student facilitators indicated that when they were able to share about their own lived experiences and see them valued by others on their campus, they felt a sense of being seen and heard. The most impactful comment here from the survey to them was from a White peer who said that their biggest takeaway was to "Learn more. Hear others."

A third and final movie club was planned with MSA in April of 2020, but in mid-March, the COVID-19 pandemic led to a shutdown of our in-person classes and events. Our Ashoka grant funding also ran out and was nonrenewable. I was devastated, but also relieved because at the time I could not imagine how I would continue promoting third spaces and movie clubs on our campus. After two months of struggling to imagine the next steps in a pandemic world, innovation finally showed up and Project Reconnect was born.

Table 6.4 Participant Takeaways after the Second Movie Club (Open-Ended and Optional)

What was your biggest takeaway from this experience?

I learned a lot about different students' ideas and experiences and am excited to know that so many people feel so strongly and passionately about this topic.

I should expand my knowledge on other issues and advocate for more groups than my own. America has done a disservice to many groups that have contributed greatly to society.

People can be very uneducated on certain subjects and you sometimes have to educate them on these topics.

People are willing to have the difficult conversations on campus that need to be had, especially on this campus. It's reassuring.

There are many different groups with many different problems throughout the world.

Compassion is very important in understanding different cultures.

Compassion and effort to understand is crucial as a participating student on this campus.

I learned more about immigration laws and dialogue across differences.

That the struggle we all face is different based on many aspects of life including geographic location and language barriers.

I owe it to my fellow humans to always strive to become more aware of their experiences.

Learn more. Hear others.

VIRTUAL MOVIE CLUBS

The name for Project Reconnect came from a desire to *reconnect* during a time of social isolation, but it was also about helping students, faculty, and staff unlearn what we think we knew and with new information through movie events and discussion around social justice. The most important feature of the new project was that it was virtual and therefore, free! I ran Project Reconnect myself during the summer months more for ease than any other reason. Each discussion took place on the 13th of each month via Zoom. This date was chosen as it connected to our first movie club around the injustices of the 13th Amendment. In June, Project Reconnect hosted a discussion around a television series called *Mixed-ish*. In July, we watched the film *Just Mercy* and in August, we discussed questions about Trevor Noah's book, *Born a Crime* (Appendix C). I used Flipgrid as a platform for Project Reconnect and uploaded videos and discussion questions myself. Each conversation drew an average of two to four other participants and I did not administer a post-viewing survey. Despite the groups being small, the conversations were robust and one student in particular attended each of the three conversations, contributing each time.

At the end of the summer, a colleague approached me and asked if I was interested in having Project Reconnect be a part of community-engaged learning for a class that she was teaching. The class focused heavily on human-centered design and building empathy and was an immediate fit. That semester I met weekly with five students completing the project in their LEAD100 class. As a group, we decided to partner with MSA—as that was the fair thing to do—and we planned an in-person event for the fall semester of 2020. Each student took on a different role: two students served as community-engaged liaisons to MSA, one student took on marketing, another took on logistics, and the fifth student was in charge of data collection. It was important to me to have their participation and the participation of the student organization. I realized that I was not comfortable hosting virtual movie events and coming up with the discussion questions myself, particularly on topics where I was not an insider. As it turned out, one of the students was also an active member of MSA and served as a bridge between the two groups of students.

The team worked closely with MSA leadership and decided to do things slightly differently. Instead of showing just one documentary or film, the students wanted to show scenes from a film and use a YouTube "cut lineup" video in order to discuss Islamophobia. I found great contrast between the two forms of media that they chose. Scenes from *Mooz-lum* (an American Independent film) discussed the 9/11 attacks and their effects on a Muslim college student very seriously while the YouTube video discussed Islamic stereotypes in a more light-hearted way. My understanding is that MSA chose bits and pieces of media that they wanted to use to tell their story instead of using just one. Fifteen participants including the Project Reconnect team and MSA Executive Board members gathered in October on Zoom as the event had to be adapted from being in person to being virtual due to the pandemic again. Survey results from this movie club are the intellectual property of the LEAD100 students and will be shared elsewhere, but they echo the findings from the previous movie club events.

CONCLUSIONS AND INSIGHTS

Two years after the initial movie club, it is time to focus on yet another transformation for the fall of 2021. What the movie club will look like now is yet to be determined. Will we room and zoom this time? Will there be an ability to have food at future events? For the next movie club, Project Reconnect will bring together students from all over our campus including Project LEAD ambassadors, LEAD100 students, the International Club executive board, and student members of The Asian Konnection in order to educate the community regarding Asian American history and promote the message of putting a stop to AAPI Hate. Insights from the previous years will hopefully make this next event meaningful.

After reading this chapter, I hope that others will get inspired to start third space movie clubs on their own campuses or in their own communities, because they offer a unique opportunity for purposeful conversations on a campus without the pressures of a classroom environment. For those looking to do so, I would like to offer some insights I have gained through this process. First is the importance of creating partnerships by reaching out to the various Academic Affairs departments. The support provided by the Office of Multicultural Affairs and the Center for Social Impact was significant especially considering logistical issues and connection with student leadership. Staff in these departments who regularly worked with student organizations were able to make connections between the movie club and students. The trust that students had in staff that they regularly interacted with contributed to their willingness to work with the movie club. Staff also helped with booking venues, ordering massive amounts of food, and thinking about other logistical issues that I, as faculty, was unfamiliar with.

Second, a keystone of third space movie clubs is also the partnership with student organizations whether that be one or many. The insider information and authenticity that members of the student leadership brought to this project are imperative. Students played an important role throughout this entire process from helping with marketing and social media to choosing the media and discussion questions. Third space movie clubs led by grassroots efforts on our campus built toward more awareness around issues of equity and inclusion and student involvement was always at the center. Based on anecdotal evidence and conversations with those involved, I know that students felt a sense of ownership of these events.

Third, one aspect of student leadership that came about organically was the ability for at least one student to be able to code switch on the implementation team or essentially play for both teams. What I mean by that is that one student was able to be part of the planning team and have lived experiences as an insider with the group trying to build awareness. For example, one student was a leader in Project Reconnect and a member of the BSA, LSA, or MSA. Although this is not always an option, there is a notable difference when it is possible. It adds a layer of authenticity to the event.

Finally, when bringing together students, faculty, and staff, one must consider power dynamics, especially in third spaces meant to disrupt them. One of the factors that sometimes, but not always, led to a more equitable space was the use of only first names in the third space movie clubs. All students, faculty, and staff introduced themselves only by their first names and why they chose to attend the event that night. Though many could tell who was who due to factors including but not limited to age, titles and roles on campus were purposely left out. All participants were reminded that rank did not amount to more space in the conversation. Rounds of structured and unstructured dialogue allowed all voices to be heard, though unstructured dialogue was preferred according to survey feedback.

Overall, Destiny was right, third spaces were different and offered an opportunity to build awareness, compassion, and empathy on our campus around issues of equity in a way that felt more authentic for our BIPOC students mostly because the people who attended these events wanted to be there and wanted to learn and grow. Third spaces also allowed for our BIPOC students to lead the conversation. At our campus, we are just getting started. Will you meet me in the third space?

SOMETHING TO READ, DO, OR CONSIDER

Consider hosting a social justice-oriented movie club at your institution. What would be the mission and vision for your own movie club? Are there student organizations on your campus that might want to participate and lead such events? What about Student Affairs? For those interested in such an idea, the first step might be to form a team consisting of faculty, staff, and students and coming up with next steps.

REFERENCES

Cochran-Smith, M., & Villegas, A. M. (2015). Studying teacher preparation: The questions that drive research. *European Educational Research Journal, 14*, 379–394.

Hallman, H. L. (2012). Community-based field experiences in teacher education: possibilities for a pedagogical third space. *Teaching Education, 23*(3), 241.

Kirkland, D. (2010). Englishes in urban contexts: Politics, pluralism, and possibilities. *English Education, 42*(3), 293–306.

Soja, E. (2004). *Postmodern Geographies: The reassertion of space in critical social theory* (2nd ed.). Verso.

Zeichner, K. (2010). Rethinking of connections between campus courses and field experiences in college- and university-based teacher education. *Journal of Teacher Education, 61*(1–2), 89–99. https://doi.org/10.1177/0022487109347671

Media utilized in the movie clubs:

Barris, K., Saji, P., & Ellis Ross, T. (2019). *Mixed-ish*. ABC.

Basir, Q., & Glover, D. (2011). *Mooz-lum*. Lionsgate.

Cretton, D. D. (2019). *Just mercy*. Warner Brothers.

DuVernay, A., & Moran, J. (2016). *13th*. Netflix.

James, S., Liu, B., Parrish, R., & Shaw, K. (2018). *America to me*. Prime video.

Krause, E., Perlmutter, A. H., & Fink, M. (2016). *Beyond borders: Undocumented Mexican Americans* (PBS Version). Independent Production Fund, Editorial Clio, Fabrica de Cine.

Noah, T. (2017). *Born a crime*. John Murray.

APPENDIX A

Movie Club Agreements

Welcome, we are glad that you are here. In this space, we will watch films/documentaries and/or read books and articles around issues of diversity and inclusion including race, gender, class, orientation, religion, ability, nationality, ethnicity, and intersections between them. Please note that some of the texts may elicit an emotional response. In order to facilitate conversation, the movie club team came up with the following agreements that were adapted from Essential Partners, a 501(c)3 organization (https://whatisessential.org/).

Agreements: *We ask that all who participate adhere to these agreed upon statements. These agreements are in place in order to allow everyone to feel welcome and heard.*

- Share the air: I will "flow up" and "flow back" in conversations as it pertains to the conversation. This will allow for all who want to share the floor with me to do so. Flowing up refers to being bold and speaking my truth while flowing back means knowing when to let others speak when I have spoken enough or have held the floor for longer than a few minutes.
- Avoid judgment without cause: I will avoid making negative attributions about the beliefs, values, and motives of other participants (e.g., "You only say that because . . ."). When tempted to do so, I will consider the possibility of testing the assumption I am making by asking a question (e.g., Can you tell me more?).
- Speak your truth: I will speak for myself. I will not ask others to represent, defend, or explain an entire group.

However, if speaking from my experience and my heart requires me to mention my group identity or connectedness to a group with purpose, I will feel empowered to do so.

- I will avoid making grand pronouncements and instead, connect what I am saying to what I know and believe to be my experiences, influences in my life, and particular sources of information I know.
- Respect confidentiality: If asked to keep something confidential, I will honor the request. In conversations outside of the group, I will not attribute particular statements to particular individuals by name or identifying information without permission.

APPENDIX B

Movie Club Sample Questions

LatinX Student Association Movie Club

- How has the political climate in the United States shaped the narrative and misconceptions about immigration and undocumented people living in the United States?
- What do you think people are chasing when they pursue the American dream?
- What was your biggest takeaway from this experience? What are you taking from what you heard here that you want to continue to think about, dialogue about, or work on in our community?"

Muslim Student Association Movie Club

- In the film, after hearing about the 9/11 attacks, the professor is on the phone and says "I'm thinking about dropping an email on behalf of Muslims on campus . . . I'm worried this could really get out of control." Additionally, during the mob attack, one of the girls screams, "We are not terrorists!" Why do you think the first instinct of many Muslims after hearing about an attack has to be in defense of themselves and their faith?
- In the movie, the characters experience great bias and discrimination. Can you describe a time when you have experienced or witnessed Islamophobia? How was it handled?
- When watching the Cut: Lineup video did you make the same assumptions as those that were guessing? Why do you think you did that? Where do you think that comes from?
- Were your ideas of what Islam looks like challenged after watching the Cut: Lineup video? Why or why not?
- What has watching these videos/having these discussions taught you about your own implicit biases and what can you do to change things going forward?
- If you identify as Muslim, is there anything else you would like to share that you would want those of us who do not practice Islam to know?

Born a Crime Questions

- Do you ever feel like you live between two (or more) cultures?
- How does language play a role in Trevor's life? Does it create barriers or provide unity? How does language play a role in your own life?
- What is grit? Does Trevor Noah possess grit? Can grit be positive and negative? If so, how?

- How does this book contribute to your own understanding of the current state of race relations in the United States?
- What was your opinion of Trevor's mom and the role she played in his life or the choices she made for her own life?
- What are some of your favorite parts of this memoir? What made you laugh out loud?

APPENDIX C

Project Reconnect Summer 2020 Timeline

Black lives matter. If you are looking for a place to learn about how to work toward being anti-racist, check out Project Reconnect. This informal book and movie club with an initial focus on racism toward the Black community gives students, faculty, and staff a chance to come together during this period of social isolation and use media for conversations related to current events. On June, July, and August 13, we will gather online via Zoom and ask that you view media before joining our conversation. We welcome you for any amount of time that you can attend, whether or not you have had time to view the media.

Here is the current lineup:

June 13, 5:00 p.m. to 6:30 p.m.: *Mixed-ish*: Episodes 1, 2, 20, and 23 (T.V. series)
July 13, 5:00 p.m. to 6:30 p.m.: *Just Mercy* (movie)
August 13, 5:00 p.m. to 6:30 p.m.: *Born a Crime* by Trevor Noah (book)

Want to join or have questions? Go to: https://flipgrid.com/projectreconnect
We will use Flipgrid to communicate with each other in between our online sessions.
We hope you will join us as we learn, grow, and change as a community. The time is right, right now.

Chapter 7

Disrupting Institutional Racism in Higher Education

Beyond the Cultural Keeping in Curriculum

Vanessa M. Rigaud and Jody Googins

INTRODUCTION

Notable efforts have been made within the last decade to incorporate diversity and cultural awareness into curriculum instruction. Nevertheless, challenges remain in the curriculum's design and intentionality that fully embrace the United States' changing demographics. The United States Census Bureau (2018) estimated that by 2020 the post-millennial population—minorities (under 18)—would be in the majority, while Whites will be in the minority. By 2060, the combined racial minority population will grow by 74 percent. The steady increase in our nation's diversity over the years has gained significant attention. However, multicultural education continues to marginalize non-Whites because it is embedded in, and couched in the perspective of, the norms of the dominant White American culture. According to Banks (2014), "Multicultural education is a reform movement designed to make some major changes in the education of students" (p. 1). Existing research suggests that cultural transformation is necessary to improve learning among the diverse student population of the twenty-first century; however, this work continues to lag behind (Aronson & Laughter, 2016; Banks, 2014; Ladson-Billings, 2006; 2014).

This chapter addresses the complexity of multicultural education/Culturally Responsive Pedagogy curriculum design, specifically in a teacher preparation program. It brings forth culturally responsive practices that can navigate race, ethnicity, class, sexual identity, gender, language, nationality, learning differences, religion, and age in the classroom. Two mini-instrumental case studies will be presented, shedding light and giving evidence to the importance of designing a curriculum with intentionality. Furthermore, it will provide strategies, discourse, and leadership in educational practices that call all learners to the table for global partnership. This chapter will go beyond the cultural keeping that prevails in classrooms in the United States and engage in culturally responsive practices, leading to a new transformation among all students.

POSITIONALITY

Our (authors Vanessa and Jody) journeys have significantly influenced our approaches to curriculum and classrooms in our teacher preparation program, which are detailed herein. We are two early career professors at a mid-sized, private institution in the United States. Vanessa began at our current institution in 2016, while Jody began in 2020. We are both former public school teachers, which informs our interest in teacher preparation and culturally responsive pedagogy (CRP). It is something we both inherently practiced before formal researching, reading, and learning gave us the theoretical foundation and language to understand and implement CRP more fully.

I (Vanessa) am completing my fifth year of teaching as a junior professor at our mid-sized, private university. My teacher preparation work in the school of education is guided by 15 years of teaching in the K-12 classroom and 10 years as a school administrator, which includes 5 years of international work in China. I am a Haitian American, Black, middle-class, cisgender woman born in the United States. The curiosity around culture and ethnicity commenced at the early age of four due to frequent family world travel. My profound love for diverse traditions and customs is woven into all of my prior teaching practices. During my years in higher education, this has been augmented with the intensity of intentionality in my current research of CRP and multicultural education.

I (Jody) am a first-year, junior professor at our mid-sized, private institution. As a former 18-year high school teacher, I am able to reflect back and acknowledge my lack of preparation for navigating the complexities of a diverse classroom, especially early in my career. I am a White, middle-class, cisgender woman. My interactions in classrooms with adolescents were always guided blindly by intuition, and it was not until I enrolled in a PhD program that I was able to put a name to my instincts, to understand the theoretical underpinnings of my daily decisions. It is through the lens of practitioner and scholar that I approach the work of modeling and integrating CRP with intentionality into my research and our teacher preparation program.

GUIDING PRINCIPLES OF CRP

In the early 1990s, Dr. Gloria Ladson-Billings (1995) introduced the concept of CRP, a pedagogical framework that centers on three guiding principles: "academic achievement, cultural competence, and sociopolitical consciousness." These guiding principles work in unison with one another—videlicet, a culturally relevant instructor cannot focus on one principle without also integrally converging on the others (Ladson-Billings, 2006). Later in 2014, after an experience with Paris' (2012) work, Ladson-Billings (2014) enhanced her theory to be more inclusive and published "Culturally Relevant Pedagogy 2.0: a.k.a. the Remix." For the purpose of this chapter, we will examine the current expansive model of CRP.

Academic Achievement

Academic achievement places the onus on instructors to cultivate the minds of their learners. CRP holds the notion that effective teaching happens when the expectations are clear and meet the learners where they are at presently (Ladson-Billings, 2006). One must examine, from students' perspectives, how their curricular content will transform their understandings of themselves and of the world.

The instructor must know the content and reflect on it deeply, understand why they are teaching it, and examine how they will teach based on what they know about the learner. Most importantly, how will this knowledge propel the learner? Hence, student learning occurs when we cultivate the mind (Ladson-Billings, 2006). To cultivate the mind, it is necessary to unpack lived experiences that allow students to engage in deep, profound metacognition and synthesis which brings in a greater depth of knowledge and comprehension of the course content. Gay (2010) explains, "When academic knowledge and skills are taught within the lived experiences and frames of reference of students, they are more personally meaningful, have higher interest appeal, and are learned more easily and thoroughly" (p. 31). This work of academic achievement is paramount to lay the foundation for a course's content delivery, and it functions in unison with the two other guiding principles of cultural competence and sociopolitical consciousness.

Cultural Competence

According to Ladson-Billings (2006), cultural competence can be explained in this way:

> [Cultural competence] refers to helping students to recognize and honor their own cultural beliefs and practices while acquiring access to the wider culture,

where they are likely to have a chance of improving their socioeconomic status and making informed decisions about the lives they wish to lead. (p. 36)

A culturally relevant pedagogy is cognizant that students need to appropriate certain skills to navigate the world around them, and of the requirement to furnish students with expertise needed to triumph in an educational system that decenters their ideas and thoughts. To achieve this competence, teachers must expose their students to the reality of culture and systemic racism that oppresses others or themselves (Delpit, 2006; Ladson-Billings, 2006). How do we expose students to a broader world and empower them to surmount these obstacles? Our greatest challenge, which we have the power to impact as educators, is to prepare a curriculum that embeds students' personal and cultural knowledge while assisting them in extending beyond their cultural boundaries in the hopes that they will be the impetus for radical change in our K-12 classrooms. Gaining cultural competence can raise a teacher's sociopolitical consciousness, the third guiding principle of CRP.

Sociopolitical Consciousness

In our current times, the topic of sociopolitical consciousness remains ubiquitous, often resulting in avoidance by teachers for fear of misrepresentation. Sociopolitical consciousness begins with teachers understanding and educating themselves around sociopolitical issues of race, ethnicity, class, sexual identity, gender, language, nationality, learning differences, religion, and age; then analyzing the causes of inequities before integrating these topics into curriculum (Ladson-Billings, 2006, p. 37). How can we move students to examine the community they serve and the reality that exists in social constructs to foster greater awareness of themselves and others? As teachers, we seek to enhance student's sociopolitical consciousness by allowing "students to recognize, understand, and critique current and social inequalities" (Ladson-Billings, 1995, p. 476).

In developing the CRP curriculum, we are commissioned to "deconstruct, construct, and reconstruct" (Ladson-Billings, 2006, p. 32) learning by means of a cultural artifact, creating spaces where students can critically analyze content through their life experiences and understanding of their community. As CRP educators, we must cultivate and prepare students to "explicitly unmask and unmake oppressive systems through the critique of discourses of power. Culturally relevant educators work not only in the classroom but also in active pursuit of social justice for all members of society" (Dover, 2013). We are called to be advocates for the children, promoting change and equity for all to learn and develop as global citizens for tomorrow. Teacher educators need to be aware of and knowledgeable about the injustices that exist in the educational system in the United States in order for them to construct and forge avenues which will lead to change in this millennium. Henceforth, the teacher preparation program becomes the conduit for the CRP in higher education.

INTEGRATING CRP INTO HIGHER EDUCATION

Aronson and Laughter (2016) describe the emergence of culturally responsive teaching (CRT) and CRP in relation to prior concepts, like *culturally appropriate* or *culturally congruent*, that emerged from school desegregation efforts in the wake of *Brown v. Board*. For the purpose of this essay, we will use CRP as a broad term, referring to both CRT and CRP. While CRP was meant to address the needs of K-12 classrooms originally, Larke (2013) argues that it has a place in higher education. Larke (2013) says that "cultural competence, critical consciousness, and academic success" (p. 40) are all components of CRT that can be of greatest benefit within higher education environments. Taking this point further, Conklin (2008) asserts that "critical, justice-oriented teacher education" (p. 654) is essential in teacher education programs, as preservice teachers have remained a largely homogenous population, primarily "white, middle-class, female, monolingual English speakers" (p. 654), while student populations have continued to diversify. In teacher preparation, both implementing CRP into course syllabi and content *and* modeling the practice of CRP are important elements because it maximizes our teacher educators' academic achievement by integrating the knowledge base, the pedagogy, *and* the thinking behind CRP into the curriculum. In addition, CRP brings different perspectives and diverse theories of thought, recognizes that others have strengths regardless of who they are, and builds empathy among the community of learners.

Teacher preparation programs have historically "been fraught with 'soft approaches' to multiculturalism, diversity, and urban education; resistance by students and even some teacher educators to such discussions; and the ignoring of issues of racism, power, and whiteness" (Picower & Kohli, 2017, p. 7). Implementing the elements of CRP in a higher education environment, and especially in teacher education programs, is a much-needed practice. Cochran-Smith, et al. (1999) argues that infusing social justice into teacher preparation programs is a "fundamentally different way of doing the daily work of teacher education" (p. 232).

The idea of *doing* social justice can be accomplished by modeling what CRP looks like for preservice teachers in our teacher preparation programs. Studies tell us that there is a "need for multicultural or culturally relevant pedagogy [in teacher preparation programs], as it has been demonstrated to have positive impacts on students of Color" (Picower & Kohli, 2017, p. 6). Conklin (2008) tells us that:

> Modeling refers to both having teacher educators practice the pedagogies they espouse and unpacking these pedagogies so that the prospective teachers have access to the thinking behind a teacher educator's practice. Prospective teachers then first experience the pedagogies from the perspective of students and then learn about the pedagogies from teachers' perspectives. (p. 661)

It is this process of "modeling" and "unpacking" that is so beneficial to preservice teachers when teacher educators model CRP in the classroom. While there are certainly preservice teachers who might be resistant to CRP, many simply have a lack of understanding. This resistance or lack of understanding can be mitigated by experiencing and reflecting on pedagogy.

MINI CASE STUDIES INTRODUCTION

As faculty, we (Jody and Vanessa) "deconstructed, constructed, and reconstructed" (Ladson-Billings, 2006, p. 32) our courses to build a framework that allows students to immerse themselves in CRP. In this section, mini case studies from both courses will be shared as examples of how CRP can be utilized to design a syllabus/curriculum. Due to the complexity of CRP, we will focus on Ladson-Billings' (1995) three guiding principles—"academic achievement, cultural competence, and sociopolitical consciousness"—and Banks' (2014) theory of "multicultural education" as the driving force for curriculum transformation.

In alignment with Ladson-Billings (2006) and Banks (2014), Larke (2013) argues that both "teaching skills and professional practices" (Larke, 2013, p. 40) need to be targeted when implementing CRP in higher education. She says that

> First, instructors should develop a multicultural education base (D1) before they are able to design a course (D2) to incorporate the tenets of culturally responsive teaching. Second, professors should engage students (E1) and evaluate their course content and student progress (E2). (p. 40)

In this way, when CRP is integrated into the course design and materials, professors can begin to embark on "social justice" instead of simply "talk about social justice" (Aveling, 2012, p. 114). The student will partake in and be empowered to commission this restorative social justice work in education.

Developing Knowledge Base (D1) and Designing a Course (D2)

Ahead of analyzing the syllabus, the instructor develops a knowledge base (D1) and awareness around cultural diversity (Larke, 2013). The instructor must have an understanding of why cultural diversity is essential to our work in higher education—in addition, the instructor must build knowledge about diversity to elevate their cultural competence by reading, attending workshops/seminars, engaging in local and community immersion experiences locally, participating in teaching/studying abroad, and partaking in professional group discussions about sociopolitical issues of race, ethnicity, class, sexual identity, gender, language, nationality, learning differences, religion, and age in the educational system.

Once the knowledge base and vernacular with diversity have been received and students have a sense of awareness, the instructor can commence the task of bringing CRP into the curriculum. An in-depth comprehension of the curriculum content, as well as knowledge of students, must be present to effectively design a course with CRP (D2). What do you know about your students that will inform this process? Upon completing an investigation of our students, we (Jody and Vanessa) discovered that many of them had little or no experience with diversity, being members of the dominant White American culture. In contrast, others were inundated with daily life experiences. How would the curriculum content integration and knowledge construction process for our two courses, Observational Methods and Assessment (Vanessa) and History and Philosophy of American Education (Jody), become the cornerstone for cultural competence in each course? Textboxes 7.1 and 7.2 provide an overview of two mini case studies where D1 and D2 were processed and implemented.

TEXTBOX 7.1. VANESSA'S MINI STUDY I ON D1 & D2: OBSERVATION METHODS AND ASSESSMENT COURSE

In late June 2017, I was given the syllabus for Observational Methods and Assessment in preparation for teaching in the fall. My aforementioned preparation in cultural diversity (D1) allowed me to turn my focus to the content of this course. Upon examining the syllabus, I began contemplating the aspects of the scientific role of observation in the classroom. Scientific observation is part of all that we do, "taking place in the interstices of daily life, bringing together shifting sets of people and raising a steady stream of questions" (Daston, p. 199). Explicit scientific observation provides an in-depth look at culture, theory, practice, and how living things exist in the environment in which we live. "Observation (inseparable from experiment) generated a continual flow of ideas—for explanations, for interventions, and sometimes even for theories" (Daston & Lunbeck 2011, p. 203). Through scientific observations, students will have the opportunity to examine the world around them and understand the nuisances that exist hidden beneath the surface.

Furthermore, according to Dee & Gershenson (2017), the human tendency of the brain is to store life experiences consciously and unconsciously, which impacts how we solve immediate problems and make decisions in swift action, which is the analytical role of cognitive function. Our past experiences of life become an imprint on our new impressions. How could I influence the germane "psychological mechanisms" of awareness, empathy, individuality, and self-determination to allow clearance for the five senses to be the compelling dynamism of observation?

Decentralizing my perspectives, I contemplated the complexity of this scientific practice and the tapestry of our diverse communities in the K-12 classrooms currently. Pondering the following questions certified what I knew but bequeathed forethought and direction. How are we preparing teacher candidates to implement the observational process in an educational world which includes race, ethnicity, class, sexual identity, gender, language, nationality, learning differences, religion, and age in the classroom? Are we providing them the mechanisms to distinguish and navigate the differences that are present before them?

In this course, the teacher candidates must be propelled to reflect and discern their own unconscious bias that may impact the scientific observation process. How can I assist them in becoming more aware of their own identities and life experiences? How does unconscious bias impede the practice of observation? Engaging in scientific observation requires teachers to calibrate their tainted lens to see the whole child and not let our unconscious bias blur vision. Consequently, it became evident that dismantling the stained lens must be initiated in this course to bring heightened awareness in the classrooms.

In my discernment, I discovered that the philosophical concept of CRP and the educational process of multicultural education could be brought in as concept-building literature in the forms of photographs, readings, and videos, stimulating conversation and dialogue framing their personal and cultural diversity. I reviewed the courses' Student Learning Outcomes (SLOs) to ensure it was aligned with the new items that I wanted to infuse into the curriculum. The adjustments of the SLOs and course descriptions were done to reflect the new CRP elements. Now, it was time to design activities and engagement around these structures.

TEXTBOX 7.2. JODY'S MINI STUDY II ON D1 AND D2: HISTORY AND PHILOSOPHY OF AMERICAN EDUCATION COURSE

When I was hired at our current institution, I was asked to teach a course called The History and Philosophy of American Education. I was given previous syllabi and a textbook, and I began preparation. I had little understanding of our institution, of our students, or of the historical context of the course. From what I could ascertain, the course focused primarily on the history of education, while exploring philosophical orientations to teaching by adding a traditional "My Philosophy of Education" essay assignment at the end. I was not sure if the course had used a critical lens in its exploration of history, or if it examined the complexities that race, ethnicity, class, sexual identity, gender, language, nationality, learning differences, religion, and age had played in the development of the educational systems and structures in the United States. Most of all, I was uncertain if the course had emphasized philosophical orientations that stemmed from ideas like critical pedagogy or CRP. Were we acknowledging that the origins of education in America were incredibly exclusionary of Indigenous people, people of color, women, the poor, and more; and were we troubling these hard truths? Had the theme of equity (or lack thereof) been infused in the course? Through what lens were we engaging in history? In "Objections to Objectivity," Zinn (2002) says, "The chief problem in historical honesty is not outright lying. It is omission or de-emphasis of important data. The definition of 'important,' of course, depends on one's values" (p. 30). What values were a part of the fabric of this course?

As much as it was essential to trouble the course content, it was equally important to me that my pedagogy, the philosophical orientations that drive my engagement with preservice teachers and inspire my teaching, was ingrained in the course. I am committed to "a pedagogy of critical, justice-oriented teacher education that focuses on modeling compassion" (Conklin, 2008, p. 654). How would I maintain the course's core content while attending to and modeling the culturally relevant practices that I believe should be at the core of teacher education programs? This is the work I came into as a new faculty member at my institution.

My aforementioned knowledge base and awareness of cultural diversity (D1) informed my efforts to design my course (D2) in a way that reflected the tenets of CRP and also supported my desire to consistently model this pedagogy, I began with the resources and texts, or the "explicit curriculum" (Eisner, 2002). While the textbook provided a broad historical and philosophical foundation, it became apparent that more perspectives and voices were needed to achieve the cultural competence and sociopolitical consciousness that Ladson-Billings (2006) stresses. Mindful of the course SLOs, I infused the course with supplementary readings to the textbook and a reading bank that would complement that core knowledge. The reading bank included excerpts of texts by hooks (1994), Freire (1998), Delpit (2006), Laura (2014), Love (2019), and Milner (2020), to name a few (see Appendix). The addition of these excerpts reflected the CRP values that I desired in my course design. The work then turned to implementing activities and engagement around these texts.

Engagement (E1) and Evaluation (E2)

In order to implement CRP effectively, student engagement (E1) is vital to the learning process. The course design plays an indispensable role in bridging the content to the working world. In the 2015 study conducted by Witkowski and Cornell, a preponderance of students stated that collaborative activities resulted in a deeper comprehension of the content and motivation throughout the course. Students are searching for learning activities that provide opportunities for reflection and connection with others in the world. CRP sets the stage for student engagement around their personal cultural frames of reference regarding the content. Education today necessitates "weaving critical reflection, active engagement, and real-world application into the learning process and educational environment" (Larke, 2013, p. 47).

The most challenging aspect of CRP development in the curriculum is the evaluation (E2). How will the students' progress and outcomes be evaluated in CRP related to the course content? CRP has to be woven into the curriculum and cannot be an extra credit assignment or a one-time offer. We begin the process with the backward design model. What are the desired SLOs in these courses, and what life experiences/projects will lead to those outcomes? In a community of practice (Wenger, 1998; Smith, Kempster & Wenger-Trayner, 2019), students need to contextualize "the learning process," giving them "an experience that enables students, as novice practitioners, to develop the kind of tacit sensibilities found among expert practitioners" (Wenger-Trayner & Wenger-Trayner, 2015, p.164). These projects are places where people interact as "an agile pedagogy for 'social learning'" (Wenger-Trayner & Wenger-Trayner, 2015, p.170). Thus, in the implementation of CRP it is helpful to view learning as a social construct. Textboxes 7.3 and 7.4 provide an overview of the two mini case studies where E1 and E2 were processed and implemented.

TEXTBOX 7.3. VANESSA'S MINI STUDY I ON E1 & E2: OBSERVATION METHODS AND ASSESSMENT COURSE

Several previous readings of the syllabus were replaced with new culturally competent texts stretching students' understanding of the role of scientific observation as educators for a diverse classroom tapestry of students (E1). The Hypothesis software, which is embedded in our Learning Management System (LMS), was used when working with a reading text "increasing student engagement, expanding reading comprehension, and building critical thinking and community in classes . . . while enabling students to respond to a text using different media and empowering them to collaborate on understanding and developing ideas about their readings" (2021). Hypothesis is an annotation LMS software that allows students and instructors to analyze digital texts collaboratively and across the web.

After being inspired by an article on Dr. Maurice Berger (2017), the Research Professor and the Chief Curator for the Center for Art, Design and Visual Culture, shared the power of photography in "Race Stories" in *The New York Times,* I began incorporating photography to share untold stories of the global majority in this course. In the first session, the power of photography sparked conversations about sociopolitical issues of race, ethnicity, class, sexual identity, gender, language, nationality, learning differences, religion, and age with no hesitation—as if the students were waiting for permission to engage in this dialogue (E1).

They shortly ascertained that their personal life experiences and stories framed preconceived ideas which could become "lenses" that might "filter" or "distort" objective empirical outcomes of the scientific observation of the child. In the Isis article "On Scientific Observation" by Danson (2008), students had robust discussions in the Hypothesis software on Canvas about "ontology of scientific observation: how expert observation discerns and stabilizes scientific objects for a community of researchers (E1). This is a question that lies somewhere between epistemology (which studies how scientific observers acquire knowledge about their chosen objects) and metaphysics (which addresses the ultimate reality of the entities observed)" (p. 98).

I embarked on this venture to create a blueprint for this course project. As I pondered, I discovered that this project would necessitate engagement from many stakeholders such as the generalist teacher, and perhaps the specialists in the area of occupational therapy, special education, or speech pathology. As I researched the current studies on scientific observation, I found several articles that emphasized that the risk of bias assessment during scientific observation compels a degree of procedural expertise (Lindahl, 2016;

Rangel & Shi, 2020). In order to frame this naturalistic observational child study, the students would need opportunities to enhance their knowledge and understanding of how children develop and learn by using different observational techniques while being aware of their personal biases and filters.

A series of activities used from "The art of awareness: How observations can transform your teaching" (Curtis & Carter, 2013) for class engagement/discussion/analysis was followed by applied observations using different techniques in the in-person course session. Hence, this gave students opportunities to enhance their knowledge and understanding of how children develop and learn by using different observational techniques and developing procedural expertise through CRP. This culminating project was marshaled with the scientific study of human development which is compatible with the educational tenets of meeting the child's needs rather than moving through a set curriculum (Jones & Cossentino, 2017).

Students were assigned a field placement where they could conduct and collect observational data. They selected one child from the initial classroom observation and launched their naturalistic observational child study. While utilizing varied observation and recording methods to collect data on their child, they also practiced putting aside their perception filter and bias in a small organized field notebook—specifically into five social justice sections—access to resources, equity, participation, diversity, and human rights. The field notebook allowed students to be aware of their personal interpretations and biases that could impact the accuracy and reliability of observation while categorizing their observations into the five social justice pillars. The evaluation (E2) of this project focused on three main topics:

- The appropriateness/quality of the various supporting observation data
- Demonstrations of their awareness of CRP woven throughout the child study
- The quality of their synthesis/assessment of the child

Accordingly, this resulted in a beautifully woven tapestry with threads of cultural competence and sociopolitical consciousness as the hallmark of CRP within the naturalistic observational child study project.

TEXTBOX 7.4. JODY'S MINI STUDY II ON E1 AND E2: HISTORY AND PHILOSOPHY OF AMERICAN EDUCATION COURSE

After infusing the course with varied perspectives and voices, I began the work of engaging students (E1) by developing "projects, papers, and other class projects that require[d] students to reflect and use their cultural frames of reference" (Larke, 2013, p. 46). Students in my course were primarily practicing teachers, attending graduate school to pursue master's degrees. The students were professionals who were eager to learn and grow; the potential to immerse ourselves in CRP through the development of a professional learning community in the classroom was apparent.

Using my experiences from my doctoral program and knowing the power of community and conversation, I chose to use the reading bank I had developed as just that: a reading bank from which students, in groups, could choose to read and discuss on a biweekly basis for the first 10 weeks of the semester. The first step was setting the students up to interact with the various texts in a meaningful way. In her text *Is Everyone Really Equal: An Introduction to Key Concepts in Social Justice Education*, a text geared for students in higher education, Sensoy and DiAngelo (2017) offer guidelines "to maximize your learning of social justice content" (p. 4). When setting the expectations for the reading groups, I took cues from Sensory and DiAngelo (2017), offering these guidelines to students when interacting with the texts in the reading bank:

1. Strive for intellectual humanity.
2. Recognize the difference between opinions and informed knowledge.
3. Let go of personal anecdotal evidence and look at broader social patterns.
4. Notice your own defensive reactions and attempt to use these reactions as entry points for gaining deeper self-knowledge.
5. Recognize how your own social *positionality* (such as your race, class, gender, sexuality, ability status) informs your perspectives and reactions to your instructor and the individuals whose work you study in this course. (p. 4)

Next, after modeling—"demonstrating in action the very practices one advocates" (Conklin, 2008, p. 660)—what a productive group discussion might look like with each individual group, and then giving the students "access to the thinking behind [my] practice" (p. 661), the students met in their small groups throughout the semester, choosing two texts per meeting.

In these same groups, after completing the supplementary reading and holding reading group meetings, students engaged in an abridged ethnographic case study. Because ethnography "seeks to describe culture or parts of culture from a point of view of culture insiders" (Hatch, 2002, p. 21) using data collection methods like "participant observation, informant interviewing, and artifact collection" (p. 21), and case studies "explore[s] a real-life, contemporary bounded system . . . over time, through detailed, in-depth data collection involving multiple sources of information (e.g. observations, interviews, audiovisual material, and documents and reports), and reports a case description" (Creswell, 2013, p. 97), it was an ideal way to integrate CRP into the study of a school district or community that was outside of the students' current experiences.

By engaging in an ethnographic case study, students were able to examine a community through a critical lens, troubling the data they uncovered that related to race, ethnicity, class, sexual identity, gender, language, nationality, learning differences, religion, and age. Students pored over demographic data; spent time observing community hubs like schools, community centers, or libraries; had conversations with people they encountered at coffee shops; and gathered artifacts like website pages, yearbooks, newspaper articles, course offerings, and marketing campaigns, to name a few. They looked for community norms and practices, marketing messages that might contain bias, or courses of study that might reveal a certain value system. Taking into account all that they had learned through their data collection process, students wrote about how they connected socioeconomic data to report card data, or racial demographics to neighborhood schools, or school personnel data to free-and-reduced lunch data. Their efforts resulted in an abridged research study, including an introduction, literature review, methodology, and findings. By studying a community that might be outside one's own experiences, students were able to build their cultural competence while fostering academic achievement and sociopolitical consciousness (Ladson-Billings, 2006). The results were beautifully composed qualitative texts that engaged in the hard work of being culturally responsive.

The difficult element is the evaluation of CRP and its impact on the students' work in their reading groups and in their research project (E2). How would I know if CRP had enhanced "academic achievement, cultural competence, and sociopolitical consciousness?" (Ladson-Billings, 2006) My goal was to gauge this primarily through student reflection. Would the students find the texts personally meaningful and independently read more in that same vein? Would the students be better equipped to navigate their diverse classrooms with the knowledge that systemic racism and oppression were inherently a part of those structures? Would the students have heightened sociopolitical consciousness because they were able to have conversations about and then investigate difficult and contentious issues that were previously outside of their experiences? These are the questions I sought to answer when reading and listening to student reflections in the wake of their reading group and research experiences.

INSTITUTIONAL TRANSFORMATION FOR CULTURAL COMPETENCE

When infusing CRP into a higher education environment, specifically a teacher preparation program, there are several important measures that can be implemented that have the potential to make a momentous impact on transforming a department, program, or institution at a course (micro) and a structural (macro) level. Tables 7.1 and 7.2 highlight some practices we have experienced at both our current institution, institutions we served previously, or institutions with which we have had experiences. These initial practices have the capacity to radically and systemically change the way we perceive teacher preparation in our current times.

Table 7.1 Institutional Transformation Practices: Program/Department

	Program/Department
Institutional prioritization	It is essential that departments or programs make a commitment to prioritize and practice *teaching for social justice*. This commitment is the foundation for the intentional work that must be done in implementing CRP program-wide.
Mission/threshold concepts	Departments or programs can establish a common mission or threshold concepts that permeate all elements of a teacher preparation program, including courses, syllabi, advising, marketing campaigns, and workshops that might be offered. In this way, the mission or values of the entity is explicit and all stakeholders are accountable to it.
Common language	At a structural level, departments or programs can work to implement common, universally understood language to be used in all facets of the department or program. This common, shared language can put all administrators and instructors in lockstep when introducing or discussing diversity and equity among themselves and with students.
Book groups	Creating book groups and/or reading common texts is a practice that can meet personnel where they are on their social justice journey. While acknowledging that administrators, instructors, and other members of a department might be at different places in their understanding of and ability to implement CRP, we can use accessible texts to continue to infuse common language and challenge oppressive norms within a department or program.
Course of Study Immersion Experiences	Departments or programs can systematically develop immersion experiences that preservice teachers and graduate students will encounter through their course of study. Immersion experiences might include opportunities to engage in communities that surround partner school districts and can be both research- and experiential-based opportunities.

Table 7.2 Institutional Transformation Practices: Individual Course/Syllabi

	Individual Courses/Syllabi
Syllabi: Inclusivity Statements	Departments or programs can work collectively, using common language and understanding gained through many of the aforementioned practices, to create an "Inclusivity Statement" or "Diversity Statement" to be included in all program/department syllabi, which would note that CRP and teaching for social justice is an institutional priority.
Syllabi: Reading Materials/Text Selection	Instructors should be encouraged to include contemporary texts in their course that examine not only the complexities that race, ethnicity, class, sexual identity, gender, language, nationality, learning differences, religion, and age present in a diverse classroom; but also representations of diverse authors and scholars.
Syllabi: Student Learning Outcomes (SLOs)	Instructors should be encouraged to formulate Student Learning Outcomes (SLOs) that "integrate culturally responsive teaching and multicultural education issues" (Larke, 2013, p. 44). In this way, assessments can directly connect to the learning outcomes, resulting in CRP being a central influence in the instruction and assessment processes in the course.
Syllabi: Topics	There should be a process of re-examining the topics instructors have chosen to highlight in a course. CRP should not be an "add-on" but should be infused throughout the duration of a course and addressed explicitly in the topics that are covered.

CONCLUSION

Maya Angelou (1995) affirmed, "We should all know that diversity makes for a rich tapestry, and we must understand that all the threads of the tapestry are equal in value no matter what their color; equal in importance no matter their texture" (p. i). Across the United States, the tapestries of our classrooms have been changing, and diversity in the classroom is increasing. Thus, higher education is required to prepare educators to become knowledgeable and skillful in meeting the needs of all children. Systemic bias of race, ethnicity, class, sexual identity, gender, language, nationality, learning differences, religion, and age must be unrooted and dismantled within our educational system.

This chapter encapsulates the complexity of multicultural design and requirement of instructor intrepidity to implement CRP with intentionality in higher education. The framework of Ladson-Billings' three guiding principles (1995)—"academic achievement, cultural competence, and sociopolitical consciousness" and Banks' (2014) theory of "multicultural education" provide a focused lens through which to examine curriculum transformation. Strategies, discourse, and leadership in educational practices that call on all learners in global partnership were highlighted in the faculty mini study cases. By sharing how two distinct courses, each with very different SLOs and subject matters, could be examined and infused with CRP, we provide a framework for all teacher educators moving forward.

Our desired outcome is to illuminate anecdotal and research-based evidence regarding the need for and importance of intentionality in CRP syllabi/curriculum designing and to bring about radical and systemic change to meet the needs of a growing body of diverse K-12 classrooms in the United States. Our students deserve the opportunity to unpack, reflect, and discern the realities of injustice that lie before them in the educational system that they will be working in at the conclusion of their studies. This intentionally comes with hard work, research, and diligence to create an environment where CRP can be explored and actualized with success. Thus, creating new social justice advocates in the teaching force that will grapple with systemic bias and create new avenues of equitable education for all children.

SOMETHING TO READ, DO, OR CONSIDER

After reading this chapter, you are now ready to engage in this magnificent work. First, you may want to read *Culturally Responsive Pedagogy: Working towards Decolonization, Indigeneity, and Interculturalism* (2017), which presents an overview of CRP theory, allowing opportunities for personal development and awareness. In addition, the text provides guidance when preparing preservice teachers and shares case studies of lived experiences. You may want to consider doing this work a semester or a year prior to teaching your course to allow ample time to prepare yourself through self-reflection and discernment, to explore the resources with other faculty, and to facilitate the embedment of CRP in your course.

REFERENCES

Angelou, M. (1993). *Wouldn't take nothing for my journey now*. Bantam.
Aronson & Laughter (2016). The theory and practice of culturally relevant education: A synthesis of research across content areas. *Review of Educational Research, 86*(1), 163–206.
Aveling, N. (2012). Indigenous studies: A matter of social justice; a matter of urgency. *Diaspora, Indigenous, and Minority Education, 6*(2), 99–114.
Banks, J.A. (2014). *An introduction to multicultural education* (5th edition). Pearson.
Cochran-Smith, M., Albert, L., Dimattia, P., Freedman, S., Jackson, R., Mooney, J., Neisler, O., Peck, A., & Zollers, N. (1999). Seeking social justice: A teacher

education faculty's self-study. *International Journal of Leadership in Education*, 2(3), 229–253.

Conklin, H.G. (2008). Modeling compassion in critical, justice-oriented teacher education. *Harvard Educational Review*, 78(4), 652–674.

Creswell, J.W. (2013) *Qualitative inquiry & research design: Choosing among five approaches*. Sage.

Curtis, D., & Carter, M. (2013). *The art of awareness: How observation can transform your teaching*. Redleaf Press.

Daston, L. (2008). On Scientific Observation. *Isis*, 99(1), 97–110. https://www.journals.uchicago.edu/doi/abs/10.1086/587535

Daston, L. & Lunbeck, E. (2011). Histories of Scientific Observation. University of Chicago Press.

Dee, T., & Gershenson, S. (2017). *Unconscious Bias in the Classroom: Evidence and Opportunities*. Google Inc. Retrieved from https://goo.gl/O6Btqi.

Delpit, L. (2006). *Other People's Children*. The New Press.

Dover, A. G. (2013). Teaching for social justice: From conceptual frameworks to class-room practices. Multicultural Perspectives, 15, 3–11. doi:10.1080/1521096 0.2013.754285

Eberbach, C., & Crowley, K. (2009). From everyday to scientific observation: How children learn to observe the biologist's world. *Review of Educational Research*, 79(1), 39–68. Retrieved June 8, 2021, from http://www.jstor.org/stable/40071160

Eisner, E.W. (2006). *The educational imagination: On the design and evaluation of school programs* (3rd edition). Merrill Prentice Hall.

Freire, P. (1998). *Pedagogy of freedom: ethics, democracy, and civic courage*. Rowman & Littlefield Publishers, Inc.

Gay, G. (2010). *Culturally responsive teaching: Theory, research, and practice*. Teachers College Press.

Genzlinger, N. (2020, March 26). Maurice Berger, Curator Outspoken About Race, Is Dead at 63. *The New York Times*. https://www.nytimes.com/2020/03/26/arts/maurice-berger-dead.html?smid=em-share

Hatch, J. A. (2002). *Doing qualitative research in education settings*. State University of New York Press.

Hypothesis. (2021, May 7). *Hypothesis for Education*. https://web.hypothes.is/education/

hooks, b. (1994). *Teaching to transgress: Education as the practice of freedom*. Routledge.

Jones, A., & Cossentino, J. (2017). What's going on with this child? Child study for the 21st century. *NAMTA Journal*, 42(2), 249–260.

Ladson-Billings, G. (1995). Toward a theory of culturally relevant pedagogy. *American Educational Research Journal*, 32(3), 465–491. https://doi.org/10.3102/00028312032003465

Ladson-Billings, G. (2006). "Yes, but how do we do it?" Practicing culturally relevant pedagogy. In J. Landsman & C. Lewis (Eds.), *White teachers/diverse classrooms: Creating inclusive schools, building on students' diversity, and providing true educational equity* (pp. 29–41). Stylus Publishing.

Ladson-Billings, G. (2014). Culturally relevant pedagogy 2.0: a.k.a. the remix. *Harvard Educational Review 84*(1), 74–84.
Larke, P. (2013). Culturally responsive teaching in higher education: What professors need to know. *Counterpoints, 391*, 38–50.
Laura, C. T. (2014). *Being bad: My baby brother and the school-to-prison pipeline.* Teachers College Press.
Lindahl, E. (2016). *Are teacher* assessments biased? – Evidence from Sweden. Education Economics,*24*(2), 224–238.
Love, B. L. (2019). *We want to do more than survive: Abolitionist teaching and the pursuit of educational freedom.* Beacon Press.
Milner, H. R. (2020). *Start where you are, but don't stay there: Understanding diversity, opportunity gaps, and teaching in today's classroom* (2nd edition). Harvard Education Press.
Paris, D. (2012). Culturally sustaining pedagogy: A needed change in stance, terminology, and practice. *Educational Researcher, 41*(3), 93–97.
Picower, B., & Kohli, R. (Eds.) (2017). *Confronting racism in teacher education: Counternarratives of critical practice.* Routledge.
Pirbhai-Illich, F., Pete, S., & Martin, F. (2017), *Culturally responsive pedagogy: Working towards decolonization, indigeneity and interculturalism.* Palgrave Macmillan.
Rangel, M., & Shi, Y. (2020). *First impressions: The case of teacher racial bias.* Working Paper.
Sensoy, O. & DiAngelo, R. (2017). *Is everyone really equal? An introduction to key concepts in social justice education* (2nd edition). Teachers College Press.
Smith, S., Kempster, S., & Wenger-Trayner, E. (2019). Developing a program community of practice for leadership development. *Journal of Management Education, 43*(1), 62–88.
U. S. Census Bureau. (2018, March 13). Older people projected to outnumber children for first time in U.S. history: 2030 Marks important demographic milestones for U.S. population. Retrieved July 2018, from United States Census Bureau: https://www.census.gov/newsroom/press-releases/2018/cb18-41-population-projections.html
Wenger-Trayner, E., & Wenger-Trayner, B. (2015). Introduction to communities of practice: A brief overview of the concept and its uses. https://wenger-trayner.com/introduction-to-communities-of-practice.
Wenger, E. (1998). *Communities of practice: Learning, meaning, and identity.* Cambridge University Press.
Zinn, H. (2002). *Failure to quit: Reflections of an optimistic historian.* South End Press.

APPENDIX

History and Philosophy of American Education Excerpt Reading Bank: includes all text excerpts used in semesters since Summer 2020

The reading bank comprised excerpts, namely the introduction and/or the first chapter of the following texts:

Being Bad: My Baby Brother and the School-to-Prison Pipeline: Crystal T. Laura (2014)

Democracy and Education: John Dewey (1916/2011)

Educated in Whiteness: Good Intentions and Diversity in Schools: Angelina E. Castagno (2014)

Experience and Education: John Dewey (1938/2015)

For White Folks Who Teach in the Hood ... and the Rest of Y'all Too: Christopher Emdin (2016)

"I Shall Create! Teaching Toward Freedom": William Ayers (2019) in Delpit, L. (ed.) *Teaching When the World is on Fire*

Is Everyone Really Equal? An Introduction to Key Concepts in Social Justice Education (2nd ed.): Ozlem Sensoy & Robin DiAngelo (2017)

Other People's Children: Cultural Conflict in the Classroom: Lisa Delpit (2006)

Pedagogy of Freedom: Ethics, Democracy, and Civic Courage: Paulo Freire (1998)

Reaching and Teaching Students in Poverty (2nd ed.): Paul Gorski (2018)

Start Where You Are but Don't Stay There: Understanding Diversity, Opportunity Gaps, and Teaching in Today's Classrooms: H. Richard Milner IV (2016)

Teaching in the Cracks: Openings and Opportunities for Student-Centered, Action-Focused Curriculum: Brian D. Schultz (2017)

Teaching to Transgress; Education as the Practice of Freedom: bell hooks (1994)

Teaching with Vision: Culturally Responsive Teaching in Standards-Based Classrooms: Christine E. Sleeter and Catherine Cornbleth (eds.) (2011)

To Teach: The Journey of a Teacher (2nd ed.): William Ayers (2001)

We Want to do More than Survive: Abolitionist Teaching and the Pursuit of Educational Freedom: Bettina L. Love (2019)

"*Why Are All the Black Kids Sitting Together in the Cafeteria?" And Other Conversations About Race*: Beverly Tatum (1997)

Why We Teach Now: Sonia Nieto (ed.) (2014)

Widening the Circle: The Power of Inclusive Classrooms: Mara Sapon-Shevin (2007)

Chapter 8

Anti-racist Research in Teacher Education

Creating Critical Online Communities

Lauren Angelone, Romena M. Garrett Holbert, and Joanne Baltazar Vakil

While the United States grows more diverse, the teaching profession remains a White woman's profession (Geiger, 2018). Efforts to address this disconnect have evolved over time, becoming well established in the form of multiculturalism (Banks, 1995) and culturally relevant pedagogy (CRP) (Ladson-Billings, 1995) in the 1990s. Though the aims of multiculturalism and CRP were broader, often the applications of these concepts took "perniciously shallow forms" (Petrovic & Caddell, 2020, p. 1), translated as "We did or read something Black" (Ladson-Billings, 2017, p. 142) in an effort to provide representative content rather than addressing the larger systemic issues that undergird racist curricula and practices.

At the time of this writing, a guilty verdict was reached in the trial of the murder of George Floyd at the hands of police. The brutal killing of Floyd sparked protests all over the world recentering the need to address anti-Black racism systemically. At the same time, a global pandemic was laying bare racial and economic disparities that further highlight systemic racism (CDC, 2021). A global pandemic, that the president of the United States, dubbed the "China virus" or "kung flu," in an effort to blame China for the spread of the novel coronavirus, which was followed by an uptick in violence against Asian Americans and Pacific Islanders (Nuyen, 2021). Just a few weeks ago a White man walked into a spa and brutally murdered eight people, six of which were of Asian descent. It is within this context, that discussions have moved from representative content to explicitly anti-racist practices. Culturally Sustaining Pedagogy (Paris & Aim, 2017) and abolitionist teaching (Love, 2019), instead, call for not just understanding the "other," but decentering whiteness, and not just reimagining schools, "but . . . build[ing] new schools that we are taught to believe are impossible: schools based on intersectional justice, anti-racism, love, healing, and joy" (Love, 2019, 11).

As teacher educators and researchers of varying intersectional (Creshshaw, 1989) identities working with predominantly White populations with their own intersections, each of the authors will share how we have grappled with White privilege (Amico, 2016) or internalized racial oppression (Pyke, 2010) in both ourselves and our students. As a result, we see a need to support more explicitly anti-racist practices in our work. As the pandemic moved our courses online, we each adapted or continued our work around technology in various ways. We saw opportunities in the online environment due to affordances like global connections made possible through social media and more time to process thoughts in online discussion boards. It is in these spaces that we envisioned creating more critical online communities, ones that could support several of the actions for teaching for an anti-racist future (Simmons, 2019), such as talking about race, acknowledging the construct of race, and engaging in vigilant self-awareness.

Although social media and online discussion boards can be used to divide and uphold systemic racism through racist algorithms (Noble, 2018), they have also supported learning and equity in multiple ways, with possibilities for thinking otherwise. Social media has been used by teachers in particular in formal and informal learning settings, as a way to connect with communities (Greenhow et al., 2020) develop teacher identities, provide mentoring (Carpenter et al., 2017) and share resources (Hsieh, 2017; Carpenter & Krutka, 2015). In online learning settings, getting to know students, building community (Lawrence, 2020), and designing more structured asynchronous discussions (Zydney et al., 2012) are strategies used to promote equity in that environment. With the emergent use of many new technologies in higher education as a result of remote learning during the pandemic and the ongoing work to break down institutionalized racism, here we present further opportunities to use technology to support the work of equity, specifically anti-racist practices within teacher education. In what follows, each of the three authors will expound upon her work that exists at the intersection of technology and anti-racist research in teacher education.

TOP POSTS AND THE (WHITE) CONSTRUCTION OF TEACHERS ON INSTAGRAM

My name is Lauren Angelone. In this first example of creating critical online communities, I will begin by situating myself as a White teacher educator. I will then share an example of an assignment around the creation of personal learning networks, which led to the study of a popular hashtag used by teachers on Instagram to understand the discourses around teachers in online spaces.

Positionality

I am a White cisgender straight female teacher educator in a teacher education program at a Catholic Predominantly White Institution in the Midwestern United States. I grew up poor but am currently living in upper-middle-class suburbs where I can quietly fit in, as long as I don't mention my upbringing. Though being female is not the dominant gender in society, it certainly is within the field of education and I would say that since starting my undergraduate teacher education program, I have always felt my own White privilege in the ways in which I was able to feel as though I fit. Though I would not have identified it as such, even as a new teacher with little experience, I felt my privilege in being embraced by other teachers, parents, and students in the suburban school setting where I spent my first years teaching. When I made mistakes or was challenged by others, I knew that my race was not a factor.

I have a PhD in Cultural Foundations, Technology, and Qualitative Inquiry and am now an assistant professor of Science Education and Instructional Technology. In my doctoral program, I was introduced to Critical Race Theory (Delgado, 2012), CRP (Ladson-Billings, 1995), the cultural construction of gendered bodies (Butler, 1990), the cultural construction and productive power of "truth" (Foucault, 1980), and so on, and I began to understand in what ways I was privileged and oppressed in different contexts, and more importantly, the way my privilege actively impacted others. In my current context, I find myself well-situated to introduce critical frameworks to future educators with whom I share many parts of my identity. Though there are areas where I feel my students must engage with a broader and more diverse world in order to understand it, I feel as though through my own awakening, I can help them to move forward by being an example and a catalyst for doing anti-racist work as (mostly) White women in their increasingly diverse future classrooms.

Personal Learning Networks

"They all have names like that." This comment, from a White preservice teacher in my Instructional Technology class in my first year as a tenure-track professor shocked me in its blatantly racist tone. The student was responding to seeing a name of a child on a sample of student work that sounded to her like it might be the name of a Black student. While the rest of the class didn't appear to respond, I stammered through a brief and sad explanation of our need to understand cultures outside of ourselves, trying to suddenly and poignantly remind students of what they should have learned about CRP. This experience and others like it prompted me to find ways to engage students in discussions of equity and justice within my Instructional Technology course.

Within this course, I decided to introduce a personal learning network (Warlick, 2009) project. A personal learning network is an informal online learning community established with the purpose of learning about a particular topic. In my first iteration, I asked each student to sign up for a new Twitter account that would be used for professional purposes. I then engaged students in biweekly Twitter chats in which I used the hashtag #TechforJustice and encouraged reading and discussion around justice and the use of technology in schools (Angelone, 2021). Over the course of the semester using the Q1/A1 format of Twitter chats, which has the moderator tweet with "Q1" to indicate the first question and the participants tweet their responses with "A1" to indicate a response to the first question, we discussed the digital divide (Tyson, 2015), queer critical media literacy and representation (van Leent & Mills, 2017), technology to support English Learners (Warschauer, et al., 2004), and engaged with educators locally and around the world. Through these chats, students demonstrated several tenets of critical media literacy (Kellner & Share, 2007) including social justice, social construction, and the politics of representation.

Though Twitter is the most popular current social media for informal teacher professional development (Carpenter & Krutka, 2015), many of my students expressed an interest in moving over to Instagram, a more visual platform introduced in 2010 and on which more of my Gen Z students were already engaging. In response to the ever-changing landscape of Instructional Technology, I spent a summer informally investigating Instagram to see if teachers were on it and how they were using it. I found the hashtag #teachersofinstagram and discovered that teachers were using Instagram in a variety of ways, though it looked and felt much different than the teacher use and chats that took place on Twitter. On Instagram, images are the central feature and images with the most likes and comments are moved into a category called "Top Posts" that are featured at the top of the search for a hashtag. Like on Twitter, teachers seemed to be using Instagram to share resources (mainly on the classroom environment) and for connection with fellow teachers (Carpenter et al., 2020). Unlike Twitter though, Instagram was noticeably more polished (likely due to the image-enhancing features built into the platform) and sometimes was created in an effort to sell products (Shelton, et al., 2020). Also because of the image-centric nature of Instagram, it was easy to see while scrolling through posts using #teachersofinstagram that there were mostly White female faces smiling back at you. This is ultimately representative of the teaching profession, with 80 percent of teachers being White and approximately 75 percent being female (Geiger, 2018).

Who Are #teachersofinstagram and What Does 'Who They Are' Do?

The following semester, I decided to use Instagram with my students using a similar format to the #TechforJustice chats on Twitter. I engaged students in similar themes with similar readings and chats. Because the chats could not follow the Q1/A1 format, we used the #xuedchat to either create new posts or discuss within a post by myself or a student chat leader. We also experimented with the story feature on Instagram, which encourages more informal and interactive sharing of images, videos, and quizzes. Student participation seemed similar to our Twitter chats in terms of previously analyzed data on engagement with critical media literacy components (Angelone, 2021).

Also during that semester, I began to investigate the hashtag #teachersofinstagram more formally, collecting data to conduct a critical discourse analysis in order to understand what discourses were dominant and therefore with which discourses my students would be engaging. Each week on Monday, I would capture the Top Posts of the #teachersofinstagram, which included nine posts. These are the posts with the most likes and comments and the ones displayed at the top of the page when you search for the hashtag. Through the collection and initial analysis of this data, I began to see that #teachersofinstagram was a community of resource sharing and connection, but it was also a homogeneous heteronormative space comprised of mostly White women. For the last Instagram chats with my students for the semester, I created a mashup image of some of the Top Posts from the semester that were generally representative of the discourses that I was finding through my analysis. I asked students the following questions: "Who do these posts tell you teachers are? Take the analysis further. Who is centered and decentered? What is seen as important and unimportant? Does this represent how you see teachers?"

In response to my questions, students found the images to represent the broad lives of teachers both personally and professionally, that teachers worked hard, and that teachers cared enough about their work to engage in Instagram in addition to their duties. Several students also noticed the lack of diversity and discussed that Instagram images were meant to be "pretty" and may not show the reality of teaching, but in general, they felt that these images represented the modern teaching profession.

I turn to Foucault (1980) to understand not only the discourses present on #teachersofinstagram but to understand that these discourses are productive. The Top Posts of Instagram are an indication of the ways in which teachers are constructed and constructing themselves, but they also do something.

Through the thousands of views and reposting through stories, they produce more teachers who see teaching this way. New teachers, like my students, join Instagram and learn more about who teachers are and what they do. If they are to join an uncritical space, dominated by apolitical discourse and polished images of a White woman's world, how will Black, Indigenous, People of Color (BIPOC) teachers see that they belong? How will there be possibilities for thinking otherwise? This is what Foucault (1991) would call the work of "a thousand things to do," (p. 174) both creating new discourses to undo others only to have more to undo. We may, for example, begin a new hashtag in order to be in solidarity with BIPOC teachers and end up doing damage that we don't anticipate. But, this is also the work of those of us in privileged positions of power in the teaching profession. We must reflect in ways that provoke us to take action to undo systems that both sustain us and deny access to others.

PROMOTING ANTI-RACIST TEACHING PRACTICES IN ONLINE FOUNDATIONS OF EDUCATION COURSEWORK

My name is Romena M. Garrett Holbert. Recent examination of my courses and instructional practices through a critical lens has prompted me to explore my own, and my teacher candidates' learning experiences as they relate to racism. To begin, I share my own positionality as a Black female tenured university teacher educator working at a predominately White institution. I then share my experience of revamping elements of the Foundations of Education courses I teach to heighten the anti-racist focus of the courses within the online-only learning context prompted by the COVID-19 pandemic. Then I unpack and describe how identifying and confronting, my own internalized racism enabled me to leverage my experiences to develop a supportive context for anti-racist teaching and learning online.

Positionality

I identify as a Black cisgender straight woman born and raised in a multicultural area of New York City until tenth grade. At the outset of my tenth grade year, my mother and I moved to a predominantly White suburb in the Midwestern United States. In this region, I obtained my college education on a National Achievement Semifinalist Scholarship. During study for my Bachelor's degree in Biological Sciences, my Masters in Education, and my doctorate in Teacher Education Policy and Leadership, my experiences of academic study were primarily led by White educators. Anti-racist research was not included among my academic studies, and instead was a focus that I adopted to support my own children in understanding their rich and multifaceted identities and capacities in a world in which others may discount them.

My experience of high school in the Midwest was markedly different from the multicultural experience of attending a specialized high school which was populated by students from a wide variety of racial backgrounds, family compositions, and economic standings in New York City. In the Midwest, particularly as a teen mother who simultaneously excelled in academics, I found covering my identities and downplaying the effort associated with my academic success to be central to obtaining positive recognition and avoiding discrimination based on stereotypical assumptions.

Enacting and Modeling Anti-racist Teaching in Foundations of Education

As courses at our institution shifted to online delivery, faculty had limited time to develop fully online instruction. I became concerned about the retention of our already limited numbers of teacher candidates of color and how anti-racist teaching aims could be employed from afar. I wondered how students might develop networks of peer support, and how productive teamed tasks and dialogue around issues such as race would be in an online format. I deliberated about what my students most needed from me, sought student input, and read anti-racist instructional design articles for educators. Simmons (2019) defined five actions for teaching for an anti-racist future: (1) engage in vigilant self-awareness, (2) acknowledge racism and the ideology of White supremacy, (3) study and teach representative history, (4) talk about race with students, and (5) when you see racism, do something. I thought back to my own experiences as a learner, as well as to my experiences as a faculty member and recognized right away that students of color may face particular challenges in the online foundations of education courses. In suddenly implemented distance learning formats with students already under stress, miscommunications would be likely and discussion of race and racism, (which undergird many of the modern and historical contexts of schools and is central to the course content), may further isolate students of color who may not have strong networks among their classmates. I thought back to my experience of being the sole representative of the "Black perspective" on *To Kill a Mockingbird* during my high school years and cringed at the thought that one of my students might have the whole class staring at them as they took on the emotional labor of explaining their feelings, clarifying the connections between the content and racism, or trying to pretend that racism didn't exist to gain and maintain the acceptance of classmates who were relative strangers. I also recognized that Black faculty in teacher education receive lower course evaluation scores than their "White" or "Other" peers (Smith & Hawkins, 2011). I came to recognize my initial fear of facilitating the "difficult dialogue" (hooks, 1994), and leveraging the transformative power of diversity in online settings as an example of how my previously unexamined internalized White racial supremacy (Pyke, 2010) could undermine the impact of my course. I pondered how I could effectively respond to Pitts' (2020) assertion that:

> Anti-racist educators understand that, in love, they must never be silent. *Ever.* Anti-racist educators understand that their positions as teachers, leaders, policymakers and social workers are positions of great privilege and power, and that they have the ability to leave this world better than they found it. (Para. 6)

Despite my role as the teacher and leader of the newly online course, my experience of often being one of few if not the only person of color present, and recognition that the course would be recorded, did not feel like a powerful stance from which to initiate in-depth discussions of racism (Shim, 2018). I wanted students to be able to engage in critical dialogue that would help them broaden their multicultural understandings of racial injustice in K-12 schools, understand relationships to structural issues, engage in solidarity building among peers, and develop strategies for change. (Kohli, 2012; Alamo, 2012). Engagement in vigilant self-awareness prompts the asking of such questions as "How does your identity provide or prevent access to necessary resources?" "How does your power and privilege show up in your work with students, take up space, or silence others?" and "What single narratives are you telling yourself about students, and how does that affect grading, behavior management, and other interactions?" (Simmons, 2019, para. 4). Asking myself these questions, I came to recognize that my work with building classroom community (Holbert, 2015) and adapting resources from restorative justice circles for classroom use (Holbert, 2019) should inform the decisions I made about designing the online course. Coupling self-awareness and acknowledgement of racism prompted me to recognize that my motivation for creating networks that would promote a healthy atmosphere for student conversations also limited retaliatory student evaluations by teaching students to enact empathy and to express concerns directly.

I implemented course structures such as daily opener check-ins in which students shared a brief statement of how they were feeling that day and why and began each class with a notecard prompt that elicited sharing regarding a perspective or lived experience relating to the topic for the day. These activities required *everyone* to share ideas, afforded an opportunity for students to become aware of commonalities among students' experiences and witnessings of oppression (Kohli, 2012) and supported empathy building and readiness for engaged dialogue. Each session concluded with a prompt eliciting a takeaway message from the lecture materials, a peer, or a new understanding constructed based on a combination of ideas. Prior to the online transition, students had responded to these prompts on individual notecards. The move to a discussion board format allowed all students to see all others' responses and afforded me the opportunity to read and respond to them in real time, thus supporting my continued aims of building community and developing empathy by allowing students to ask questions of one another and to relate the experiences and perspectives to the course materials and activities within each session.

Pedagogical practices implemented during the shift included the formation of base groups for student interaction on major projects, activity completion in breakout rooms, and engagement in circle conversations on topics their peers or I advanced across the entire term. Within the groups, students were supported to develop group norms and shared expectations for participation, to define what respect looks like within their group, and developed a process for advancing constructive criticism or expressing dissatisfaction or concern. Additional data-based materials and videos directly related to race were included among course materials and were the focus of structured breakout group conversations that prompted a critical lens toward historical and systemic understandings of racism. Students were to analyze and discuss in their groups, often using a circle question format focused on listening to understand.

Individual and collaborative student work showed that students were able to take on new perspectives that evidenced heightened understandings of the existence and impacts of racism within and surrounding educational settings through the practices employed. Students also discussed having developed closer, more personal, and more impactful relationships with individuals and perspectives they may not have engaged in their typically highly homogenous prior educational settings. The solutions that students generated as they considered issues of racism frequently included a mix of self-directed actions such as checking one's own biases, other-directed actions including effective responses to the witnessing of social inequalities, and intergroup collaborative actions representing community engagement for the benefit of society (Alimo, 2012). Authentic engagement supported by dialogue was often suggested by students as a way to support the development of critical consciousness. My students' recognition that people should be aware of social inequality, understand their place in that inequality, and take action against oppressive elements in society and their assertions that engagement with dialogue and questioning that supports these aims (Freire, 1970), was a signal of the success of my course revisions. Importantly, many students also recognized the importance of addressing racism and its impacts even in settings in which visual differences could not identify the presence of more than one racial group. Students who evidenced less significant development toward an anti-racist stance of their own consistently listened to and engaged respectfully with peers who shared ideas that were new or challenging to them.

Looking back with the wisdom of a critical lens, I now recognize the internalized racism my initial hesitations represented (hooks, 1994). Through course redesign, I explored and overcame responses emergent from internalized racism such as the tendency I recognized in my high school self to downplay my effort toward success as an attempt to fit in. Having confronted and taken action against my own internalized racism facilitated the study and teaching of representative history and effective dialogue about race within my online classroom context (Simmons, 2019). Confronting internalized racism enables Black teacher educators to act against oppression effectively to challenge the alienation, disenfranchisement, and discrimination faced by teacher candidates of color (Shim, 2018), increase access to authentic stories of lived experience available to teacher candidates, and inspire solidarity and change to positively impact the experiences of the P-12 learners they will ultimately serve (Alamo, 2012).

LEVERAGING TWITTER AS A CRITICAL TOOL TO SUPPORT ANTI-RACIST EDUCATIONAL PRACTICES

My name is Joanne Baltazar Vakil. Recently discovering and participating in critical online communities has enlightened me with the complex facets in identifying and addressing issues of racism in the K-12 and higher education classrooms. I will first share my positionality as an Asian American middle school teacher and university teacher educator. Then I will detail my own insecurities in overcoming internalized racism and positioning myself as a leader in guiding preservice teachers (PSTs) toward anti-racist discourses in online spaces.

Positionality

I identify as an Asian American, specifically a Filipino/Pin@y, Muslim revert, cisgender woman reared in a predominantly White, New England suburb. My first interaction as a student with an Asian American educator occurred during the first semester of my doctoral studies in STEM Education. It was in this professor's class where I first heard the verbalization of discomfort an Asian American felt walking into a restaurant filled with only White customers. I certainly related to the professor's personal experience, but found it an unusual, even irrelevant, topic to address in the course that was being taught.

My journey in anti-racist research did not begin until my third semester when I was further illuminated with the concept of internalized racism (Pyke, 2010). Having been one of only a handful of Asian Americans in my high school, it never occurred to me that my longing to look and be like the rest of the girls in my class was the result of an "individual inculcation of the racist stereotypes, values, and ideologies perpetuated by the White dominant society" which led to feelings of self-doubt, but thankfully not to "disgust, and disrespect for one's race and/or oneself" (Pyke, 2010, p. 553).

As a middle school teacher, students held a variety of assumptions about my origins. I once received a beautiful, wooden, floral hand fan with the reasoning, "because you are Japanese." In the university setting where one faculty member initially approached me and asked if I could pronounce my first name slowly. An accumulation of moments like these had me almost give up on correcting and clarifying my identity to others. However, my newly formed understanding of implicit bias, White gaze, "psychosocial dominance,"—the dominant culture's imposition of its definition of subordinates (Baker, 1983), and the model minority myth, which aggrandizes Asian Americans as a "beacon to highlight the prototypical American success story, a group to be admired and emulated by others" (Ng et al., 2007, p. 95), has afforded me more insight and courage in introducing critical frameworks to my PSTs.

Connecting to the Teaching Community

As a former instructor for Math Methods courses in two different Midwestern universities, I was introduced to the idea of incorporating social media as part of the homework. Comparing the connectivity between me, the students, and others outside of class over the semesters, I found an increasing value in the implementation of social media into weekly assignments. During the first day of class, I requested that each student set up a "professional," rather than personal, Twitter account. Each week, two or three students were designated as moderators to our class hashtag. This collaborative group oversaw the Q1/A1 format, encouraging classmates to reflect on assigned readings and informally engage in dialogue with each other. Topics addressed ranged from implementing strategies to develop early number sense and geometric thinking to considering the power and status of math and its influence on teacher identity (Aguirre et al., 2013). Students also exchanged thoughts and examples on how they could develop an advocacy disposition (Chao et al., 2016) by practicing openness to others' cultures and arguments, self-awareness and critical self-reflectiveness, and committing to culturally responsive mathematics teaching that holds "high expectations for all children" (White et al., 2012, p. 35).

As student moderators oversaw, engaged, and summarized tweet responses to their questions, a sense of camaraderie developed as classmates shared their personal encounters with math stereotypes, math anxiety, and their understanding of mathematical agency. The weekly content lead toward "unpacking issues of equity and social justice in the classroom" (Vakil & Chao, 2019, p. 1291). In addition, I was in the position to repost relevant tweets from other educators and math organizations outside the university.

Overall, students considered the weekly Twitter assignments less taxing than a more traditional, linear discussion board post. Students began to view this platform from the perspective of an emerging teacher, one whose teaching and learning could benefit from in-service teachers in the online community actively tweeting about their classroom practices. Indeed, participants who I interviewed realized the impact Twitter had in enabling them to make "connections with other teachers around [the] world," resulting in an extended forum to "advocate for things that are important" (Vakil & Chao, 2019, p. 1293).

Extending Twitter Assignments to Raise Anti-racist Consciousness

Despite the relative success in engaging and informing students by using Twitter, I had failed to extend the activity to a more heightened awareness of racism. This was a challenge for me. Similar to my first Asian American professor who felt uncomfortable in the restaurant, I felt "intimidated by the sea of White faces" each time I walked into a lecture hall or classroom (Vakil, 2021). I was a member of an underrepresented racial group in a field dominated with over 82 percent White teachers (Aud et al., 2010) and tended to distance myself as the Asian American instructor in order to secure some form of acceptance from my students as a legitimate teacher educator, expert in her field, despite the Brown skin and scarf.

Yet now, with the alarming rise in viscous hate crimes toward Asian Americans, I am reawakened. My own childhood memories of being taunted as a "chink," hearing the unendearing chants of "ching-chong-ching-chong" in my school's hallways and playground, resonate with the surge of bullying of Asian Americans and Pacific Islander (AAPI) students, which the White House Initiative on AAPI (2018) "reported the highest rate of classroom bullying, 20 percent higher than any race or ethnic group." What has further emboldened me has been hashtags such as #miseducAsian. As my own students felt connected to teachers outside of their physical communities, I too was able to establish online connections with other Asian American educators. Slow Twitter chats provided us with a safe space to discuss how we can recenter curriculum from an Asian American perspective and how our own histories can disrupt the dominant narratives taught in school. The forum of Twitter affords multiple avenues for critical discourse and can offer teacher candidates not only pedagogical ideas for the classroom, but also promote the awareness of the struggles of racism, stereotyping, and feelings of invisibility that many Asian minority students face.

CONCLUSION

In our work as anti-racist teacher educators, we each recognized our own identities as highly intersectional (Crenshaw, 1989) and as influencing the approaches we took to educating our teacher candidates. Our examination of our online teaching practices led us to more deeply agree with the assertion by Crenshaw that "[i]ntersectionality is not just about listing and naming your identities—it is a necessary analytic tool to explain the complexities and the realities of discrimination and of power or the lack thereof, and how they intersect with identities" (1989, p. 3). We recognized the important impacts of teaching explicitly about race and supporting future teachers in recognizing the ways in which race, perceptions, and related beliefs create or limit opportunities for learning and advocacy (Simmons, 2019). Exploration of our pedagogies, and the personal histories that undergird them helped us to recognize that we were each empowered by the creation of safe spaces that took into account our intersectional identities and bolstered our confidence and capacity with regard to engagement in conversations about race. We sought to engage our teacher candidates in critical conversations which they would come to view "dynamic cultural dexterity as a necessary good, and [see] the outcome of learning as additive rather than subtractive, as remaining whole rather than framed as broken as critically enriching strengths rather than replacing deficits" (Paris & Alim, 2017, p. 1). Such dialogue serves to prepare our teacher candidates for engagement in abolitionist teaching in which Whiteness is de-centered and healing, love and joy are key foundations (Love, 2019). These critical conversations are an essential starting point in making Whiteness visible, "but it cannot end there" (Love, 2019, p. 130).

Simmons' (2019) five actions for teaching for an anti-racist future—(1) engage in vigilant self-awareness, (2) acknowledge racism and the ideology of White supremacy, (3) study and teach representative history, (4) talk about race with students, and (5) when you see racism, do something—provided a framework and guideposts in our preparation for and enactment of anti-racist pedagogies with our teacher candidates. We found that strong positive interdependence was central to our students' engagement with challenging race-related constructs. When our teacher candidates felt welcomed and included they were maximally willing to share personal stories and engage in critical discussions. Within our teaching and modeling spaces, we as anti-racist teacher educators hold the power to listen to our students, to prompt their peers to listen to and engage with one another's unique vantage points. We have become increasingly committed to providing students opportunities to articulate and discuss identities that are important to them. Within such a context, we are best positioned to prompt learning through dialogue, engagement, and action—to move our classroom outcomes from moments to movements.

One direction for movements is to encourage students to pursue affinity groups through hashtags on social media. Hashtag feminism is an example of the ways in which social media can connect people to not only create dialogue but to bring about change.

> Feminists are not just creating discourse around issues online, they are taking these concerns to the street for even greater impact. #SlutWalk, #WeareallPussyRiot, #Bringbackourgirls, #DestroytheJoint and #SayHerName are four widely spread worldwide feminist hashtags that have had an impact both on and off-line. (Boling, 2019, p. 971)

For Joanne, #miseducAsian and #AbolitionistTeaching have provided a source of insight and socio-emotional support particularly after watching the barrage of news reports of elderly Asian Americans being brutally attacked and beaten, and the Atlanta women being targeted and fatally shot. A global connection to other educators of Asian descent emboldened us to redesign the direction of future Twitter assignments. No more can we as teacher educators stand and think this topic of racism might not be so relevant to Math or Instructional Technology. We must strive to bring to the forefront abolitionist teaching, "the practice of working in solidarity with communities of color . . . to eradicate injustice in and out of schools" (Love, 2019, p. 2). By introducing students to social justice hashtags, we can promote the development of our teacher candidates' critical consciousness, an integral aspect to CRP (Ladson-Billings, 2017), with possibilities for on the ground activism.

SOMETHING TO READ, DO, OR CONSIDER

- Read: Bettina Love's *We Want to Do More than Just Survive: Abolitionist Teaching and the Pursuit of Educational Freedom* (2019)
- Do: Participate in a social justice hashtag on social media.
- Consider: Plan a lesson based on one of Simmons' (2019) five actions for teaching for an anti-racist future.

REFERENCES

Aguirre, J., Mayfield-Ingram, K., & Martin, D. (2013). *The impact of identity in K-8 mathematics: Rethinking equity-based practices*. National Council of Teachers of Mathematics.

Amico, R. P. (2016). *Anti-racist teaching*. Routledge.

Angelone, L. (2021). #TechforJustice: Twitter chats and critical media literacy. In E. Langran & L. Archambault (Eds.), *Proceedings of society for information technology & teacher education international conference* (pp. 1402–1408). Online, United States: Association for the Advancement of Computing in Education (AACE). Retrieved April 7, 2021 from https://www.learntechlib.org/primary/p/219336/.

Aud, S., Fox, M., & Kewal Ramani, A. (2010). Status and trends in the education of racial and ethnic groups. NCES 2010-015. *National Center for Education Statistics*.

Baker, D. G. (1983). *Race, ethnicity and power*. Routledge Kegan Paul.

Banks, J. A. (1995). Multicultural education: Historical development, dimensions, and practice. In J. A. Banks & C. A. M. Banks (Eds.). *Handbook of research on multicultural education* (pp. 3–24). Macmillan.

Boling, K. S. (2019). #ShePersisted, Mitch: A memetic critical discourse analysis on an attempted Instagram feminist revolution. *Feminist Media Studies, 20*(7), 966–982. DOI: 10.1080/14680777.2019.1620821

Butler, J. (1990). *Gender trouble: Feminism and the subversion of identity*. Routledge.

Centers for Disease Control and Prevention. (2021, April 19). *Health equity considerations and racial and ethnic minority groups*. Centers for Disease Control and Prevention. https://www.cdc.gov/coronavirus/2019-ncov/community/health-equity/race-ethnicity.html

Carpenter, J. P., Cook, M. P., Morrison, S. A., & Sams, B. L. (2017). "Why haven't I tried Twitter until now?": Using Twitter in teacher education. *Learning Landscapes, 11*(1), 51–64.

Carpenter, J. P., & Krutka, D. G. (2015). Engagement through microblogging: Educator professional development via Twitter. *Professional Development in Education, 41*(4), 707–728.

Carpenter, J. P., Morrison, S. A., Craft, M., & Lee, M. (2020). How and why are educators using Instagram? *Teaching and Teacher Education, 96*(2020), 1–14. https://doi.org/10.1016/j.tate.2020.103149

Chao, T., Murray, E., & Gutiérrez, R. (2016). *"Classroom practices that support equity-based mathematics teaching."* [Research Brief.] National Council of Teachers of Mathematics, http://www.nctm.org/Research-and-Advocacy/Research-Brief-and-Clips/Classroom-Practices-That-Support-Equity-Based-Mathematics-Teaching/.

Crenshaw, K. (1989). Demarginalizing the intersection of race and sex: A Black feminist critique of antidiscrimination doctrine, feminist theory and anti-racist politics. *University of Chicago Legal Forum*, 1989(1), 139–167.

Foucault, M. (1980). *Power knowledge: Selected interviews and other writings*. 1972-1977 (1st ed.). Pantheon Books.

Foucault, M. (1991). *Remarks on Marx: Conversations with Duccio Trombadori*. Semiotext(e).

Geiger, A. W. (2018). *America's public school teachers are far less racially and ethnically diverse than their students.* Pew Research Center. https://www.pewresearch.org/fact-tank/2018/08/27/americas-public-school-teachers-are-far-less-racially-and-ethnically-diverse-than-their-students/

Greenhow, C., Galvin, S., Brandon, D., & Askari, E. (2020). A decade of research on K-12 teaching and teacher learning with social media: Insights on the state-of-the-field. (Open Access) *Teachers College Record, 122*(6), 1–72.

Holbert, R. M. G. (2015). Classroom community and possible selves: Implications for Midcareer Teacher Seminars. *Teachers and Teaching: Theory and Practice, 21*(1), 44–60.

Holbert, R. M. G. (2019). Using the circle question format to promote pre-reading for Individual and collaborative critical thinking. *College Teaching (online ahead of print 25 Jan 2019).*

hooks, b. (1994). *Teaching to transgress: Education as the practice of freedom.* Routledge.

Hsieh, B. (2017). Making and missing connections: Exploring Twitter chats as a learning tool in a preservice teacher education course. *Contemporary Issues in Technology and Teacher Education, 17*(4). Retrieved from https://www.citejournal.org/volume-17/issue-4-17/current-practice/making-and-missing-connections-exploring-twitter-chats-as-a-learning-tool-in-a-preservice-teacher-education-course

Kellner, D., & Share, J. (2007). Critical media literacy is not an option. *Learning Inquiry, 1,* 59–69.

Kohli, R. (2012), Racial pedagogy of the oppressed: Critical interracial dialogue for teachers of color. *Equity and Excellence in Education, 45*(1), 181–196.

Ladson-Billings, G. (1995). Toward a theory of culturally relevant pedagogy. *American Educational Research Journal, 32*(3), 465–491. https://doi.org/10.3102/00028312032003465

Ladson-Billings, G. (2017). The R(E)volution will not be standardized. In Django Paris & H. Samy Alim (Eds.), *Culturally sustaining pedagogies: Teaching and learning for justice in a changing world* (pp. 141–156). Teachers College Press.

Love, B. (2019). *We want to do more than survive: Abolitionist teaching and the pursuit of educational freedom.* Beacon Press.

Ng, J. C., Lee, S. S., & Pak, Y. K. (2007). Contesting the model minority and perpetual foreigner stereotypes: A critical review of literature on Asian Americans in education. *Review of Research in Education, 31*(1), 95–130.

Noble, S. U. (2018). *Algorithms of oppression: How search engines reinforce racism.* New York: NYU Press.

Nuyen, S. (2021). *Anti-Asian attacks rise during pandemic.* National Public Radio. https://www.npr.org/2021/03/17/978055571/anti-asian-attacks-rise-during-pandemic-read-nprs-stories-on-the-surge-in-violen

Pyke, K. (2010). What is internalized racial oppression and why don't we study it? Acknowledging racism's hidden injuries. *Sociological Perspectives, 53*(4), 551–72.

Shelton, C., Schroeder, S., & Curcio, R. (2020). Instagramming their hearts out: What do edu-influencers share on Instagram? *Contemporary Issues in Technology and Teacher Education, 20*(3), 529–554.

Shim, J. M. (2018). Inquiry into (In) ability to navigate dissidence in teacher education: What it tells us about internalized racism. *International Journal of Teaching and Learning in Higher Education, 30*(1), 127–135.

Smith, B., & Hawkins, B. (2020). Examining student evaluations of Black college faculty: Does race matter? *Journal of Negro Education, 80*(2), 149–162.

Tyson, P. (2015). The digital divide and inequities for students with disabilities: Needed… a bridge over troubled waters! *Journal of the American Academy of Special Education Professionals, Spr-Sum,* 151–162.

Vakil, J. (2021, in press). Faculty lounge flashpoints and an Asian, Muslim GTA's navigation in the classroom. *Women, Gender, and Families of Color, Graduate Students of Color Special Online 2020.*

Vakil, J., & Chao, T. (2019). Mathematics teacher education in the age of Twitter: A critical tool in elementary math methods. In S. Otten, A. G. Candela, Z. de Araujo, C. Haines, & C. Munter (Eds.), *Proceedings of the fort-first annual meeting of the North American Chapter of the International Group for the Psychology of Mathematics Education.* University of Missouri.

Van Leent, L., & Mills, K. (2018). A queer critical media literacies framework in a digital age. *Journal of Adolescent & Adult Literacy, 61*(4), 401–411.

Warlick, D. (2009). Grow your personal learning network: New technologies can keep you connected and help you manage information overload. *Learning & Leading with Technology, 36*(6), 12–16.

Warschauer, M., Grant, D., Del Real, G., & Rousseau, M. (2004). Promoting academic literacy with technology: Successful laptop programs in K-12 schools. *System, 32,* 525–537.

White, D. Y., Murray, E. C., & Brunaud-Vega, V. (2012). Discovering multicultural mathematics dispositions. *Journal of Urban Mathematics Education, 5*(1), 31–43.

White House Initiative on Asian Americans and Pacific Islanders. (2018). Retrieved from https://sites.ed.gov/aapi/

Zydney, J. M., deNoyelles, A., & Seo, K. K.-J. (2012). Creating a community of inquiry in online environments: An exploratory study on the effect of a protocol on interactions within asynchronous discussions. *Computers & Education, 58,* 77–87. https://doi.org/10.1016/j.compedu.2011.07.009

Chapter 9

One Man's Journey as a Black and White Educational Researcher

Self-determination through a Biracial Perspective

Brett A. Burton

I have elected to present this particular chapter as an autobiographical inquiry. My experiences as a biracial child (Black father and White mother) where I was born five years after the U.S. Supreme Court case of *Loving v. Virginia*, which legalized interracial marriage, inspired me to discuss my past and present racial experiences and research (Cole & Knowles, 2000, p. 14). I believe now is the optimal time to share my experiences as I have lived as a biracial individual in a country obsessed with race for almost half a century. It's important to remember that "The history of race in America is a history of discrimination and intimidation, intertwined with a history of progress" (Lukianoff & Haidt, 2018, p. 140). In addition, I will discuss the connection between my biracial identity experiences and self-determination theory which has been instrumental in my development as an educator and researcher.

I am the son of an interracial couple, a Black father and White mother. Life was hard for my parents, who eventually had three biracial children before turning 26. I was born in 1972, my sister B.M. was born in 1974, and my baby sister R.L. was born in 1976. My White, Irish-Catholic mother and Black-Baptist father were 18 years of age and in their senior year of high school. In 1972, interracial marriage was uncommon and not socially acceptable, especially when one considers that interracial marriage was legalized in 1967 by the U.S. Supreme Court, *Loving v. Virginia*. Because interracial marriage was in the infancy stages of social acceptance by American citizens, my parents endured many hardships, creating stress and tension in our family. The adversity my father and mother faced was from external and internal forces.

The external adversity revolved around prejudice and racism in the community by receiving piercing looks, glares, and under-the-breath comments as they entered a doctor's office or grocery store. The internal adverse forces my father endured questions his allegiance to the struggle of Black people in the United States. Can a Black man married to a White woman be viewed as a person committed to the Black struggle for equality and opportunity? The internal adverse condition was just as harsh and intense as the external forces. Furthermore, both mom and dad came from limited financial resources. On the other hand, the internal adversity came from grandparents (mother side) who were not initially accepting and concerned about the racism and hardships my mother would experience by being married to a Black man. Also, my father dealt with demons stemming from not knowing his father, which created bitterness toward the world. My grandmother had three children by three different men in a decade. My father was the oldest of three. Essentially, my father was raised by his grandmother and her husband, who migrated from Vicksburg, Mississippi, to Chicago, IL, in 1960 for better opportunities and employment. His life was difficult for many reasons. First, the lack of a father in his life was challenging. Second, he was a Black male who attended mostly White public schools. Third and foremost, he impregnated a White Catholic female, eventually married her, and had three interracial children.

All of the factors combined created a roller coaster childhood for my sisters and me. There were consistent verbal holiday arguments between my parents, especially at Christmas time. My father would typically argue with my mother every Christmas morning as he did not want to attend my mother's family's Christmas party. What I always found interesting is that he would complain and resist going, but when our family arrived he would be a happy and positive individual, even smiling for family pictures. There were many occasions my father would come home from work, and we never knew what type of mood my father would be in after working in the factory. At times my father would be in a good mood but other times we would feel his wrath. My dad would blame my mother for being stuck working in the factory and having limited options for work as the burden of family and marriage weighed on him. However, my parents persevered and remained together for over 20 years before eventually divorcing in 1993. Since adversity was unavoidable, my parents had to rely on one another to navigate their own identities as individuals and as interracial couples. They had to collaborate and create a family structure that would shield us from the racist perils of the world. My parents understood what it's like to be an interracial couple. However, they did not know or experience what our lives would be like as biracial children.

Furthermore, my mother and father had to prepare us for a country that has been judgmental and critical of biracial marriages and individuals. Both of my parents instilled important life skills in all three of their children.

They expected each of us to work hard and be self-determined. I could not have predicted the attributes of self-determination that have played in my life as a biracial adult and will discuss the impact later in this chapter. As the emphasis of anti-racist pedagogy comes to the forefront in educational systems and institutions, scholars may find it beneficial to explore the role of self-determination theory in conquering the racism biracial children and adults experience in educational institutions (Rockquemore & Brunsma, 2008).

PROBLEM STATEMENT

Racial identity scholars suggest that biracial students begin to question their identity when they first appear on a college campus (Zook, 2019; Renn, 200). As a result, biracial students pursue understanding their racial identity through courses in racial-ethnic studies, student organizations, and peer relationships (Renn, 2000; Clayton, 2020). Although some biracial students may negate their racial backgrounds from two different racial groups, others attempt to embrace and accept their identities as belonging to different racial groups. As a result, the self-identified biracial students may experience rejection among peers belonging to monoracial groups, confusion with their racial identity, certain levels of unique microaggressions, and feelings of isolation at the university (Cooney & Radina, 2000; Clayton, 2020; Zook, 2019). Also, in the United States Census in 2013, about nine million Americans chose two or more racial groups and have experienced racial slurs (61 percent White-Black), poor service in restaurants (57 percent White-Black), and unfairly stopped by police (41 percent White-Black) (Pew Research Center, 2015, p. 8). As research has demonstrated, biracial individuals are negatively affected by these unique racial challenges. In that case, this chapter may provide a template for others to challenge moments of racism.

LITERATURE REVIEW

In 1967, the U.S. Supreme Court legalized interracial marriage in *Loving v. Virginia*. This case may have been the catalyst for the increased biracial population in the United States. After *Loving*, the multiracial population "increased from 310,000 (in 1970) to 1.4 million (in the early 1990s)" (Rockquemore and Brunsma, 2008), and currently stands at over nine million (Pew Research Center, 2015).

Biracial individuals expand across many racial categories and combinations. The Pew Research Center (2015) defines multiracial adults as those who select two or more races for themselves; those who do not select two or more races for themselves but report that at least one of their parents was not the same race as the one they selected for themselves, or select two or more races for at least one of their biological parents, respondents who do not fit the definition of biracial based on their own or their parents' racial background, but indicate that at least one of their grandparents was not the same race as themselves or their parents, or select two or more races for their grandparents. (p. 13)

The United States Census Bureau currently recognizes the following racial categories: White, Black, Asian, American Indian or Alaska Native, and Native Hawaiian or Pacific Islander. Specifically, the U.S. Census Bureau will disaggregate racial groups by using terminology such as "White alone or in combination" or "Black alone or combination" and a specific category defining "two or more races" (https://www.census.gov/topics/population/race.html). Although there are various racial combinations for biracial groups, this particular chapter will specifically focus on biracial individuals with one Black parent and one White parent.

Biracial individuals that are the offspring of an interracial couple may experience racism. As an almost half-century biracial man, I ask myself two questions in 2021 about race relations? "Will racism ever end? What role can educational research play in eradicating racism?" It was apparent that George Floyd's death became the catalyst of the anti-racist movement currently taking place in the United States. As protestors marched in the streets demanding justice and defunding the police, I could not help to wonder about the implications of this very powerful and emotionally triggering movement. I also wondered how biracial individuals, specifically when racial combinations are Black and White, navigate the current polarizing mindsets with race relations. The challenge for biracial individuals is that they may be perceived as being the "buffer" between Whites and Blacks when race relations are tumultuous (Rockquemore & Brunsma, 2008, p. 10). As social activist groups such as Black Lives Matter and Make America Great Again (MAGA) strive for power and control, biracial individuals are placed in the middle.

Biracial Experience

Historically, racism against biracial individuals has been present since the days of slavery in the United States. As American slave owners began to rape and impregnate female slaves, the biracial population began to grow, forcing the reckoning of a slave force whose phenotype was growing Whiter by the year (Chiong, 1998). To protect the institution of slavery and the purity of the monoracial system, legislators in the southern states had to reaffirm their position of superiority; hence the "one-drop rule" was created and sustained in this country (Chiong, 1998, p. 11). Davis (1991) defines the one-drop rule as a racial categorization rule that applies only to Blacks. No other race, claiming that if an individual has one drop of Black blood, he/she is defined as Black (p. 13). After the Civil War, the South and the United States transitioned into the Jim Crow era, reinforcing a systemic racist structure absentia slavery. The United States was able to tighten its grip on systemic racism against Blacks and biracial by leveraging the U.S. Supreme Court and in the case of *Plessy v. Ferguson*, 1896.

In this essential case, Homer Plessy, a biracial man from Louisiana who was one-eighth Black and seven-eighths White, attempted to sit in a first-class passenger seat on a train reserved for White citizens only. The rail conductor asked Homer Plessy to move and sit in the colored-only section. He declined this directive and was subsequently arrested and jailed. Mr. Plessy filed a petition stating that his 14th Amendment Right, otherwise known as the Equal Protection Clause, was violated. The court claimed that the 14th Amendment did not pertain to social situations but was intended for political and civil rights. This historic case clarified that "separate but equal" and affirming that an individual with one-eighth Black blood shall be defined as Black (*Plessy v. Ferguson*, 1896). This historical case eventually created a system that permitted and sanctioned racist practices and claimed that racial groups should remain separate and biracial individuals with any trace of Black blood should be defined as Black citizens. Due to the systemic racist obstacles, biracials endured during this time, some individuals made efforts to pass their racial status as White (Rockquemore & Brunsma, 2008, p. 42). Biracial individuals with a phenotype that appeared White have an easier time with passing (Rockquemore & Brunsma, 2008). However, all biracial individuals possess different phenotypes and may have different skin tones or complexions. Therefore, biracial individuals with a light-skinned tone may elect to pass as White or keep their racial identity ambiguous. Racial "passing" is defined as when a Black or biracial light-skinned individual passes their racial identity as White (Smith, 1994). When a biracial individual makes the decision to "pass" as White, they are making a conscious choice to deny their own biracial heritage, which can lead to identity and psychological challenges (Cooney & Radina, 2000).

One would presume in today's age that having "one drop" of blood from any racial group doesn't qualify a person to identify with one sole racial group. However, according to Sharfstein (2007), "the American insistence on absolute White racial purity is presumed to be the brightest of bright-line rules, synonymous with racism and central to the evolution of racial identity and resistance in the United States" (p. 594). The insistence on racial purity in the United States may deter biracials from embracing their sense of belonging to the different racial groups and subsequently will be rejected by monoracial friends or peers (Wardle & Cruz-Jansen, 2004).

One example of the lengths biracial individuals may conceal their racial identity and conceal their true racial identity pertained to Anatole Broyard. Anatole was born to light-skinned Creole parents in New Orleans, Louisiana, in the 1930s (Broyard, 2007). Anatole's parents elected to pass for "White" as they believed they would be better positioned to secure employment in New York City in the 1930s. When Anatole grew up in Brooklyn, New York, he expressed that children from both Black and White racial groups did not accept but actually rejected and insulted him. Anatole decided to pass as White and lived the rest of his life as a White male, who eventually became a writer and editor for *The New York Times* (Broyard, 2007).

In addition, Anatole married a White female and raised his children and family among the upper elites that belonged to such White privilege societies as the Connecticut Yacht Club. Not until Anatole died in 1990 did his adult children become aware that he was Black and they are biracial. Even though Anatoles' story goes to the extreme length of a biracial individual concealing their racial identity, it is pertinent to provide context to the biracial challenges in the current racial climate. As a biracial man, I can relate to the perils that Anatole Broyard experienced. Still, instead of opting to pass, I elected to take a different approach toward harmonizing my own racial identity. I leaned on my family that instilled a value of teaching me to be self-determined through hard work, effort, and persistence. Before I describe my present self, it is paramount to provide the background on self-determination theory (SDT).

Self-Determination Theory (SDT)

Scholars have explored Deci and Ryan's (2000) SDT and the potential impact it may have on human motivation (Center for Self-Determination Theory, n.d.). SDT attempts to frame the variables that simplify "intrinsic motivation, autonomous extrinsic motivation, and psychological wellness," which impact learning organizations such as schools (Ryan & Deci, 2020, p. 54). I posit that SDT may play an instrumental role in supporting biracial individuals in navigating a racial duality where they may experience challenges (Deci and Ryan, 2000). To conceptually grasp the SDT framework, it is important to explain the three components of the motivational theory and how they interact. Ryan and Deci (2020) posit that individuals may be intrinsically motivated. With the right support, they will "learn, master, and connect with others" (Introduction section). The primary three facets of SDT are autonomy, competence, and relatedness (Ryan & Deci).

Autonomy

One important aspect of SDT is that individuals will encounter two different types of motivation. Deci (2017) claims that motivation is binary as most people will experience autonomous motivation or controlled motivation. Autonomous motivation is described as motivation that arises when people choose and perform a task for pleasure and enjoyment (Deci, 2017). An example of autonomous motivation would be when a student has an assignment such as a science project. The teacher allows the student to select and create a project based on 150 options. Controlled motivation is when an individual performs a task because they seek to avoid a consequence, punishment or are coerced to do something (Deci, 2017). An example of controlled motivation is when a teacher dictates that they must create a diorama on cellular formation for their science project. This would be controlled because the student was given a directive and does not have a choice. The next aspect of Deci and Ryan's SDT is relatedness.

Relatedness

Deci (2017) defines relatedness as the need for individuals to have a sense of belonging to a relevant group. The other aspect of relatedness is that an individual needs to be cared for by others (Deci). An example of relatedness would be like having a "romantic partner or best friend" that an individual can rely on for support and listen to them (Deci & Flaste, 1995, p. 119). When I reflect on the relatedness aspect of SDT, I believe I was blessed to have many close friends from all racial backgrounds. However, my closest friend was a White young man that was an amazing athlete and confidante. We developed this close friendship through 6:00 a.m. morning weight training workouts which were four days a week before the school day. My friend and I developed a strong relationship because we had similar goals which fostered friendly competition that lead to holding one another accountable while supporting one another. The time we spent over those four years in high school as teammates, competitors, and more importantly friends allowed us to confide in one another when we faced adversity with divorce, death, or failed relationships. The relatedness aspect has truly provided me the capacity to cope with personal and professional hardships because my positive relationships with friends and family support me with moving forward.

Competence

Deci & Flaste (1995) claim that "feeling competent" is a human necessity and compels individual motivation (p. 64). Competence pertains to mastery and having the ability and aptitude to achieve one's goals (Martela & Tapani, 2018). An example of competence would be when a "C" student sets a challenging goal such as making the honor roll in school, requiring a minimum of "B" letter grades in all subject areas. The student intentionally decides to spend more time studying for exams, completing homework, and improving their daily attendance. Before the goal, the student seldom turned in homework or studied, and their attendance was inconsistent. Because the student previously earned "C" letter grades without much effort, setting a goal of earning "B" letter grades is an "optimal challenge" (Deci & Flaste, p. 66).

Life as an Oreo

This autobiographical chapter aims to frame my biracial identity experiences and the impact SDT assisted me in overcoming moments of racism and to evolve into an education professor and researcher. To understand my perspective, it is important to share my past experiences and present perspective.

My Past

I was born into a world where race matters. I cannot recall the first time another person called me "mixed," "yellow," "red," "oreo," "chocolate, vanilla swirl," or "n-word." I just knew that my parents were different from all of my friends' parents in that no one in my neighborhood had one Black and one White parent. When my mother registered me for kindergarten in 1977 in a public elementary school 40 miles west of Chicago, she checked both racial identity boxes for Black and White. At the time, I was pretty oblivious to the relevance and importance of racial identity. My elementary school had a very diverse student population, and I had Puerto Rican, Mexican American, Black, and White peers. The economically marginalized neighborhood I resided in was mostly Puerto Rican, Mexican American, and Black. Most of the parents in the area worked at local factories and attained a high school diploma at best. I have to admit that I was very fortunate to live in a diverse neighborhood because I don't recall experiencing any racism from my Latinx peers and friends. My friends' Latinx parents assumed I was Puerto Rican due to my curly brown and blondish hair and a tan complexion. I played baseball, rode bikes, participated in a bowling league, and was very much embraced by all peers and families until we moved to the other side of town after my fourth grade school year.

When I was ten years old, my parents started noticing changes in the neighborhood as the crime rate increased and our street became more transient and unsafe. My parents sold our "eastside" home and purchased a house on the "westside" of the city. When my family moved to the west side of town and enrolled all three children into the local public school, I noticed an immediate difference among my peer group. The students and families were predominantly White, middle to upper class. The parents were commonly in management positions at the local factories or commuted to Chicago to work at a downtown corporation. During my fifth grade school year, I started to become very aware of my racial identity. It was the first time I experienced blatant racism from peers and school leadership.

In October 1983, I vividly remembered playing a game called Four Square before school. Four Squares is a game played with a rubber athletic ball about the size of a soccer ball, and each player stands in one of the Four Squares. The game's goal is to move into Square four because the player in the fourth square is allowed to create the rules for the game. Many of the children at this school arrived early and were allowed to play Four Square, kickball, dodgeball, and so on, out on the school grounds. However, the game of Four Squares was by far the most competitive. Typically, the students were unsupervised until approximately 20 minutes before the first bell. I remember this particular morning because I was competing in Four Squares and worked my way into the fourth square. During my tenure as the Four Square champ, I remember a student in the sixth grade named Danny decided to leave his dodgeball game to play Four Square. Danny came from a pretty large blended family. He was third oldest in his family out of five boys and two girls. Danny was not an intimidating boy but more or less, a White young boy that enjoyed inciting his classmates by making fun or pulling pranks on them. His motive was very typical and that was to get some sort of emotional reaction out of his victim. As Danny was standing in line and waiting to enter square one, I heard him make a racist comment to another student standing in line waiting a turn. Danny said to the student next to him, "Brett must be winning because he's playing by 'n---' rules."

Once I heard that statement come out of Danny's mouth, I lost my temper and went after him. Students who heard the comment and were playing Four Square began to laugh as Danny ran around the play area trying to escape the thrashing I was about to place on him. When I was running after him, a teacher noticed that I was upset and chasing Danny for some reason. The teacher yelled at me and said, "Brett Burton, stop what you are doing and come here now!" When I heard the teacher, I stopped chasing Danny and approached the teacher with my fists balled and eyes watering. The teacher asked me to explain why I was so angry, which I did at this time. The teacher sent me into the building to wash my face, get a drink of water, and calm down. On the way into the building, I remember the teacher telling me to ignore Danny in the future and stay away from him. Based on the teacher's comments I inferred that I wasn't going to receive justice in any form, meaning no consequences for Danny. Furthermore, I remember thinking that the teacher was going to downplay this racist action, which would mean that I would have to take matters into my own hands in the future, something I was more than prepared to do. When I went home that afternoon, I waited for my father to return home from his factory job in a neighboring city.

When my father arrived home, I explained to him what transpired at school today and how Danny said that I was playing by "n--- rules." My father said, "Brett, I told you, your sisters, and mother that by moving over here that we would be dealing with this racial stuff. This side of town has always had racial problems, so this is nothing new. My advice to you is always be twice as good as other people and make sure you don't mess up. As a Black male, you don't get second chances like White kids." My father's message to me was pretty direct, and I was immediately aware that as a biracial individual I could not make mistakes like other White students, and I had to perform at a higher level than Whites in school, athletics, etc. to have an opportunity at success. As a biracial adolescent my father's message was clear and it is something I continue to carry to this day. After that comment, my father took his work clothes off and showered before we ate dinner. Unfortunately, this racial experience became one of many forms of racism I would experience in junior high, high school, and college. The next vivid memory of racism I experienced evolved during my freshman year of college.

In 1990, I attended a state university located in the western part of the state of Illinois. Although I experienced levels of racism during my elementary, middle, and high school years, I became more conscious of my racial identity during my freshman year of college. As previously stated multiracial or biracial individuals start to understand their racial "identity in college" (Renn, 2000, p. 400). One of my first semester classes freshman year was African American History 100: my professor was an, African native, and a long-standing professor in the Department of African American Studies. I vividly remember a class lecture where the professor discussed biracial or multiracial individuals in the United States and racial classification. The professor explicitly stated that biracial, specifically any biracial person with African American blood, is categorized as "Black." He claimed that the rationale behind this statement is because America will never embrace the biracial individual as a separate racial group, and mulattos are better served by claiming "Black" and denying their White heritage. This lecture created a personal identity conflict inside. I have always honored both of my parent's racial identities and identified as Black and White. However, this professor challenged my racial identity and stated that I must claim "Black" only. I recall thinking as a 19-year-old college student that his statement was racist. During this time, I did not realize that the emphasis on biracial individuals identifying as Black only is a common mindset within the White power structures of society White (Campion, 2019, p. 199). Scholars have stated that biracial individuals' presence in the United States is not "a new phenomenon" (Rockquemore and Brunsma, 2008, p. 3), but individuals are identifying as biracial have created a cultural issue (Rockquemore and Brunsma). I believe I understood the professor's perspective with the message that biracial individuals should solely identify as Black. Based on the U.S. Supreme Court case of *Plessy v. Ferguson, 163 U.S. 537 (1896), an individual with any Black blood should be categorized as Black, regardless of Black or White blood percentages.* During my freshman year of college, I believe this experience became the catalyst of my unapologetic acknowledgment of identifying as a biracial man. As a biracial professor, I believe my ability to navigate the person of color identity, and the White identity has shaped my perspective as an instructor and educational researcher. Perhaps this radical movement in my thinking and rejecting the pressure to select membership to one race provided me the courage to never allow any individual or system to define me. The next aspect of this chapter is to discuss my present biracial self in the context of a retired public school principal and current educational administrator professor and researcher that leverages self-determination as a means to overcome explicit and implicit racism.

My Present

My viewpoint of racism is binary. I have lived almost 50 years as a biracial male who has experienced acceptance and rejection from Black and White racial groups. Regardless of the situation where I was embraced or denied, I remained steadfast in my ability to understand that the only means for me to engage, achieve, and evolve with this racial identity in a country obsessed with race is to be self-determined. When I was asked to participate in the anti-racist book project, I was forced to reflect on my past and present racial experiences as a biracial man. I was fully aware that my life experiences were unique as I have no perspective on living as a monoracial individual. However, my binary racial perspective has provided me insight with almost five decades of experience to understand the characteristics I have acquired in life that have positively impacted me. When I was seeking ways to frame this chapter, I started to recall a theory that I have researched and read over the years connected to my existence, survival, and resiliency as a man of color—the SDT created by Deci and Ryan (2000). Throughout my life span, I have learned that biracial individuals, specifically from Black and White parents, are in the throes of determining how to navigate the racial tension reignited by George Floyd's death on May 25, 2020. Floyd's death sparked interest in examining systemic race issues that have caused substantial and historical harm to the Black community for more than a century. The current conversation also expanded to the biracial community. It spurred interest among this population, particularly when the biracial combination was Black and White.

The *Today Show* provided advice to the biracial community that was challenged to balance supporting the Black Lives Matter (BLM) Organization and how they participate in the movement when part of their racial identity is White. Dr. Gaither (2020), a biracial assistant professor at Duke University, has studied multiracial experiences for over ten years and received a vast amount of emails and social media messages from biracial individuals seeking advice on how to fight White supremacy when their physical appearance may be perceived as White. Some of the biracial individual's inquiry to Dr. Gaither (2020) asked if they needed to select a side, referring to a racial side as the murder of George Floyd blurred racial lines. Gaither's response to the abundance of biracial inquiries she received was that biracial individuals should acknowledge their privilege but comprehend that it's important to foster "change, when and where you can" (Gaither, 2020). Meaning, biracial individuals have the fortune to reside in a country where they have first-hand experiences of being Black and White. Therefore, being biracial may be considered a strength and provide opportunities to create positive changes in the anti-racist movement. One possible means to explore the strengths of biracial individualism in a systemically racist culture is to assist biracial individuals in leveraging Deci and Ryan's (2000) SDT.

Biracial individuals, at times, will experience racism from both Black and White individuals and face the greatest exclusion from belongingness than any other racial group (Latson, 2019). As an education professor and researcher, I believe the implementation of SDT deserves to be further investigated to support biracial students in navigating their racial journey and identity.

SDT and Biracialism

Based on my personal experiences, I posit that SDT and biracialism warrant further investigation in educational research. As a biracial professor and researcher, I serve in a higher education system where 75 percent of all professors are White, 6 percent Black, and 1 percent or less are biracial (National Center for Education Statistics, 2020, https://nces.ed.gov/programs/digest/d20/tables/dt20_315.20.asp). Therefore, I intend to present evidence supporting the impact SDT may have on supporting biracial individuals at the university. This section will connect my own biracial experience to the three SDT aspects of autonomy, competence, and relatedness.

Autonomy and Biracialism

Through my past and present self, I have determined that autonomy with support from family and teachers has been instrumental in my development as an educational leader and researcher. I have experienced racism from both Black and White individuals. The racist experiences have been the catalyst for me to strive and understand both sides of racism. However, I haven't been consumed with resolving this conflict as much as I am inspired to use it as a means to motivate myself as an educator, researcher, and responsible citizen. Deci and Flaste (1995) claim that autonomy is about "feeling a true willingness to behave responsibly, in accord with your interests and values" (p. 134–135). Because of my lack of acceptance at times from both racial groups, I looked for moments within myself to determine my value. Throughout my childhood, it was athletics and school. As an educator and researcher, I have found value in being a relational leader and researcher. As Ryan and Deci (2020) state that "autonomy support is thus a central element in cultural competency-that is, in being able to effectively work with people from diverse backgrounds and value systems, whose frame of reference influence their motivations and valuations" (p.5). Due to the lack of racial acceptance at times, I became more sensitive to and looked for moments that would allow me to connect with individuals from various racial groups in various settings and systems. The moments I had as a building principal provided autonomous decision-making opportunities. For example, as a principal and assistant principal I would lead school improvement or crisis teams as part of my administrator duties. The leadership role afforded autonomous decision-making which increased professional moments where I was able to recruit or appoint a team with racial differences to serve in a building leadership capacity. My ability to collaborate with individuals from different racial backgrounds, enhanced my cultural competency and gave me the courage and insight to create school leadership teams comprised of teachers from various racial backgrounds. Even though autonomy is paramount in SDT, it cannot stand alone as the ability to relate to others from different racial backgrounds is just as vital.

Relatedness and Biracialism

Scholars have claimed that biracial individuals who try to please both racial groups to gain acceptance will experience frustration, rejection, and isolation (Quillian and Redd, 2009; Cooney and Radina, 2000). As a biracial adolescent, I was compelled to relate to my peers from both racial groups and experienced angst from rejection. When I experienced rejection from my Black and White contemporaries, I consistently leaned on my family for support. Often, my nuclear family support was sufficient and helped me process the rejection. However, as I matured and became older, I was able to leverage my family relationships to help guide my ability to be "independent and autonomous" among my peers that belonged to both racial groups (Deci & Flaste, 1995, p. 89). Being independent and autonomous helped me focus on my actions and goals, which gave me more confidence in my biracial identity, which transcended into accepting others regardless of their racial background. The ability to embrace individual differences among racial groups has fostered my capacity to relate and accept others regardless of race or any other differences. My ability to lean and relate to my family has allowed me to examine race relations as a construct that may consume a person's identity and a sense of purpose and value if one allows it. One of the many challenges that I have experienced in the past through present times is not allowing the negative racial rhetoric of selecting a side to deter my values and beliefs about race. My life experiences and journey to this point, fostered by the acquired attributes of autonomy, relatedness, and competence, have shielded me in a sense from the current racial climate. A biracial individual possessing the "relatedness" characteristic may have the capacity to overcome racism by understanding both racial perspectives. Herman's (2004) study revealed that biracial individuals have "differential opportunities" (p. 732). Meaning, because biracial individuals may associate and assimilate into different racial groups, they have a unique insight on race relations that are different when compared to single-race individuals. This relatability characteristic integrated into a person's biracial identity may provide an opportunity to bring people together to appreciate differences within a system.

Competence and Biracialism

The acquisition of competence continues to be a work in progress throughout my life as a biracial individual, so I wanted to merge biracialism and competence as the last aspect of this autobiographical chapter. Competence has played a pivotal role in understanding myself as a biracial male in a culture where race continues to matter. During this autobiographical journey, I realize that the racist moments I experienced throughout my life supported my competence with understanding my place in the world and race relations to a certain extent. The struggle of being denied and not accepted by either racial group motivated me to "engage in various activities to expand [my] own sense of accomplishment" (Deci & Flaste, 1995, p. 65). When I reflect, I would claim that my experiences became the catalyst for my desire to excel professionally, scholarly, and personally. I wanted to demonstrate to the world that a biracial individual could attain goals despite the constant question of racial identity. I used the psychological need for competence as a means to become one of the few school leaders of color in a suburban school district that had a history of possessing a glass ceiling for Black, Indigenous, People of Color (BIPOC) educators striving to become leaders. Once I secured a school leadership position, my desire for competence increased, and I enrolled and completed a doctoral degree at a large university. During my doctoral experience, I was the sole male of color out of 16 doctoral candidates. I was the first student to complete their dissertation. Again, my need for competence was driven by my racial experiences and possessing autonomy and relatedness.

CONCLUSION

As I conclude this chapter, it is paramount to state that no two biracial experiences are the same. Many factors in my life supported me in navigating a biracial existence, specifically support from my family, parents instilling a work ethic, and intrinsic motivation to strive and meet my full potential. I posit that the negative racial moments I experienced and continue to experience are challenging. Throughout my personal and professional journey, SDT has been instrumental in helping me understand how I evolved from a biracial, unaccepted, working-class individual to a retired school leader and current anti-racist educational professor and researcher. My hope is that other biracial individuals that encounter racism can use my story and the integration of SDT to overcome any latent, blatant, and systemic racism.

As I approach 50 years of age as a biracial individual, my counsel to younger biracial people is to be authentic and resist the temptation to be defined by others. I would recommend that biracial individuals seek and join athletic teams, or school clubs and activities if available. The extracurricular organizations may provide the opportunity to collaborate and develop social ties based on a common goal which may enhance an individual's ability to be autonomous. These school opportunities will foster an individual's development in collaborating and communicating with others that may have differences in race, culture, gender, and so on. In addition, I advise biracial individuals to seek family or friendships that will help foster relatedness. Racism will never cease to exist and biracial individuals will more than likely experience racism from two different racial groups at some point in time. One of the keys to conquering racism for me was to lean on my family relationships and close friends when this happens. I have found through my experience that having this support is critical in overcoming the difficult times and incidences of racism. Equally as important, I discovered through my journey that as I developed skills with autonomy and relatedness, my level of competence on racial dynamics and systems increased. I recommend that biracial adolescents should use and frame their negative and positive racial experiences as a form of educational lessons. Racism is difficult, challenging, and catastrophic if a biracial individual accepts the notion that they are less than others. The key for biracial individuals in conquering racism is to possess autonomy, relatedness, and competence.

SOMETHING TO READ

I would encourage scholars that have interest in learning more about the biracial experience to read *The Color of Water: A Black Man's Tribute to His White Mother* (1996/2006) by James McBride. The author provides a description of his life as a biracial individual growing up in Brooklyn.

REFERENCES

Broyard, B. (2007). *One drop*. Little Brown and Company.
Burton, B. (2014). *A quantitative analysis of resiliency and academic achievement among multiracial students*. (Publication No: 3624769). [Doctoral dissertation, Northern Illinois University]. ProQuest Dissertations and Theses Global.
Center for Self Determination Theory. (n.d.). *Overview*. Retrieved April 7, 2021, from https://selfdeterminationtheory.org/the-theory/
Clayton, K. A. (2020). Biracial identity development at historically white and historically black colleges and universities. *Sociology of Education*, *93*(3), 238–255. doi:10.1177/0038040720926216
Cole, A. L., & Knowles, J. G. (2000). *Researching teaching: Exploring teacher development through reflexive inquiry*. Allyn & Bacon.
Cooney, T., & Radina, M. (2000). Adjustment problems in adolescence: Are multiracial children at risk? *American Journal of Orthopsychiatry*, *70*(4), 433–454.
Davis, J. (1991). *Who is Black? One nation's definition*. Penn State University Press. DOI 0271021721
Deci, E., & Flaste, R. (1995). *Why we do what we do: Understanding self-motivation*. Penguin Books.
Deci, E. L., & Ryan, R. M. (2000). The 'what' and 'why' of goal pursuits: Human needs and the self-determination of behavior. [Article]. *Psychological Inquiry*, *11*(4), 227.
Gaither, S. (2020, June 30). *My message to Black people questioning their role in Black Lives Matter*. Today. https://www.today.com/tmrw/biracial-people-questioningtheir-role-Black-lives-matter-t185441
Herman, M. (2004). Forced to choose: Some determinants of racial identification in multiracial adolescents. *Child Development*, *75*(3), 730–748.
Latson, J. (2019, May 7). The biracial advantage. *Psychology Today Magazine*. *Psychology Today Magazine May 2019*.
Lukianoff, G., & Haidt, J. (2018). *The coddling of the American mind. How good intentions and bad ideas are setting up a generation for failure*. New York: Penguin Books.
Martela, F., & Tapani, J. (2018). Autonomy, competence, relatedness, and beneficence: A multicultural comparison of the four pathways to meaningful work. *Frontiers in Psychology*, 9, 1157. https://selfdeterminationtheory.org/wp-content/uploads/2019/08/2018_MartelaRiekki_FrontiersInPsych.pdf

National Center for Education Statistics (2020). *The condition of education 2020: Characteristics of postsecondary faculty* [Data set]. https://www.nces.gov/programs/coe/indicator/csc

Pew Research Center. (2015). *Biracial in America: Proud, diverse and growing in numbers.* Washington, DC: June

Plessy v. Ferguson, 163 U.S. 537. (1896). https://supreme.justia.com/cases/federal/us/163/537/

Quillian, L., & Redd, R. (2009). The friendship of multiracial adolescents. *Social Science Research, 38*(2), 279–295.

Renn, K. A. (2000). Patterns of situational identity among biracial and multiracial college students. *The Review of Higher Education, 23*(4), 399–420.

Rockquemore, K. A., & Brunsma, D. L. (2008). *Beyond Black.* Lanham, MD: Rowman and Littlefield Publishers, Inc.

Ryan, R., & Deci, E. (2020). Intrinsic and extrinsic motivation from a self-determination theory perspective: Definitions, theory, practices, and future decisions. *Contemporary Educational Psychology.* https://doi.org/10.1016/j.cedpsych.2020.101860

Ryan, R. M., & Deci, E. L. (2000). "Self-determination theory and the facilitation of intrinsic motivation, social development, and well-being". *American Psychologist, 55*(1), 68–78. CiteSeerX 10.1.1.529.4370. doi:10.1037/0003-066x.55.1.68. PMID 11392867.

Sharfstein, D. J. (2007). Crossing the color line: Racial migration and the one-drop rule, 1600-1860. *Minnesota Law Review, 91*(3), 592–656.

Wardle, F., & Cruz-Janzen, M. (2004). *Meeting the needs of multiethnic and multiracial children in schools.* Pearson Education.

Zook, K. B. (2019, September 23). Universities are still struggling to provide for mixed-race students. *Multiracial in America.* Universities Are Still Struggling to Provide for Mixed-Race Students | by Kristal Brent Zook | ZORA (medium.com)

Chapter 10

Children's Literature

Guiding Change

Teresa Young, Vanessa M. Rigaud, and Sara Fitzgerald

Sharing good stories is an important part of any classroom. Children's literature helps us expand our experiences, knowledge, and worldview, takes us to new places, and guides us through happy and sad times. A good book can transform all of us. Short, Lynch-Brown, and Tomlinson (2018) state:

> Literature is not written to teach something, but to illuminate what it means to be human and to make the most fundamental experiences of life accessible—love, hope, loneliness, despair, fear, and belonging. Literature is the imaginative shaping of experience and thought into the forms and structures of language. Children read literature to experience life, and their experiences inside the world of a story challenge them to think in a new way about their lives and world. (p. 4)

Literature can change us. We know the impact of delightful stories. We realize that text, fiction, and nonfiction, can be transformative. And, so we define children's literature as literature that illuminates the lived-through experience. According to Short, Lynch-Brown, and Tomlinson (2018):

> Children's literature is defined as high-quality trade books for children from birth to early adolescence, covering topics of relevance and interest to children through prose and poetry, fiction, and nonfiction. They are the books that children see as reflecting their life experiences, understandings, and emotions. (p. 4)

THE VALUE OF CHILDREN'S LITERATURE: PERSONAL AND ACADEMIC

Books can transport us to unfamiliar places, expand our understanding, and change our thinking. The books we share with children in our classroom should promote these ideas. They should represent diversity, including topics about race, ethnicity, gender, language, religion, socioeconomic background, and ability. Children should see themselves in the stories that they read. Moreover, books can help children understand experiences and consider wider perspectives. Yokota (2009) states, "Reading about the diversity within the United States and the diversity of the world provides readers with settings and perspectives that allow them to imagine and consider a wider world beyond their own" (p. 66). The books we share with children should incorporate a wide array of topics presented through multiple lenses. As stated by Young, Bryan, Jacobs and Tunnell (2020), "A classroom context where reading is valued has an atmosphere that says, 'Books are important'" (p. 14). Important because of how books can impact us as readers, individually and as a community of readers, inside and outside of the classroom.

As educators reflect on the importance of sharing meaningful and impactful literature with children, they must consider how to select books and how to plan for instruction. What informs their decisions about books? How do they evaluate the literature they will use in their classroom? When selecting books, how do they provide a wide range of stories that are meaningful for students, help them to appreciate the literature, connect to them personally, and expand their experiences and knowledge? In the opinion of Short, Brown-Lynch and Tomlinson (2018) literature holds many values both academically and personally; literature has significance in children's lives. Specifically, they identify the following values of literature.

1. Enjoyment: read for the sheer enjoyment of reading.
2. Personal and cultural identity: stories connect us to our past, to the roots of our cultural identities, and to the human condition.
3. Imagination and transformation: by seeing the world through a new perspective and considering ways of living other than their own, children are encouraged to think creatively and divergently. Stories can provide children with alternative pathways for understanding their past or imagining their future.
4. Knowledge and insights: good books offer information and wisdom and so combine the heart and mind, reason, and emotion.
5. Understanding and empathy: literature helps children gain an appreciation for the universality of human needs across history and place, which

makes it possible for them to understand what connects us as human beings as well as what makes each of us unique.
6. Literary and artistic preferences: students come to understand and recognize the literary and artistic styles of many authors and illustrators.
7. Literature has value in academic learning: reading, writing, literature across the curriculum and appreciation and visual culture (pp. 5–8).

Teacher educators must share great stories and so we focus on how to use literature for all the aforementioned values, and specifically, reflect on ways to share literature to expand personal and cultural identity, which relates to a recent study in an early childhood children's literature course. Short, Lynch-Brown and Tomlinson (2018) state, "Readers grow in their identities by finding themselves and their families and communities within books and exploring the multiple connections of their identities, including race, ethnicity, nationality, gender, religion, language, disability, region, family structures, and social class" (p. 6). We reflected on a recent study of favorite books and memories of students enrolled in a children's literature course at two universities, one in the United States and one in Ireland (Fitzgerald et al., 2020). This international research was an extension of a previous project that examined students engaged in literature circles from both universities. As one part of that project, students from each institution created a video introducing themselves and sharing their favorite children's book. From these responses, we sought to find commonalities in children's literature book selections and student rationales between universities. Part of the research questions focused on finding cultural connections from students' favorite books and comparing students' responses from each university. As part of our research, we selected the following definition of culture to guide our analysis specifically because it aligned with our understanding of culture:

> Culture is a way of life, the total human-made environment, the values and beliefs, the symbols, the interpretations, and the viewpoints of a given social group (Banks, 2008). Culture determines the way in which each person thinks, feels, and behaves. The culture of a group is evident through values, nonverbal communication, language, interpersonal relationships, dress codes, parenting, gender roles, social customs, and humor of its people. (Seefeldt et al., 2014, p. 177)

"When investigating the cultural connections, the participants in Ireland showed a higher percentage of interrelatedness between their favorite book and cultural connections. The interrelatedness was much lower among the U.S. participants. This study suggests that among Americans, participants were more evasive and made less cultural connections" (Fitzgerald et al.,

2020, p. 18). We realize more research is needed to examine how social class, ethnicity, race, gender, and religion might impact their understanding of cultural context and the role literacy plays in helping students appreciate how books can show how their culture is represented and to better recognize others and their worlds.

In this chapter, we discuss how selecting high-quality children's books, ones that expand students' experiences and broaden their cultural understandings, is a critical responsibility for teachers. Students need to see themselves in the books and stories that they read. The classroom environment, materials, and instruction in the classroom should send a message to students that books are valued and important. Children need knowledgeable teachers who know how, and just as importantly, know why they select books to share with students. "The goal of those who write, publish, and promote multicultural and global children's literature is to help young people learn about, understand, and ultimately accept those different from themselves, thus breaking the cycles of prejudice and oppression among peoples of different cultures" (Short et al., 2018, p. 172). Therefore, the books we use for read alouds, curricular connections, book displays, independent reading should reflect the diversity of the students' communities and welcome exploration and discussion. In the next section, we situate our discussion within a social justice, critical literacy, and multiculturalism framework to explain why this knowledge is important to teacher educators and how this erudition guides their philosophy of instruction, including book selections and using materials. We outline the criteria for selecting books for the classroom, and then provide a list of good reads with instructional suggestions and guiding questions.

SOCIAL JUSTICE

Social justice can be defined as a process of reconstructing society in accordance with principles of equity, recognition and inclusion with the aim of achieving full and equitable participation of people from all social identity groups in society that is mutually shaped to meet their needs (Adams & Bell, 2016). Literature provides a powerful way through which to explore social justice. Texts can serve as mirrors and windows (Bishop, 1990) and can transform human experience as a result of enabling readers to reflect on their own lives as part of a larger human experience (Tschida et al., 2014). A book can act as a mirror whereby it reflects back to the reader portions of their identity, culture, and/or experience resulting in the reader seeing something of themselves in the text and therefore acting as a form of validation (Tschida et al., 2014). All children have a right to books that reflect their own images (Bishop, 2012) so that children can make connections with what is being read and thus understand personal experiences to a greater extent. Moreover, "Children from marginalized cultural groups must have opportunities to see themselves reflected in literature" (Tschida et al., 2014, p.29) in order to foster a greater sense of belonging in the world around them. However, for many readers their identities, cultures, and/or experiences are not reflected in children's literature. Consequently, for some children this near invisibility suggests that books and literature, while often pleasurable, are in some sense apart from them (Bishop, 2012). Furthermore, Tschida, Ryan and Ticknor (2014) assert that "Books are sometimes the only place where readers may meet people who are not like themselves, who offer alternative worldviews" (p. 29). Thus, books can also act as windows by providing less familiar worlds to children (Bishop, 2012) allowing for a vicarious experience to supersede the limits of the readers' own lives and identities and to enable children to spend time observing those of others (Tschida et al., 2014). It is imperative that books act as both mirrors and windows by providing children the opportunity to see something from their own world reflected in the book in order to make connections between their own world and that portrayed in the book while also providing children the opportunity to learn about, understand and ultimately accept and respect other worlds and the lives of others that may be different to their own.

The role of an educator regarding social justice is multifaceted. Educators must delve into the messages and socialization from which they operate daily (Kissinger, 2017) and confront and critically reflect on any personal prejudices and be opened to accepting all personal and cultural differences of the students and families in their classroom. Jiménez (2021) maintains that teachers "must learn to recognize, appreciate, and celebrate identities that are different from their own across multiple matrices of race, ethnicity, language, gender, sexuality, ability, religion, and class" (p. 157). In addition, a focus on social justice within education "encourages students to critically examine oppression on institutional, cultural, and individual levels in search of opportunities for social action in the service of social change" (Hackman, 2005, p. 104).

CRITICAL LITERACY

Critical literacy, which is an instructional approach that epitomizes a theoretical perspective, promotes democracy by acknowledging and challenging the influence that issues such as power and equity can have on literacy by enabling students to examine and question the construction of texts. Critical literacy engages in an ideological critique of the world portrayed in media, literature, textbooks, and functional texts (Shor & Freire, 1987). According to Stevens and Bean (2007), "Critical literacy views text meaning making as a process of construction with a particularly critical eye toward elements of the particular historical, social, and political contexts that permeate and foreground any text" (p. 6).

Critical literacy acknowledges the significant role that education plays regarding the socialization and transmission of culture and social facts. According to Luke (2012), "Critical literacy has an explicit aim of the critique and transformation of dominant ideologies, cultures and economies, and institutions, and political systems" (p. 5). It is about helping readers understand their reading practices and realize that their responses to texts are not really individual or personal but are socially constructed (Hall, 1998). Acquisition of this type of literacy creates "a citizenry critical enough to both analyze and challenge the oppressive characteristics of the larger society so that a more just, equitable, and democratic society can be created" (McLaren, 1988, p.214). When given the opportunity to engage in critical literacy students learn about the transformative potential of literacy and they discover that words, their words, can have the power to effect change (Powell et al., 2001). Consequently, critical literacy is about envisioning how students might be active, influential, and critical users of texts and discourses to enable them to understand the role of texts within social contexts with the hope of achieving subsequent action and thus change.

MULTICULTURAL LITERATURE AND CRITERIA

As the children's representation in classrooms continues to expand and become more culturally and linguistically diverse, as teacher educators we find ourselves tasked with providing experiences that closely mirror their lives. Yokota (2009) contends that "we—and they—are challenged to consider a wide range of perspectives and to take a global perspective on a variety of social, economic, scientific, political, and intellectual issues" (p. 66). One way to engage in this diversity in our classrooms is through literature, specifically a well-designed multicultural literature program. An excellent piece of literature can enhance our understandings and knowledge about the world and events that have happened in our history (Landa & Stephens, 2017).

Multicultural literature is defined as literature about people from diverse cultural, linguistic, socioeconomic, religious backgrounds, gender, sexual orientation, and disabilities (Banks, 2003). It is a powerful tool that sheds light on others' cultures and holds up a mirror to students' own culture (Yokota, 2009; Beck 2005). In multicultural literature, we can introduce students to current cultural issues, promoting and developing global awareness. By vicariously experiencing the stances and sentiments of others through literature, students begin to look at the world more critically to appreciate better the global community surrounding them. Thus, "the examination of values, beliefs, and events in personal and collective lives, and the recognition of literacy . . ." becomes "an empowering rather than silencing force in classrooms" (DeNicolo & Franquiz, 2006, p. 168). In multicultural literacy, the educator fosters opportunities to question social injustices, builds critical conscientious, and self-awareness while partaking in inclusive learning practices to guide change into the fabric of our daily lives.

As previously noted, literature can have a significant impact on students in our classrooms providing them the ability to "see how different social spheres support different and competing perspectives that must ultimately interact and inform one another" (Beck, 2005, p. 399). How you select, discuss, and plan with multicultural literacy may have a profound effect upon assisting or hampering reader response in discussions of literature due to the instructional approaches employed and literature selection, which impinge upon the quality of learner response (Mart, 2019). We outline our approach to evaluating picture books shared in the classroom as an avenue to enhance children's interaction with the narrative or content and build diversity of thought among the global community of learners. We ascribed to Yokota's (2009) criteria for evaluating and selecting the best multicultural and international literature.

1. *Do the author and illustrator present authentic perspectives?*
2. *Is the culture portrayed multi-dimensionally?*
3. *Are cultural details naturally integrated?*
4. *Are details accurate, and are the interpretations current?*
5. *Is the language used authentically?*
6. *Is the collection balanced?* (p. 67)

These criteria have been utilized to create a checklist to evaluate a multicultural literacy text's potential effectiveness in the classroom. In addition, we consider criteria used to evaluate picture books such as are the literary elements prevalent and woven throughout the story; is their excellent writing that is complemented by the illustrations; and are the stories developmentally appropriate and extend the student experience? "To be avoided, however, are books that perpetuate erroneous information or have hurtful images" (Yokota, 2009, p. 67). By sharing excellent multicultural and international books, children have the opportunity to experience a rich understanding of themselves and others. "When multicultural literature and literature-related activities are infused into the curriculum in developmentally appropriate ways, children uncover commonalities and differences within and among diverse groups of people. They learn to value both the differences and the commonalities" (Harper & Brand, 2010, p. 224).

In this section, we highlight several books we feel exemplify excellent multicultural and international books. Our scheme includes selecting books we have used in the classroom or listed as outstanding literature that can extend cultural understandings, promote global perspectives, and transform human experiences.

Subsequently, a checklist (Table 10.1) was created using Yokota's six criteria and enhanced with additional clarifying sub-questions (2009). In our selection process, we have identified several books meeting all six criteria

Table 10.1 Criteria for Selecting Multicultural Literature

Questions	Validation
Does the text present authentic perspectives?	yes no
☐ Is there an appreciation of human experiences present in the text? ☐ Are the illustrations, gender roles, and information about the culture accurate? ☐ Is this written from an insider's viewpoint? ☐ Is the author a member of the culture presented in the text?	
Is the culture portrayed multi-dimensionally?	yes no
☐ Are the interactions between characters with a cultural group or between two or more cultural groups genuine? ☐ Are the characters authentic, not stereotyped? ☐ Is the culture portrayed accurately?	
Do the cultural details integrate naturally in the text?	yes no
☐ Is the dialogue realistic and meaningful to the text? ☐ Does the setting include authentic scenes from the culture? ☐ Is the text rich in cultural detail?	
Are details accurate, and are the interpretations current?	yes no
☐ Are the themes and values consistent with the specific culture depicted? ☐ Is the setting consistent with either a historical or contemporary period?	
Is the language used authentically?	yes no
☐ Are the language patterns and perspectives of that culture accurate? ☐ Are the ideas and thoughts expressed in an authentic language?	
Is the collection balanced in literacy?	yes no
☐ Are the characters balanced concerning physical, social, and emotional attributes? ☐ Does the text invite the reader to reflect, critically analyze, and respond? ☐ Does the text-align with the criteria for the genre in which it is written? ☐ Does the text provide insight into a problem or provide some hope for the future?	

Note: This table illustrates the additional sub-questions and Yokota's (2009) criteria for evaluating and selecting the best multicultural and international literature.

and suggested classroom ideas and guiding questions to spark conversation and extend the learning. Moreover, reading and discussing the books provide educators with an opportunity to engage students in reflection and to synthesize the literature through the lens of social justice.

SUGGESTED BOOK CHOICES FOR MULTICULTURAL CHILDREN'S LITERATURE

Martinez-Neal (2018) *Alma and How She Got Her Name.* Alma is not sure she liked her name until her Daddy tells her the story of how she got her name. Martinez-Neal weaves cultural details throughout the story as Alma's name is revealed. The illustrations complement the brief, but rich history. *Classroom idea and guiding questions: This outstanding book may provide an opening for children to talk about their names and for the teacher to learn more about the students, their families, and cultural connections. The author's notes at the end of the story add authenticity and remind us to ask our students, "What is the story of your name?"*

Hood (2018) *Shaking Things Up, 14 Young Women Who Changed the World.* This book is a collection of 14 poems representing extraordinary women. The author accurately portrays the struggles of the women and invites us to reflect on why these obstacles existed during the specific time, and even today. From a fire fighter, paleontologist, to a war correspondent and librarian these poems illuminate, through words and illustration, the contributions of these outstanding women. *Classroom idea and guiding questions: Review the timeline and engage students in additional research about one of the women in the poems. Ponder with your students why these women's lives are extraordinary? How did the timeframe help shape their stories? Is the world different now?*

Woodson (2018) *The Day You Begin.* A celebration of you. In this artistically and authentically presented picture book, Woodson tells the story of belonging and identity, maybe not at first, but finding a place where you find uniqueness celebrated and commonalities discovered. Woodson in her text and illustrations portrays authentic interactions between the characters through dialogue and sharing the characters' thoughts. She opens the possibilities to discuss ways to be empathetic and build an inclusive community. *Classroom idea and guiding questions: An activity to use with this book is for children to tell something special or unique about themselves. Additionally, consider engaging children in specific examples throughout the text that may be upsetting or reveal biases. For example, the child with the lunch that is different than the other children, but not different to her. Discuss how we can learn from each other. At the beginning of the year, build community by discussing with students how special we are in the classroom, community, and world.*

Mora (2018) *Thank you, Omu!* How do you celebrate community? In the author's notes, Mora tells the reader that in Nigerian language, "omu" means queen; however, for this author it meant grandma. And so, the character, Omu shares her favorite food with the neighborhood—as a gesture of love and community. The wafting smells of a simmering stew represented in lines and movements across the page and provide a glimpse of the neighborhood. It may remind students of their own experiences, or it may provide a window into another way of sharing with neighbors and friends. Mora, through collage illustrations, introduces us to a community and highlights the generosity of many. The text highlights the importance of sharing, leaves us with a hopeful ending, and a celebration of love and giving. *Classroom idea and guiding questions: Share this book in the classroom to discuss members of a community and how they work together. How did the author and illustrator present the community? The members? Who else might be included? What message did you learn?*

Scott (2020) *I Talk like a River.* Creating a moving balance between words and pictures, Scott and Smith vividly capture an insider's perspective of a boy whose words get stuck in his mouth. The illustrations extend the text and provide a place to explore the boy's emotions as he sits in a classroom knowing he talks differently than other children. The illustrations coupled with the words render an emotional response that is authentic and real but may not be easily understood by the reader. *Classroom idea and guiding questions: Bubbling, churning, and crashing—how do these words help the character describe how he speaks like the river? How can we explore his feelings and help us better understand his social and emotional attributes? How will this understanding bring about different ways to respond to the situation and be more supportive of a child who stutters or has a disability? Discuss the author's note at the end of the story to extend the responses.*

Fullerton (2017) *Hand over Hand.* The gentle watercolor through the book illustrates beautiful quiet, an authentic Filipino fishing village. The setting presents an accurate depiction of the Philippines. In this vignette, Nina pushes against gender role expectations that "Girls can't fish. Their place is on the shore!" with persistence and patience. The gentle and tender intergenerational relationship between Nina and Lolo captures the Filipino authentic culture's heart-warming traditions and history. *Classroom idea and guiding questions: This story can be used in conjunction with exploring Asian cultural studies and gender roles. Nina's grandfather says, "A boat is not the place for a girl. Your job is on the shore." Why might the grandfather (and the other fishermen) think this way? Reflect on a time when you were told you could not do something. How did you react? What reasons were given as to why you could not do it?*

Faruqi (2015) *Lailah's Lunchbox: A Ramadan Story*. Faruqi shares her own experiences as a young Muslim girl immigrating to the United States, confronting her fears, and finding new acceptance in her school. The themes and values are consistent with the Muslim religion, Islam. Lailah is finally of age to participate in Ramadan and finds herself grappling with the alluring smells of food and generous offers of her classmates to share lunch when she wants to fast. The illustrations provide an authentic, rich decorative arabesque artwork on the borders of each page which give cultural importance to patterns found in the Arabic world. *Classroom idea and guiding questions: This book provides an opportunity to study the Arabic traditions/customs and investigate world religions. Why did Lailah decide not to give her teacher her mother's note about fasting on Ramadan? How do you think she was feeling? Does your family have any cultural traditions like fasting? Describe the tradition and how it is celebrated?*

Love (2019) *Julián is a Mermaid*. The author provides a magnificent story about gender non-conforming child receiving love and affirmation in his desire to dress up as a mermaid. The heart-warming marine fantasy tale in which a special relationship the love between Abuela and Julián allows for acceptance. *Classroom idea and guiding questions: This wonderful book gives children the opportunity to celebrate their individuality. How did Julián transform himself into a mermaid? How did Julián feel when his Abuela first saw him dressed up like a mermaid? Why do you think Julián wanted to dress up like a mermaid?*

Ho (2021) *Eyes That Kiss in the Corners*. The poetry of language in this story illuminates beauty found in the fantastical beasts and landscapes from Chinese culture. The little Asian girl discovers her uniqueness within herself and her family. The themes and values are consistent with the Asian culture depicted, and the character is balanced among physical, social, and emotional attributes. The softly painted illustrations coupled with lyrical text provide the reader with rich human experiences of acceptance and familial love. *Classroom idea and guiding questions: The Eyes That Kiss in the Corners allows children to appreciate their differences with self-admiration and confidence. Who does the little girl draw strength from? Who do you draw strength from?*

Morales (2018) *Dreamers*. Yuyi Morales shares her own experiences as a young Mexican mother immigrating to the United States and finding her way in a new and unfamiliar place. This personal story would resonate with anyone that has ever moved to a new place and gives hope to people dreaming of a new and better life and finding their place in an unfamiliar land. It is a simple story combined with beautiful illustrations that reminds the reader that we are all dreamers and that each one of us has different strengths that we bring with us wherever we go. *Classroom idea and guiding questions: Dreamers is an excellent book for which to start a discussion with children about times when they felt uncomfortable and/or when they were somewhere unfamiliar to them and provides a stimulus for children to talk about ways in which people can integrate into new and sometimes uncomfortable environments. Have you ever gone somewhere new and felt that you didn't belong? How did this make you feel? What did you do to feel part of your new surroundings?*

Sorell (2018) *We are Grateful: Otsaliheliga*. This information book provides an authentic insight into the Cherokee culture by delineating various celebrations and events celebrated by the Cherokee people. Traci Sorell writes this from an insider's perspective providing an authentic and contemporary view of Cherokee culture. Such a book highlights the importance of celebrating one's cultural traditions and history and the importance of expressing gratitude for them. *Classroom idea and guiding questions: This book provides an excellent platform for children to think about and discuss various traditions celebrated within their own culture while also enabling commonalities and differences between cultures to be examined. Do commonalities exist between the diverse cultures and/or traditions celebrated in the classroom? Why is it important to accept different cultures in our community and world?*

Yousafzai (2017) *Malala's Magic Pencil*. This true story is based on one young Palestinian girl's wish for a better world. It gives an accurate portrayal of the challenges experienced by young children, particularly girls, under Taliban rule. This is a beautifully illustrated book including both authentic and vivid images. Such a book provides hope for young children that they too can make a difference in their world however big or small this may be. *Classroom idea and guiding questions: This is a powerful book that allows for discussions to take place about fairness and equality and highlights for children how even young people can have a voice, stand up against injustices and help make a difference in their world. How can you make a difference in your community/world? Who has contributed to making a difference in your community / our world?*

Phi (2017) *A Different Pond*. This beautiful book written from an insider's perspective portrays a Vietnamese refugee's perspective of struggles, particularly financial struggles, experienced as a result of moving to the United States. The book centers on a simple fishing event that provides a powerful glimpse into a father and son relationship and the difficulties of building a new life in a different land. Using descriptive language Bao Phi sensitively describes how small family moments can provide opportunities for stories and cultural traditions to be shared. The vibrant and realistic images and use of water color drawings create authentic scenes that grab the reader's attention.

Classroom idea and guiding questions: A Different Pond is a lovely book for which to invite reflection and to engage children in a discussion about times that they have spent with family members and/or where family stories have been shared and presents the opportunity for children to tell their own family stories. How have family stories been shared with you? How do your own family stories and/or traditions shape who you are? Why might it be important that family stories are passed on from generation to generation?

CONCLUSION

Notable efforts have been made within the past decade to incorporate diversity and cultural awareness into literacy practices. The availability of multicultural literature has expanded over the years. However, sometimes well-intentioned teachers find themselves in perplexing circumstances while reading a literature text which results in stereotyping, condescending, or patronizing among students. To avoid these obstacles, a teacher must carefully analyze the text and use critical tools to become aware of what makes excellent multicultural literature. "This intentionality calls for educators to be diligent in not merely being inclusive, but in considering the "why, what, and how" of including literature that reflects diverse perspectives" (Yokota, 2009, p. 68). Selecting children's literature that will expand students' experiences and awareness and provide an avenue for discussion and learning about diversity and cultural understandings, is an essential obligation for teachers. However, Yokota (2009) states, "We need to go beyond merely being inclusive. A key to doing so is adopting a specific 'intentionality' in what we do when we consciously seek to expand our awareness and understanding of a diverse world and its many different perspectives" (p. 68). Students need to see themselves in the books they read and make connections to the content they are learning. We envision that the checklist and classroom connections will lead to enriching and insightful conversations and be a useful start to sharing outstanding multicultural and international books with students. As educators, it is evident to us that we need to be cognizant of the cultural values and beliefs shared with children in the classroom, acknowledging that students come from differing backgrounds. Their lens will be unique because their lived-experiences will force them to engage in critical personal reflection about race, ethnicity, nationality, gender, religion, language, disability, region, family structures, and social class leading to action and transformation. As we reflect on the impact of children's literature, we must be aware of the messages communicated in the classroom through the texts we share and that they may be similar or vastly different, and thus opening the pathway for change to occur.

SOMETHING TO READ, DO, OR CONSIDER

Consider reading one of the picture books. Add to the questions we outlined. Try reading the book with your students.

REFERENCES

Adams, M., & Bell, L. A. (2016). *Teaching for diversity and social justice.* Routledge.
Banks, J. A. (2003). Teaching literacy for social justice and global citizenship. *Language Arts,* 81(1), 18.
Beck, A. (2005). A place for critical literacy. *Journal of Adolescent & Adult Literacy,* 48(5), 392–400.
Bishop, R. S. (1990). Mirrors, windows and sliding glass doors. *Perspectives,* 6(3), ix–xi.
Bishop, R. S. (2012). Reflections on the development of African American children's literature. *Journal of Children's Literature,* 38(2), 5–13.
DeNicolo, C. P., & Franquiz, M. E. (2006). "Do I have to say it?": Critical encounters with multicultural children's literature. *Language Arts,* 84(2), 157–170.
Hackman, H. (2005). Five essential components for social justice education. *Equity and Excellence in Education,* 38(2), 103–109.
Hall, K. (1998). Critical literacy and the case for it in the early years of school. *Language, Culture and Curriculum,* 11(2), 183–194.
Harper, L. J., & Trostle-Brand, S. (2010). More alike than different: Promoting respect through multicultural books & literacy strategies. *Childhood Education: Journal of the Association for Childhood Education International,* 86(4), 224–233
Fitzgerald, S., Rigaud, V., & Young, T. (2020). Children's literature: Learning about our favorite books. *The Ohio Journal of Teacher Education,* 34(2), 4–25.
Jiménez, L. M. (2021). Mirrors and windows with texts and readers: International social justice at work in the classroom. *Language Arts,* 98(3), 156–161.
Kissinger, K. (2017). *Anti-bias education in the early childhood classroom hand in hand, step by step.* Routledge.
Landa, M. S., & Stephens, G. (2017). Promoting cultural competence in preservice teacher education through children's literature: An exemplary case study. *Issues in Teacher Education,* 26(1), 53–71.
Luke, A. (2012). Critical literacy: Foundational notes. *Theory into Practice,* 51(1), 4–11.
Mart, C. T. (2019). Reflections on discussions of literature: A language learning environment to promote speaking skills. *The Journal of Social Sciences Research,* 5(4), 846–850.
McLaren, P. L. (1988). Culture or canon? Critical pedagogy and the politics of literacy. *Harvard Educational Review,* 58(2), 213–234.
Powell, R., Chambers Cantrell, S., &Adams, S. (2001). Saving Black Mountain: The promise of critical literacy in a multicultural democracy. *The Reading Teacher,* 54(8), 772–781.

Seefeldt, C., Castle, S., & Falconer, R. (2014). *Social studies for the preschool/primary child.* (9th Ed). Pearson.
Shor, I., & Freire, P. (1987). *A pedagogy for liberation.* Westport: Bergin & Garvey.
Short, K., Lynch-Brown, C., & Tomlinson, C. (2018). *Essentials of children's literature.* Pearson.
Stevens, L. P., & Bean, T. W. (2007). *Critical literacy: Context, research and practice in the K-12 classroom.* Sage.
Tschida, C. M., Ryan, C. L., & Ticknor, A. (2014). Building on windows and mirrors: encouraging the disruption of "single stories" through children's literature. *Journal of Children's Literature, 40*(1), 28–39.
Yokota, J. (2009). Learning through literature that offers diverse perspectives: Multicultural and international literature. In D. Wooten & B. Cullinan (Eds.), *Children's literature in the reading program: An invitation to read* (3rd ed.) (pp. 66–73). International Reading Association.
Young, T., Bryan, G., Jacobs, J., & Tunnell, M. (2020). *Children's literature briefly.* Pearson.

APPENDIX

Suggested multicultural children's literature

Faruqi, R. (2015). *Lailah's lunchbox: A Ramadan story* (L. Lyon, Illus.). Tilbury House Publishers.
Fullerton, A. (2017). *Hand over hand* (R. Benoit, Illus.). Second Story Press.
Ho, J. (2021). *Eyes that kiss in the corners* (D. Ho, Illus.). HarperCollins.
Hood, S. (2018). *Shaking things up: 14 women who changed the world* (S. Alko, S. Blackall, L. Brown, H. Hooper, E. W. Martin, O. Mora, J. Morstad, S. Palacios, L. Pham, E. Robinson, I. Roxas, & M. Sweet Strickland, Illus.) HarperCollins.
Love, J. (2019). *Julian is a mermaid.* Walker Books.
Martinez-Neal, J. (2018). *Alma and how she got her name.* Candlewick Press.
Mora, O. (2018). *Thank you, Omu!* Little, Brown and Company.
Morales, Y. (2018). *Dreamers.* Holiday House.
Phi, B. (2017). *A different pond* (T. Bui, Illus.). Capstone Young Readers.
Scott, J. (2020). *I talk like a river* (S. Smith, Illus.). Neal Porter Books.
Sorell, T. (2018). *We are grateful: Otsaliheliga* (F. Iessac, Illus.). Charlesbridge.
Woodson, J. (2018). *The day you begin* (R. Lopez, Illus.). Nancy Paulsen Books.
Yousafzai, M. (2017). *Malala's magic pencil* (Kerascoët, Illus.). Brown Books for Young Readers.

Chapter 11

Preservice Teachers' Understanding of Culturally Responsive Teaching and Learning

Fears of Working in a Diverse Classroom

Winston Vaughan

The school system in the United States over the years has become very diverse with respect to race, ethnicity, and language. Today's classrooms call for teachers who are well prepared to instruct the diverse student population. Unfortunately, many classroom teachers often have life experiences that are different from the students in the classroom. Many teacher candidates enter education programs with a set of preconceived notions about teaching and learning based on their own experiences (Nieto & Bodie, 2018). With respect to language, the number of linguistically diverse students in U.S. schools is the highest in over a century (Wright et al., 2015). Nieto and Bodie (2018) also suggest that school predictions indicate population growth in reference to students that speak native languages other than English. In 2006, the U.S. Department of Education estimated that more than five million children in U.S. schools, or more than 10 percent overall, are English Language Learners (National Clearinghouse for English Language Acquisition, 2006). Likewise, it has been documented that the rise of students whose first language is not English has also been challenging for educators. Banks (2015) states that one-third of our nation's schools are students of color. Further projections show that by the year 2050 a high percentage of the student population will be students of color (Banks, 2015; Nieto & Bodie, 2018). Research also suggests that with the changing demographics in our schools, teacher education programs must prepare teachers with the knowledge, skills, and dispositions that will enable them to be more culturally responsive in the classroom, enabling them to reduce the fears and the challenges of a changing school population (Delpit,1995; Gay, 2000; Ladson-Billings, 1995; Nieto & Bodie, 2018). Likewise, research also indicates that most preservice teachers want to teach students who are like themselves in familiar settings, and they are often uncomfortable interacting with families from ethnic and language minorities (Gomez, 1996; Zeichner & Baker, 1995). Most preservice teachers are white, monolingual middle-class females who are part of a society in which whiteness is seen as the norm (Banks, 2015; Howard, 2011; Sleeter, 1995).

On the other hand, research suggests that in order to raise the cross-cultural cognizance and sensitivity to diversity of preservice teachers, opportunities should be provided for them to examine and reflectively clarify and share the foundations of their own cultural frames of reference (race, class, ethnicity, and religion) (Bennett, 1993; Brown, 2005; Gollnick & Chinn, 2009). Likewise, Banks (2006) and Sleeter (1995) advocate for diversity training with self-examination exercises which will require them to examine their own cultural identities before exploring the culture of others. This will help them to eliminate the fears they may have of working with students in diverse classrooms. This is of significance because preservice teachers need to be knowledgeable and possess the skills and dispositions needed to work in diverse classrooms.

White preservice teachers enter the teacher education programs with limited experience with diversity and embrace the idea that all schools are like the schools they attended. Because of this, students enrolled in teacher education programs frequently expressed the fear of diversity and the resistance to dealing with race and racism (Gay & Howard, 2000). Preparing teachers for diverse classrooms can be very challenging. There are usually concerns with regards to race, ethnicity, and culture between teacher and students (Ladson-Billings 1994; Sleeter, 1992).

On the other hand, White in-service teachers usually indicate the fear of engaging different ethnic groups and multicultural content in the classroom. They also express fears of how they can teach multicultural education, and at the same time meet the standards of academic excellence (Gay & Howard, 2000). According to Vacarr (2001), in the diverse classroom, many teachers are unprepared for the discoveries that await them. It is suggested that it is the responsibility of teacher educators to step out of our comfort zone, reveal our own ignorance, and engage our students in exploring transformative possibilities.

According to Gay and Howard (2000), it has been a common occurrence for students in teacher education programs to express various forms of subtle resistance to embracing the multicultural imperative for quality teaching and learning, and to work diligently to develop the knowledge and skills needed for its effective implementation. This resistance takes many different forms, including fear, denial of the verity of ethnic and cultural diversity in teaching and learning, and reluctance to confront issues of racial, ethnic, and cultural diversity directly and substantively.

Elementary preservice teachers frequently declare that they are afraid of engaging different ethnic groups in their classrooms. According to Gay and Howard (2000), investigating these fears can result in discovering issues of racial prejudices, lack of knowledge of ethnic and cultural diversity, and doubts about teaching ethnic others.

Today's classrooms call for teachers who are well prepared to teach diverse student populations. Unfortunately, classroom teachers today remain White and middle class, while the demographics of the school systems are changing. If we are going to meet the needs of these students, preservice teachers must be properly trained to work in these settings so that fears of teaching in diverse settings will be managed and understood. They should also strive to develop the knowledge, skills, and dispositions that will enable them to be culturally responsive teachers in the classroom.

According to Grant and Gillette (2006), preservice teachers should be taught the importance of culturally relevant pedagogy. They suggest that culturally relevant pedagogy can be utilized as a conduit for preservice teachers so that they can relate to and make connections with diverse communities. These may include race/ethnicity, sexual orientation, and linguistic diversity.

CULTURALLY RESPONSIVE TEACHING

Culturally responsive teaching and learning should be the goal of every preservice teacher in today's schools. If they understand the backgrounds of their students, and the various histories they bring to the classroom, they can embed that pertinent information into their daily teaching experience. If practiced correctly, teachers will be able to understand their students better, build caring relationships and make a difference in their lives. Within the area of cultural diversity as it relates to education, there are two leading frameworks. These include culturally relevant pedagogy (Ladson-Billings, 1994) and culturally responsive teaching (Gay, 2010). Culturally relevant pedagogy, according to Ladson-Billings (1994), empowers students intellectually, politically, socially, and emotionally, using cultural referents to impart knowledge, skills, and attitudes extending also to collective empowerment.

Ladson-Billings (1994) also posits that culturally responsive teaching is a pedagogical strategy that recognizes the importance of including students' cultural references in all aspects of learning. She suggests some of the characteristics of culturally responsive teaching which includes:

- Student-centered instruction
- Communication of high expectations
- Learning within the context of culture
- Culturally mediated instruction

- Reshaping the curriculum
- Teacher as facilitator
- Positive perspectives on parents and families

It is also implied that if teacher educators prepare preservice teachers with these factors in mind, they will become more effective culturally responsive teachers, while developing the skills necessary for working in diverse classroom settings.

Culturally responsive teaching, as described by Gay (2010), encourages teachers to embrace the cultural knowledge, prior experiences, frames of reference, and performance styles of ethnically diverse students to make learning encounters more relevant and effective for them.

In this chapter, I will explore preservice teachers' perspectives of culturally responsive teaching as advocated by Gay (2000). Teacher candidates investigate what it means to be a culturally responsive teacher in the classroom, highlighting some of the fears they might have with respect to working in diverse classrooms. Various strategies will be suggested to help alleviate the fears indicated.

COURSE DESCRIPTION

This course, "Cultural Diversity in Educational Settings," is one of the courses designed to meet the diversity requirements set by the state at a mid-western university. All students majoring in Early Childhood Education, Special Education, Middle Childhood Education, and Montessori Education are required to take this course to meet the requirements for graduation. In this course, students explore the literature pertaining to race/privilege, class/privilege, ethnicity, gender, disabilities, sexual orientation, religion, stereotyping racism, and discrimination and the impact on the process of schooling. They also investigate the changing demographics in our schools today while investigating various pedagogical strategies that will meet the needs of students in diverse classroom settings. They also engage in various reflective exercises and discuss concepts from a racial and cultural perspective to better understand the concept of diversity and how it can influence the education process.

METHOD

Procedure

Students enrolled in a cultural diversity course in the fall semesters of 2019 were asked to respond to two prompts as part of their final class assignments.

The first prompt required them to define what it means to be a culturally responsive teacher and identify some characteristics of a culturally responsive teacher. The second prompt required them to share three fears or concerns they might have working in schools with diverse populations.

Data Analysis

Data from students' responses were collected and analyzed using a qualitative methodology. Using qualitative methodology, data were analyzed using a system of open coding (Corbin & Strauss, 2007) in which the data was deconstructed and categorized to identify reoccurring themes. As themes emerged, common themes were grouped into categories that would be specific to students' responses.

Findings

In this analysis, students were required to respond to two prompts. The first was based on defining culturally responsive teaching and identifying some characteristics of a culturally responsive teacher. Common themes that emerged from students' responses were:

- Reshaping in the curriculum
- Using multiethnic materials
- Setting high expectations
- Fostering relationships
- Respect for students

Preservice teachers in their response articulated a good understanding of what it means to be a culturally responsive educator, and the various characteristics that it entails. In this section, I will discuss the various themes that emerged from the analysis of students' responses.

Reshaping the Curriculum

One of the most important aspects of teaching from a culturally responsive perspective is the curriculum. Reshaping the curriculum was highlighted as one of the ways to be a culturally responsive teacher. Having a curriculum that is inclusive, holistic, and integrative will enable students to get a better understanding of the knowledge being taught while embracing ethnic and cultural content into the lessons taught. It is critical that all cultures be included in the curriculum. Sharing different perspectives, opinions, and experiences allow students to gain an understanding of the various differences in society as well as in the society and try to embrace them. One student advocated a curriculum that included James Banks's four Approaches to Multicultural Education (Contributions, Additive, Transformation and Social Action/Decision Making). It was suggested that these approaches would create the ability for culture to be pervasive with in the curriculum as well as student empowerment. Another student suggested that as times change, so must schools. However, schools must provide a curriculum that is inclusive for all students. Also, one must be mindful of curricular materials that are being used by the teachers which should attend to inclusiveness, awareness, and respect and acceptance of others. Yet another student commented that the curriculum in any school should be integrative, meaningful, and centered around the different cultures that students bring to school. It should include topics and issues related to students' backgrounds to help create connections to real-life situations. In addition, another student stated that when teachers reshape the curriculum and incorporate the students' cultural backgrounds, they are providing instruction that is more meaningful to students, which in turn helps them to reach their full potential.

Multiethnic Materials

The use of multiethnic materials was another area that students identified as part of culturally responsive teaching and learning. Multiethnic materials, if used correctly, can provide a primary window into a student's cultural background. Students will be able to see themselves represented in lessons taught in the classroom by connecting them to real-life situations. This will make learning more meaningful and enjoyable especially with minority students. Using diverse materials represented in various textbooks, videos, activities, and other diverse resources in the teaching and learning process can help students become more well-rounded and culturally diverse learners. One student suggested that the use of multiethnic materials can generate questions from students and allow them to engage in discussions about various cultures that they may otherwise not consider. The use of multiethnic materials can also improve teacher and student roles, increase motivation, and foster acceptance and tolerance of various cultures in our society and the classroom. It can also help students to develop more positive self-esteem, more collaboration with peers, and gain a better understanding of their culture and the culture of others.

High Expectations

Having high expectations for students is one of the criteria given by students to embrace the concept of culturally responsive teaching and learning. As teachers go about their daily tasks, setting high expectations should be a priority. Teachers should not only set high expectations, but they should be a high level of accountability and responsibility. With respect to high expectations, the teacher should build confidence in students. This can be achieved through developing an atmosphere of caring in the classroom and speaking positively about students in and out of the classroom. Students should also be allowed to contribute by voicing their opinions and learning in a validating environment. The teacher should also be engaged in giving specific feedback to students with the idea of having this to guide future teaching and learning and provide support to the students through relationships and a caring environment. One student stated that teachers should have high expectations for students in the classroom without discrimination or lowering standards based on race, socioeconomic status, gender, or religion. Another student suggested that teachers should set high standards and expectation for all students, and school resources and opportunities should be offered to all students regardless of race, social class, gender, or disability.

Respect

Having respect was another theme that emerged. As a teacher in today's classroom, it is of utmost importance to understand, respect, and embrace the various cultures and histories that students bring to the classroom. Teachers, because of their position, bring certain aspects of authority and legitimate power to the classroom. However, it is important to create a classroom atmosphere that fosters mutual respect. One student suggested that you might have students in the classroom that may be different from you in terms of race, ethnicity, social class, and sexual orientation. It is therefore important to understand each child in the classroom in order to make them feel comfortable and allow them to reach their full potential. By understanding their culture, you can get a better sense of why students are reacting or behaving in certain ways. Another student stated that a culturally responsive teacher is one who is respectful to students of all cultural and ethnic backgrounds. Respecting one's culture allows for students and parents to feel safe and comfortable in the classroom. A third student posited that teachers must be respectful of the students and their culture in the classroom. Teachers should strive to build an awareness of the various cultural differences they might encounter during their daily experiences. A final student agreed that teachers must respect the students in the classroom as well as the various cultures they bring to the classroom. They should have an awareness of the pluralistic society that exists in our society today and try their best to gain a better understanding.

Doing this will help teachers to gain mutual respect in the classroom with respect to teacher and student, as well as student and student relationships.

Respecting the students and their cultures in the classroom is very important because every student comes from a different background with different histories. Because of this, they may tend to feel alienated if their culture is ignored. According to Nieto and Bodie (2018), students whose cultures are unacknowledged or misunderstood in the classroom, are likely to feel alienated, unwelcome, or out of place.

Fostering Relationships

Another key aspect of culturally responsive teaching is fostering relationships with students as well as parents. Relationships can contribute to helping teachers understand what students bring to the classroom. If students know that you respect them and care about who they are, they will respond in positive ways in the classroom. Teachers should therefore try to come up with ways to build trust with their students. They should provide opportunities where students can share their histories and stories with each other. Banks (2015) suggests using what he called a critical autobiography of students to help understand what students bring to the classroom, and to help build classroom relationships so that they can have a good understanding. According to Hamre and Pianta (2010), what goes on in the classroom with respect to the organization of the various features in the classroom environment to meet the social needs of students can positively impact social interactions and relationships. Relationships in the classroom can be based on teacher-student relationships as well as student-peer relationships. One student believed that it is impossible to understand your students and their backgrounds if you do not build relationships with them. Children's values, strengths, and histories will become apparent once teachers get to know their students. Another preservice teacher suggested that relationships should go beyond the students to include parents and the community as well. Building strong relationships with students, families, and the community can help teachers to gain a better understanding of the students' backgrounds. This student also suggested that strong relationships will help teachers set high standards for the students and hold them accountable.

The second prompt required preservice teachers to identify three fears or concerns they might have with respect to teaching in schools with diverse populations. Three themes that emerged from their responses were.

- Race and ethnicity
- Sexual orientation
- Language (English Learners)

Race and Ethnicity

One theme of concern that emerged from student responses was race and ethnicity. Working with students from other backgrounds can be challenging for teachers, especially those with limited diverse experiences. Lacking diverse experiences in reference to race and ethnicity may present challenges for them in working in an ethnically diverse classroom. Students seemed to have a fear of relating to students who may be different from them racially and ethnically. One student wrote that there was a fear of not understanding and making connections with students coming from different backgrounds because of limited experience working diverse classrooms. There is also the fear of stereotyping students unintentionally because of the disconnect between teacher and student. Another student stated that being afraid of being prejudice unconsciously. She felt that having been raised in a mostly White society she may tend to act and do things that may be offensive to others in prejudicial ways without even realizing it.

Sexual Orientation

Sexual orientation was another fear or concern emphasized by preservice teachers. In the past few years, with the legalization of same-sex marriages and the increase in transgender students, teachers may be challenged to embrace the concept of gender-inclusiveness in the classroom. Some teachers because of their morals, values, and beliefs may struggle with the idea of having LGBTQ students in the classroom. Preservice teachers expressed fears with respect to sexual orientation for various reasons. One preservice teacher wrote that the world is evolving and we as teachers must adapt to change. However, she argued that children are not mature enough to understand what sexual orientation entails and there is a possibility that she might confuse them even more. Fears and concerns regarding how to address the needs of transgender students were also expressed. Another student expressed concerns of how to address the making of Mother's Day cards with students who have two dads, or when students raise questions about having two dads or two moms. Overall, some preservice teachers view this as not only part of their fears but major concerns for them without the proper training.

Language (English Learners)

The language barrier was a fear indicated by preservice teachers. As we peruse the literature, there is growing evidence that indicates that preservice teachers are not being adequately prepared to work with ELs. In the U.S. school system, we use the English language to educate students. However, there is an increasing number of students in classrooms whose first language is one other than English. The possibility of providing resources to meet the linguistic and learning needs of these students depends on the ability of the school districts to do so. Preservice teachers expressed concerns about not being able to meet the needs of these students because of the lack of training and the availability of resources. One student expressed concerns of having a language barrier between herself and the students may hinder her ability to form relationships with students. This can create a situation where students may have a hard time understanding concepts taught in the classroom and being excited about learning because of this disconnect. Another student indicated that the greatest fear is working with students who language is not English. The idea of communication and the lack of resources may result in her failing to provide the proper instruction for the students and not being able to help them reach their full potential.

DISCUSSION

The findings that emerged from this study clearly showed that preservice teachers understood what it means to be a culturally responsive teacher. They clearly articulated what it means to be a culturally responsive teacher and clearly identified some of the basic characteristics. Themes that emerged from students' responses were aligned with the characteristics suggested by Ladson-Billings (1994). Similarities were communication of high expectations, learning within the context of culture, culturally mediated instruction, and reshaping the curriculum. Preservice teachers seem to embrace the concepts of using cultural knowledge, frames of reference, and performance styles of ethnically diverse students to make learning encounters more meaningful, relevant, and effective for them as advocated by (Gay, 2010). These were all evident in emerging themes, such as the use of multiethnic materials, having respect for students, as well as setting high expectations for students.

Most students expressed some form of fears and concerns in their responses. Some students mention general concerns which included writing lesson plans, communicating with parents, not being understood by parents, and delivering instruction. However, three themes as mentioned earlier, emerged which were common to most students.

Over the past few years, conversations about sexual orientation and identity in the classroom have increased. Classrooms today consist of students who openly identify as gay, lesbian, or transgender. Grant and Gillette (2006) suggest the importance of having preservice teachers exposed to culturally relevant pedagogy. They suggest that culturally relevant pedagogy can serve as a conduit for preservice teachers so that they can relate to and make connections with diverse kinds of families. Preservice teachers here, expressed several concerns about how to work effectively in these situations especially in the lower grades without the necessary training. In recent years, there have been calls by several teacher educators for the inclusion of sexual orientation, and homophobia as part of the teacher education programs (Robinson & Ferfolja, 2002; Szalacha, 2004). However, this area continues to be fraught with tension because of the various ideologies that continue to exist within U.S. society.

As we examine the demographics of our schools today, one will find that the numbers of EL students have been increasing tremendously. According to Wright, Boun, and García (2015), the number of linguistically diverse students in U.S. schools is the highest in over a century. Nieto and Bodie (2018) also suggest that the population of students that speak languages other than English is evident in school enrollments. Likewise, García (1990) posits that the influx of non-English-speaking students and the lack of language minority teachers make it impossible to place students in classrooms with teachers who are compatible with their language. Preservice teachers in this study expressed concerns about working in classroom where there is linguistic diversity because of the lack of preparation. Apart from that, concerns centered on not being able to communicate with student and parents, and not being able to help them reach their full potential. There were also concerns about differentiation of lessons to meet the needs of all students, balancing time between the English learners and the English-speaking students, while at the same time preparing students to be ready for the various high-stakes tests required.

Finally, the racial and ethnic diversity of the student population has increased significantly over the years as research continues to indicate that most teachers in our school system continue to be White, middle-class females. Research also suggests that teachers' knowledge, awareness, and attitudes toward students of ethnically and culturally diverse students may influence student learning (Jackson, 1995; Ladson-Billings, 1994; Sleeter, 2001). Preservice teachers in this study, who were majority White, expressed various fears and concerns when it comes to race and ethnicity. Some of those concerns were about the misunderstanding of students and making connections with them because of limited exposure to minority students, unintentional stereotyping due to the lack of preparation, and offending students through unconscious bias.

CONCLUSION

From this study, we can conclude that this group of preservice teachers expressed some fears and concerns about working in classrooms with diverse student population due to the lack of preparation. As preservice teacher educators, it is our responsibility to help students to understand the changing demographics of our school system and prepare them to meet these changes for them to feel more confident while working in diverse school settings. Opportunities must be created to allow preservice teachers to be fully prepared so that they will grow and feel more comfortable in the classroom while meeting the needs of their students. Allowing preservice teachers to self-reflect with reference to their diversity experiences and providing field experiences in diverse classroom will help them develop the knowledge, skills, and dispositions needed to work with diverse populations. Kissen (2002) suggests that teacher educators must make preservice teachers aware of their own stereotypes and assumptions when it comes to sexual orientation. Likewise, Elsbree and Wong (2007) suggested engaging preservice teachers to the realities of homophobia as a way of helping them become more aware of the various issues facing society.

As we prepare preservice teachers for the future with the current changing demographics in our schools, teacher educators must be constantly vigilant with respect to courses and curricular materials offered to their students. Preservice teachers need to be properly prepared to work with students in diverse settings. They need to be equipped with the knowledge skills, and dispositions needed to function effectively while meeting the needs of their students.

Finally, anti-racism is the process of unlearning racist ideologies and engaging in practices that will help to bring about changes to society that ensures equity for all. The school system in the United States reflects a society which is rooted in systemic racism (Nieto& Bodie, 2018). Culturally responsive teaching alone cannot bring about the changes needed to reform the school system. Culturally responsive teaching/learning in classrooms is part of the larger anti-racist efforts to combat systemic problems that are prevalent in the education system. These problems can be due to a Eurocentric curriculum that is being taught (Gay, 2010), teaching strategies being used, along with ethnic, racial, and linguistic misunderstandings between teachers, students, and parents.

Engaging preservice teachers with instruction based on culturally relevant pedagogy, and culturally responsive teaching and learning will help them alleviate some of the fears and concerns they may have. If preservice teachers go into the field with a solid knowledge base about culturally responsive teaching and learning, they may be able to break down some of the barriers (racial, cultural, linguistic etc.) that now exist within the U.S. school system, while simultaneously functioning more effectively in diverse classroom settings.

SOMETHING TO READ, DO, OR CONSIDER

- Teachers need to constantly reflect on their own biases and behaviors that they may bring to the classroom.
- Always set high expectations for your students.

- Recognize that students bring different cultures, histories, and behaviors to the classroom.
- Recognize and respect all students' cultural backgrounds.
- Always engage in instruction that is meaningful and considers the various cultural backgrounds of the students.

REFERENCES

Banks, J. A. (2015). *Cultural diversity and education: Foundations, curriculum, and teaching* (5th ed.). Pearson.

Bennett. C. (2003). *Comprehensive multicultural education: theory and practice* (5th ed.). Allyn & Bacon.

Brown E. L. (20005). Service Learning in teacher education: Creative strategies for alternative routes to certification. *Equity and Excellence in Education, 38*(1), 61–74.

Delpit, L. (1995). *Other people's children: Cultural conflict in the classroom*. The New Press.

Elsbree, A. R., & Wong, P. (2007). The Laramie Project as a homophobic disruption: How the play impacts preservice teachers' preparation to create anti-homophobic schools. *Journal of Gay and Lesbian Issues in Education, 4*, 97–117.

Gay, G. (2010). *Culturally responsive teaching: Theory, research, and practice* (2nd ed.). Teachers College Press.

Gay, G., & Howard, T. C. (2000). Multicultural education for the 21st century. *The Teacher Educator, 36*(1), 1–16.

Grant, C. A., & Gillette, M. (2006). A candid talk to teacher educators about effectively preparing teachers who can teach everyone's children. *Journal of Teacher Education, 57*, 292–299.

Gollnick, D. M., & Chinn, P. C. (2009). *Multicultural education in a pluralistic society* (8th ed.). Merrill.

Gomez, M. L. (1996). Prospective teachers' per-spectives on teaching other people's children. In K. Zeichner, S. Melnich, & M. L. Gomez (Eds.), *Currents of reform in pre-service teacher education* (pp. 109–132). New York: Teachers College Press.

Haberman, M. (1995). Selecting "star" teachers for children and youth in urban poverty. *Phi Delta Kappan, 76*(10), 777–781.

Hamre, B. K., & Pianta, R. (2010). Classroom environments and developmental processes: Conceptualization and measurement. In J. Meece & J. S. Eccles (Eds.), *Handbook of research on schools, schooling, and human development* (pp. 25–41). Routledge.

Haviland, V. S. (2008). Things get glossed over: Rearticulating the silencing power of whiteness. in education. *Journal of Teacher Education, 59*(1), 40–54.

Howard, T. C. (2010). *Why race and culture matter in schools: Closing the achievement gap in America's classrooms*. Teachers College Press.

Keengwe, J. (2010). Fostering cross-cultural competence in preservice teachers through multicultural education experiences. *Early Childhood Education Journal, 38*(3), 197–204.

Kissen, R. M. (Ed). (2002). *Getting ready for Benjamin: Preparing teachers for sexual diversity in the classroom.* Rowman and Littlefield.

Kumashiro, K. (2004). Uncertain beginnings: Learning to teach paradoxically. *Theory into Practice, 43,* 111–115.

Ladd, G. W., & Burgess, K. B. (2001). Do relational risks and protective factors moderate the linkages between childhood aggression and early psychological and school adjustment? *Child Development, 72*(5), 1579–1601.

Ladson-Billings, G. (2009). *The dreamkeepers: Successful teachers of African American children* (2nd ed.). Jossey-Bass.

Meehan, B. T., Hughes, J. N., & Cavell, T. A. (2003). Teacher– student relationships as compensatory resources for aggressive children. *Child Development, 74,* 1145–1157.

National Clearinghouse for English Language Acquisition. (2006). *The growing numbers of limited English proficient students: 1993/94-2003/04.* Washington, DC: Office of English Language Acquisition, U.S. Department of Education.

Nieto, S., & Bodie, P. (2018). *Affirming diversity: A sociopolitical context of multicultural education.* Pearson Education Inc.

Robinson, K. H., & Ferfolja, T. (2002). A reflection of resistance: Discourses of heterosexism and homophobia in teacher training classrooms. *Journal of Gay and Lesbian Social Services, 14,* 55–64.

Sherwin, G., & Jennings, T. (2006). Feared, forgotten, or forbidden: Sexual orientation topics in secondary teacher preparation programs in the USA. *Teaching Education, 17,* 207–223.

Sleeter, C. E., (1995). White pre-service students and multicultural education coursework. In J. M. Larkin & C. E. Sleeter (Eds.), *Developing multicultural education curricula* (pp. 81–94). State University of New York Press.

Sleeter, C. (1992). *Keepers of the American dream: A study of staff development and multicultural education.* The Falmer Press.

Wentzel, K. (2010). Students' relationships with teachers. In J. Meece & J. S. Eccles (Eds.), *Handbook of research on schools, schooling, and human development* (pp. 75–91). Routledge.

Wright, W. E., Boun, S., & García, O. (2015). Introduction: Key concepts and issues in bilingual and multilingual education. In W. E. Wright, S. Boun, & O. García (Eds.), *Handbook of bilingual and multilingual education* (pp. 1–16). Wiley-Blackwell.

Zamudio, M. M., Russell, C., Rios, F. A., & Bridgeman, J. L. (2011). *Critical race theory matters.* Routledge.

Zeichner, K., & Baker, B. (1995). Processes for leadership and change: Teacher leadership for urban schools. In M. J. O'Hair & S. J. Odell (Eds.), *Educating teachers for leadership and change.* Teacher education yearbook, Vol. III (pp. 71–76). Corwin Press.

Chapter 12

Moving toward an Anti-racist Feminist Global Lens

Delane A. Bender-Slack

I am a mid-western, White middle-class female educator. I am also a feminist, globally minded, social justice activist. With a background in English Language Arts (ELA) teaching, women's studies, and literacy, I engage in an ethic of caring and the Jesuit ideals of accompaniment and solidarity, working on being a better ally and co-conspirator. I thrive on challenging and meaningful work. I approach the world as my classroom—where I go to learn and teach. I practice reflexivity in my research, and I am consistently reflective about my teaching, learning, and living. I am collaborative by nature, keenly inquisitive, and saddened by the idea that I will leave this world before I can learn all that I desire to learn. From teaching in the middle school, high school, and university contexts, I have been plagued with the desire to do right by students and the greater collective of the local and global community. I recognize my privilege and negotiate the power that I do have. After many years in the field of education, I have developed a critical eye for its injustices, a strong sense of responsibility, and enduring optimism. This chapter addresses all three of those as it analyzes tools for justice, locating our responsibilities, all in the context of hope.

Calls for culturally responsive pedagogies (CRT) in U.S. classrooms are complicated by the influx of international students with their variety of linguistic and cultural backgrounds. This chapter addresses the intersection and tensions between culturally responsive teaching and globalizing classrooms, using the lens of feminist standpoint theory (see figure 12.1).

Specifically, I conceptually examine the intersection of culturally responsive teaching practices with students' global competencies through specific feminist standpoint epistemological moves and political claims. These intersections will impact the pedagogical and liberatory potential of such moves because within its current structures, we cannot resolve injustices. "Denial

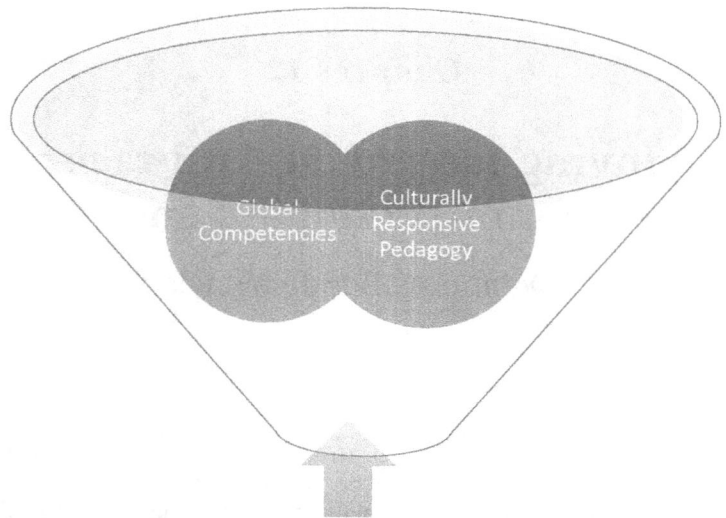

Figure 12.1 **Theoretical and Practical Conceptualization.** *Source*: Created by author.

is the heartbeat of racism, beating across ideologies, races, and nations. It is beating within us" (Kendi, 2019, p. 9). Rather than research in denial, I hope to confront the heartbeat of racism in how I conceptualize and utilize current educational theories and practices in order to engage in anti-racist work.

I, and many others in the field of education, have made the claim that in the United States, there is a need to internationalize our classrooms (Banks, 2014; Bender-Slack, 2019, 2020; Cushner, 2012; Deardorff, 2015; Mansilla & Jackson, 2011; Shaklee & Baily, 2012; Short; 2016; Snowball, 2007; Stearns, 2000). Due to cultural, social, political, and economic reasons, teaching students to develop the skills, attitudes, and behaviors of living in a global society will contribute to their success as well as improve their contributions as global citizens. "The fundamental change for children is that the world is visibly present in their daily lives through technology, mass media, economic interdependency, and global mobility" (Short, 2016, p. 3). Therefore, the progression toward global knowledge, intercultural competence, and language acquisition is crucial for today's students to function productively and harmoniously in tomorrow's ever-increasing global society, but also in today's classrooms in the United States because of the shifting demographics of students (Bender-Slack, 2019). For the sake of this chapter, "the terms global and international are used interchangeably, all with a focus of integrating and infusing the international, the intercultural, and global into the formal and informal curriculum as it relates to students at home and looking outward" (Bender-Slack, 2019, p. 11).

Why examine the intersection of cultural responsiveness and internationalization in classrooms? "First, the idea of, need for, and practice possibilities of culturally responsiveness are 'going global,' conceptually, geographically, demographically, and epistemologically" (Gay, 2018, p. xxx). Classrooms across the country, from the urban centers to rural towns have been globalized by immigration, economic need, and social ties. "High percentages of ethnically and racially diverse students have a diasporic connection to places, people, and experiences that are more genuinely worldwide than previous generations" (Gay, 2018, p. xxxi). Second, while culturally responsive teaching has addressed local and even national cultural differences, the international topics and demands complicate that to a higher degree. Third, internationalization may impact how teachers have understood and can understand elements of culturally responsive teaching. Examining the intersection of cultural responsiveness and internationalization in classrooms from a feminist lens allows for a more complex and relevant conceptual analysis.

FEMINIST LENS

Using a feminist lens to attend to linguistic differences with regard to international students is a starting point to understand how language has implications for one's lived reality. Gender is inherent in the structures of language, constructed as dichotomous categories that are hierarchically arranged in relation to one another. This standpoint is vital for feminists who perceive the female-male distinction as the binary opposite (Crotty, 2003). If the structures of language are charged with power, and its related sociocultural norms, this can be problematic in everyday events and in the interpretation of those events. Feminist theory, which I will use as a lens in this chapter, seeks to transform power relations. Given the use of women's bodies to maintain and perpetuate women's oppression, the gendered bodies in classrooms are central. From an intersectional perspective, the surveillance, policing, and violence done to bodies are inscribed by class, race, and gender.

Feminist standpoint theory is one of many feminist theories it is possible on which to draw. Rather than thinking of a standpoint as simply an interested position (interpreted as bias), "a standpoint . . . carries with it the contention that there are some perspectives on society from which, however well-intentioned one may be, the real relations of humans with each other and with the natural world are not visible" (Hartsock, 2019, pp. 106–107). Specifically, feminist standpoint theorists make three fundamental claims: knowledge is socially situated; marginalized groups are socially situated in ways that provide the ability to increase their awareness and ask questions better than (or different from) the nonmarginalized; and research focused on power relations should begin with the lives of the marginalized.

Beginning with a Marxist analysis of standpoint, Hartsock (2019) used the sexual division of labor to argue for a feminist standpoint. With regard to women's labor, the elements of the analysis included the following: dual contribution to subsistence in capitalism (working more in the workplace and working at home); involvement in processes of change and growth—not just production; reproductive labor, including motherhood as an institution; different experiences of self; and the complex relational world inhabited by women reinforced by the process of socialization. This gendered lens of the division of labor comprises the intersection of race as well.

An intersectional lens is helpful to feminist standpoint in a number of ways. "Intersectional paradigms make . . . important contributions to understanding the connections between knowledge and empowerment" (Collins, 2000, p. 227). Intersectional paradigms provide a view of the mutually constructing systems of oppression. The intersection of race, class, gender, and sexuality provides new interpretations of people's experiences and sheds light on how domination is organized.

The organization of domination can be understood as structures that support inequity. "The term matrix of domination describes this overall social organization within which intersecting oppressions originate, develop, and are contained in the United States, such domination has occurred through schools, housing, employment, government, and other social institutions that regulate the actual patterns of intersecting oppression that Black women encounter" (Collins, 2001, pp. 227–228). It is useful to start with Black women—or more globally Black, Indigenous, Women of Color—when making this analysis.

I chose to examine elements of culturally responsive pedagogies (what teachers are called to enact) with global competencies (what students are called to enact). As a White feminist researcher, I used feminist standpoint theory with an intersectional paradigm as a way to better understand the intersection of the two (culturally responsive teaching and global learning).

GLOBAL LEARNING

The transformation toward globalization in all facets of life is an ongoing movement. Whether economic, social, political, or, as we have recently discovered during the pandemic, health, globalization impacts our lived realities. Globalization impacts schools and schooling as well, so teachers must be equipped to attend to this movement with radical global moments in the classroom. "Globally competent youngsters will be prepared to further such understanding through inquiry, by recognizing perspectives, communicating with diverse audiences, and acting in competent ways" (Mansilla & Jackson, 2011, p. 7). Is engaging in culturally responsive pedagogies sufficient to addressing the needs of students to become globally competent? I will propose here that more must be done, that we must go beyond pedagogies.

Schools are laden with current cultural and justice issues. "Layering upon the already troubled nature of some schools, the complexity of immigration, the tensions that arise with students of multiple countries, perspectives, attitudes, and experiences, hamper teachers' ability to teach effectively" (Shaklee & Baily, 2012, p. 3). There are a number of constructs that provide a way for educators to understand global competencies. In fact, Tichnor-Wagner et.al (2019), provide six different global competence frameworks and the organization by which they were created such as the OECD PISA Global Competence Framework, UNESCO's Global Citizenship Education Key Learner Outcomes, and World Savvy's Global Competence Matrix. All use a multifaceted construct for global competence and coalesce around similar domains (behavioral, cognitive, and social-emotional). For the sake of this chapter, I will utilize the following four global competencies by the Asia Society (Mansilla & Jackson, 2011), which demonstrate the types of students we hope to cultivate in global classrooms:

1. Students investigate the world beyond their immediate environment, framing significant problems and conducting well-crafted and age-appropriate research.
2. Students recognize perspectives, others' and their own, articulating and explaining such perspectives thoughtfully and respectfully.
3. Students communicate ideas effectively with diverse audiences, bridging geographic, linguistic, ideological, and cultural barriers.
4. Students take action to improve conditions, viewing themselves as players in the world and participating reflectively.

These four competencies are both broad and succinct, while attending to the behavioral, cognitive, and social-emotional domains.

Viewed along a continuum, global competence is something individuals move along, never reaching true global competence. Still, these competencies are a helpful guide for teachers wanting to internationalize their classrooms and for students who want to develop globally competent dispositions, skills, and strategies. This section about global learning positioned students at the center; the next section will center teachers.

CULTURALLY RESPONSIVE TEACHING

Due to "the enduring presence of institutional racism and the culture of whiteness in the academy" (Picower & Kohli, 2017, p. 6) and throughout K-12 schooling, there is radical work to be done. First, we need to "disrupt the discourse in the larger teacher educational spaces that normalized whiteness, White supremacy, and class hostility toward urban youth and youth of Color" (Camangian, 2017, p. 32). Understanding the discourses, who has access, and how they intersect is a critical first step in being able to disrupt them.

Although I attended Catholic K-12 schools until going to college at a state university, I began my teaching career in a public school that was quickly transitioning from rural to suburban with the selling of vast acres of verdant farmland to construct brick and glass office buildings and sprawling shopping centers. I believed in the democratic ideals of public schooling. However, "that public education, though a noble ideal, rather than 'level the playing field,' often served instead to exacerbate inequalities, particularly around race, ethnicity, social class, language, and other differences" (Nieto, 2017, pp. 23–24). And this makes me angry at the White, patriarchal structure and my complicity in it. Since the vast majority of public school teachers in the United States are White, middle-class women, they/we have been doing the job of the patriarchy every long day in every classroom across the country as members of the dominant race group, maintaining control over others without critically questioning concepts like meritocracy and color-blindness.

Culturally responsive teaching was developed as a way to meet the needs of students in order to create equity in the learning experience of all students. Culturally responsive pedagogy is commonly described as consistently having these eight elements (Gay, 2018, pp. 36–45):

- *Validating*: using the cultural knowledge, prior experiences, frames of reference, and performance styles of ethnically diverse student to make learning encounters more relevant to and effective for them.
- *Comprehensive and Inclusive*: providing an extensive range and variety of topics, issues, groups, and perspectives that fall within the purview of educating for and about ethnic, racial, cultural, social, linguistic, and national diversity.
- *Multidimensional*: encompassing curriculum content, learning context, classroom climate, student-teacher relationships, instructional techniques, classroom management, and performance assessments.
- *Empowering:* enabling academic competence, personal confidence, courage, and the will to act.
- *Transformative:* respecting students' cultures and using them as resources for teaching and learning.

- *Emancipatory*: making authentic knowledge about different ethnic groups accessible to students, lifting the veil of presumed absolute authority from conceptions of scholarly truth typically taught in schools.
- *Humanistic*: being concerned with the human welfare, dignity, and respect of the various individuals and groups who comprise the United States and the world.
- *Normative and Ethical*: incorporating cultural diversity into educative processes intended for ethnically, racially, and socially diverse students.

Teachers who engage in culturally responsive pedagogy keep these practices at the forefront of their curriculum, instruction, identity, and relationships with students and communities.

Culturally responsive theory and practices provide a lens and toolbox with which educators can partially address inequities in learning spaces. My concern is that when not done effectively, it maintains institutionalized racism, leaving it in place. When K-12 teachers and university faculty have not engaged in the intellectual endeavor, emotional labor, and political work necessary to understand and confront the systemic oppression of White supremacy in schools and communities, culturally responsive pedagogy lacks its radical possibilities. "White faculty and faculty of other diverse identities also have to step up to the plate. Creating welcoming and diverse colleges of education and preparing all teachers to be supportive, creative, and critical educators should be everyone's business" (Nieto, 2017, p. 27). As White allies rather than White saviors, White educators must use culturally responsive teaching to be part of the solution.

My identity shapes not only how I see the world but will also inform how I utilize the elements of culturally responsive teaching. Reflexivity is one way to address this. "Does how we respond to the racial contradictions facing us help shape the experiences we have" (Camangian, 2017, p. 29)? There are numerous racial contradictions (as they relate to class, gender, ethnicity sexuality, nationality, and ability) vying for space and discourse in every classroom. As educators and researchers, who we are, what we do, and how we respond will not only shape our experiences but will shape the experiences of our students and readers. That is a heavy responsibility. In the Catholic Jesuit university where I work, for example, we need to design teaching and research that is "more aligned with the needs of the local poor and working class communities the SOE (School of Education) had long ignored" (Camangian, 2017, p. 33).

If we are not purposefully ignoring this work, then we may be doing so out of ignorance—from our various standpoints. The result, however, is the same. In the academy, we have the advantage of time to think and write about what can help us to be part of the solution. Those who experience oppressions in different ways may not have that luxury. In the following section, I will examine the intersection of culturally responsive teaching practices and student global competencies, using feminist standpoint epistemological and political claims.

FEMINIST STANDPOINT ANALYSIS

The following section consists of two parts. First, I will use the feminist standpoint epistemological and political claims, provided by Hartsock (2019) as a framework, through which I describe how culturally responsive pedagogies might inform the global competencies. On the left side of each of the five figures below will be the culturally responsive teaching element, and on the right side will be the global competency or competencies that could be addressed through that teaching element.

Second, I will highlight those elements of culturally responsive teaching that resist a feminist standpoint lens. Specifically, I will analyze three of the elements of culturally responsive teaching that I would like to highlight as being problematic, which are described as Multidimensional, Normative and Ethical, and Emancipatory.

Part One: The Claims

Claim #1: *Material life not only structures but sets limits on the understanding of social relations* (Hartsock, 2019).

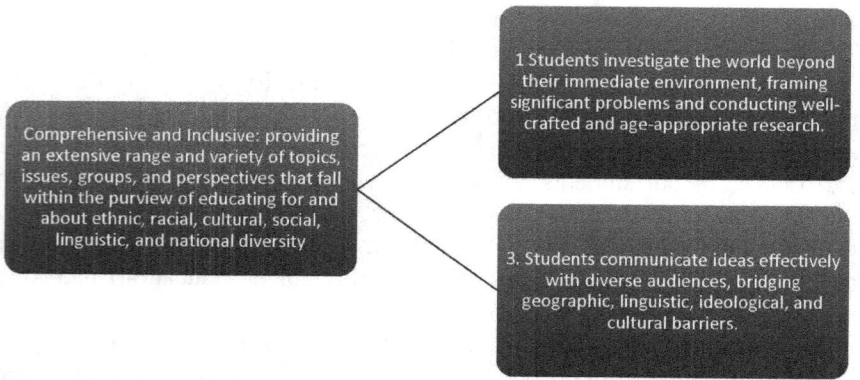

Figure 12.2   Claim 1: Framing of CRT and GC. *Source*: Created by author.

This element of culturally responsive teaching, Comprehensive and Inclusive, provides a way for students to meet global competencies one and three. For example, if teachers provide an extensive array of topics and issues, then students will have access to resources that enable them to investigate the world beyond their immediate environment, helping them frame significant problems and conducting their own research. If teachers provide a range and a variety of groups and perspectives in education for and about ethnic, racial, cultural, social, linguistic, and national diversity then students will be better able to communicate ideas effectively with diverse audiences, bridging geographic, linguistic, ideological, and cultural barriers.

"As socially transformative educators and teacher educators, we will always be faced with inequities and resistances" (Camangian, 2017, p. 34), providing us much fodder with which to work. However, material life sets limits on what we can understand. For example, despite the national barriers that separate women of African descent, Black women's experiences demonstrate marked similarities that "illustrate how the persistence of the legacy of colonialism with its racial/ethnic, sexist and class biases have resulted in a system of 'global gendered apartheid'—a global economic system characterized by the exploitation of the labour of women of colour everywhere" (Collins, 2000, p. 232). My experiences as a White woman limit what I can understand with regard to Black women's lived experiences. In her seminal essay about transforming silence to action, Lorde (2007) writes, "But primarily for us all, it is necessary to teach by living and speaking those truths which we believe and know beyond understanding. Because in this way alone we can survive, by taking part in a process of life that is creative and continuing, that is growth" (p. 43). Consequently, doing the daily work of aspiring to be an anti-racist ally and co-conspirator is critical.

Claim #2: *If material life is structured in fundamentally opposing ways for two different groups, one can expect that the vision of each will represent an inversion of the other, and in systems of domination the vision available to the rulers will be both partial and perverse* (Hartsock, 2019).

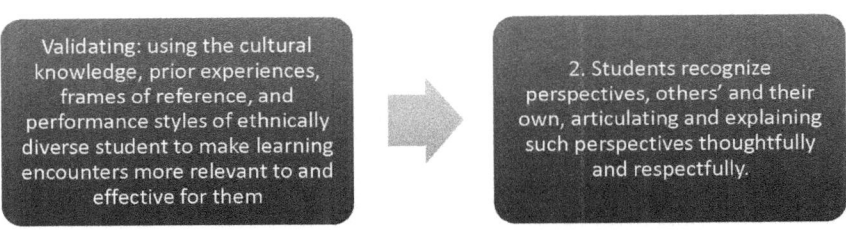

Figure 12.3 Claim 2: Framing of CRT and GC. *Source*: Created by author.

This element of culturally responsive teaching, Validating, provides a way for students to meet global competency two. If White teachers use cultural knowledge, prior experiences, frames of reference, and performance styles of ethnically diverse students to create relevant and effective learning encounters, this validation will help students recognize others' perspectives as well as their own. Viewing race as a social construct is a beginning. If White teachers want to teach about race, they first have to do the internal work of reflecting on their own complicity in a school system based in White supremacy as they do the daily work of becoming/being a good ally. Howard (2017), self-identifying as a professor of Color, described his observations like this: "While I do believe that White teacher educators can effectively talk about and teach to race, my experience is that most of my White colleagues are only able to superficially address topics related to race" (p. 38). That does not mean White educators can neglect teaching about race; there is no neutrality in the struggle to end racism. It means that White educators have to work to understand and teach race at a deeper, more complex level.

Moreover, as a White woman, I recognize that my vision is both partial and perverse. My work as a feminist researcher is to practice reflexivity. "Reflexivity generally means attempting to make explicit the power relations and the exercise of power in the research process" (Ramazanoglu & Holland (2004, p. 118). Reflexivity in feminist research is practiced as research questions are developed, throughout the design of the research study, and during the processes of data collection and analysis.

From epistemological claim #2 of feminist standpoint, in this system of domination, men see women in a way that is partial and perverse. This concurs with the idea that "feminist Marxists and materialist feminists more generally have argued that the position of women is structurally different from that of men, and that the lived realities of women's lives are profoundly different from those of men" (Hartsock, 2019, p. 106). However, well-intentioned, men can work alongside women for gender equity, but they cannot lead the movement. Consequently, White educators and scholars can work for racial equity, but they cannot lead the movement.

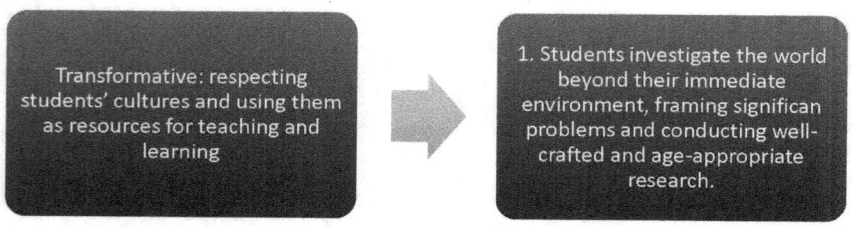

Figure 12.4 Claim 3: Framing of CRT and GC. *Source*: Created by author.

Claim #3: *The vision of the ruling class (or gender) structures the material relations in which all parties are forced to participate, and therefore cannot be dismissed as simply false* (Hartsock, 2019).

This element of culturally responsive teaching, Transformative, provides a way for students to meet global competency one. If teachers respect students' cultures and use them as resources in the classroom, students will be better able to frame significant problems. Before respecting or using those cultures, however, one must first understand them—and their place in larger institutions like education. "Scholars tend to posit whiteness as an ideological, political, legal, and social fiction that places so-called whites in a position of hegemony over other non-dominant groups" (Beech, 2020, p. 3). As long as Whiteness is centered as the default in education, little can be transformed.

It is helpful to understand the structures in which all are forced to participate, creating a matrix. "Regardless of how any given matrix is actually organized either across time or from society to society, the concept of a matrix of domination encapsulates the universality of intersecting oppressions as organized through diverse local realities" (Collins, 2000, p. 228). Those intersecting oppressions evident in schooling (in ways we label, test, and discipline students), cannot be simply dismissed as false.

Feigning that race doesn't matter does not change the material relations in which all parties are forced to participate. Howard (2017) states that "many preservice and inservice teachers adopt colorblind approaches to their teaching," claiming it is not significant, "yet for young Black boys it is significant, [in fact] to deny it is to be quite dismissive of their realities (p. 38). White teachers radically engaging in a culturally responsive pedagogy strive to understand Black boys' material realities, not negate or ignore them. "To be antiracist is to focus on ending the racism that shapes the mirages, not to ignore the mirages that shape peoples' lives" (Kendi, 2019, pp. 54–55).

Claim #4: *The vision available to the oppressed group must be struggled for and represents an achievement which requires both science to see beneath*

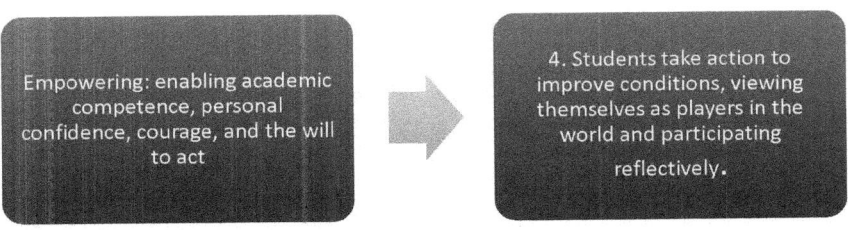

Figure 12.5 **Claim 4: Framing of CRT and GC.** *Source*: Created by author.

the surface of the social relations in which all are forced to participate, and the education which can only grow from struggle to change those relations (Hartsock, 2019).

This element of culturally responsive teaching, Empowering, provides a way for students to meet global competency four. If teachers enable students' academic competence, personal confidence, courage, and the will to act, then students will be able to take action to improve conditions, be empowered to act on their world, and reflect on their participation. This culturally responsive teaching element and global competency appear to fit seamlessly, which is why it is vital to highlight the importance of struggle. White people can often choose not to engage in that struggle, but BIPOC will find struggle necessary and unavoidable. Collins (2000) describes survival for students of Color as a form of resistance. Resistance *is* action. BIPOC have struggled to survive in the educational system for over a century in the U.S. Students' resistance can be used as a starting point from which students learn, educators teach, and scholars research. Acting via struggle is not easy or simple. We must recognize that features and forms of culture are always embedded in teaching and learning—and that U.S. schooling is Eurocentric (Gay, 2018). This creates struggles for BIPOC negotiating cultural and sociopolitical differences within the system.

Though struggles occur within a system, radical change of the system itself is the ultimate goal. "Being a permanent outsider within can never lead to power because the category, by definition, requires marginality. Each individual must find her own way, recognizing that her personal biography, while unique, is never as unique as she thinks" (Collins, 2000, p. 289). Resisting this individualistic view and embracing a collective lens will give us the strength to struggle to change social and structural relations.

Claim #5: *As an engaged vision, the understanding of the oppressed, the adoption of a standpoint exposes the real relations among human beings as inhuman, points to the present, and carries a historically liberatory role* (Hartsock, 2019).

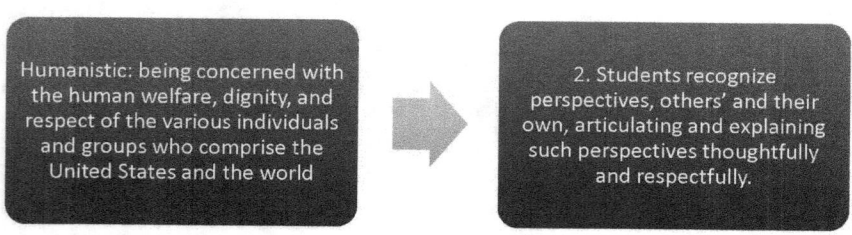

Figure 12.6 **Claim 5: Framing of CRT and GC.** *Source*: Created by author.

This element of culturally responsive teaching, Humanistic, provides a way for students to meet global competency two. If teachers are concerned with human welfare, dignity, and respect of all individuals and groups locally and around the world, then students will be able to thoughtfully and respectfully recognize their own and others' perspectives. "The field of education is anchored in White rage, especially public education" (Love, 2020, p. 21), but what if instead public education was anchored in our shared humanity? If according to the fifth feminist standpoint epistemological claim, we expose the real relations as being inhuman, then our radical work is to change those material relations. Human dignity and respect is a place to begin this work in order to create an equitable, human education system.

Anti-racist and abolitionist approaches may provide a solution. "Abolitionist teaching stands in solidarity with parents and fellow teachers opposing standardized testing, English-only education, racist teachers, arming teachers with guns, and turning schools into prisons. Abolitionist teaching supports and teaches from the space that Black Lives Matter, all Black Lives Matter, and affirms Black folx' humanity" (Love, 2020, p.12). It begins with our shared humanity because when one suffers and struggles, the community suffers and struggles.

Part Two: The Problematic Elements

In this section, I want to highlight those elements of culturally responsive pedagogy that resist a feminist standpoint lens. There are three of the elements of culturally responsive teaching that I would like to highlight as being problematic: multidimensional, normative and ethical, and emancipatory.

- Multidimensional: encompassing curriculum content, learning context, classroom climate, student-teacher relationships, instructional techniques, classroom management, and performance assessments.

I would like to explore various interpretations of multidimensional. First, while one might argue that the global competencies are multidimensional taken as a whole, they neglect specifically mentioning critical elements of education such as curriculum, learning context, student-teacher relationships, or performance assessments. They do address classroom climate, learning context, and instructional techniques. For example, if students communicate ideas effectively with diverse audiences, that would impact the classroom context. If students are investigating the world beyond their immediate environment, one could infer that the instructional techniques used would be critical to that endeavor. As previously mentioned, a standpoint carries with it the assertion that there are some perspectives on society the real relations of humans with each other and with the natural world are not visible (Hartsock, 2019, p. 107). Consequently, teachers who do not have certain perspectives will not have access to many of the real relations or dimensions.

Second, the multidimensional element does not address levels of reality. For example, Hartsock (2019) explains:

> The concept of a standpoint structures epistemology in a particular way. Rather than a simple dualism, it posits a duality of levels of reality, of which the deeper level of essence both includes and explains the "surface" or appearance, and indicates the logic by means of which the appearance inverts and distorts the deeper reality. In addition, the concept of a standpoint depends on the assumption that epistemology grows in a complex and contradictory way from material life. (pp. 106–107)

Not only are their multiple dimensions on the surface level, there are deeper levels that are distorted by that surface level. Critical theories are not relativistic with regard to what is true. Culturally relevant teaching and global education are often reduced to tolerance, respect, and acceptance of the status quo without challenging injustices, oppression, violence, and trauma that structure the reality of those who are marginalized.

Lastly, multidimensionality in regards to culturally responsive pedagogy includes educational components such as curriculum content, learning context, classroom climate, student-teacher relationships, instructional techniques, classroom management, and performance assessments. However, schooling is only part of the equation. "Educational researchers know that without a long-term strategy to eradicate the causes of racial and economic isolation—such as discrimination, predatory lending, housing displacement, the gender wage gap, rising healthcare costs, and unemployment (which leads to the 99 percent being no better than indentured servants to the 1 percent) (Love, 2020, p.19), schooling will not radically change. Therefore, any heroic efforts made to restructure schools or engage radical pedagogical techniques in the classroom will be unsustainable.

- Normative and Ethical: incorporating cultural diversity into educative processes intended for ethnically, racially, and socially diverse students

Interestingly, the global competencies do not allude to, or even mention, power dynamics or institutionalized power. Therefore, although what is normative and ethical may be resisted by addressing the competencies, the current structures and practices are not confronted. Moreover, this idea of analyzing the normative and ethical is intended for ethnically, racially, and socially diverse students, but the global competencies show no diversity with regard to the students for which these are intended. "All contexts of domination incorporate some combination of intersecting oppressions, and considerable variability exists from one matrix of domination to the next as to how oppression and activism will be organized" (Collins, 2000, 228). How do the students who are engaging in these competencies matter? What does the work look like in all-White classrooms and communities? Race still matters because they, too, are active members in an unjust world. In CRT, to whose cultures are we responding? Are we still centering Whiteness?

Moreover, feminist standpoint theory's political basis is foundational to the women's movement in that it undermines social sciences' embedding of White male standpoint as hidden subject and agent (Smith, 2000). So, too, must we undermine the White supremacy embedded in the practices of schooling. Teaching and learning in schools today already begins in an institutionalized racist location, which cannot be ignored. Classrooms are political spaces, racially charged in ways that damage all students. "The most threatening racist movement is not the alt right's unlikely drive for a White ethnostate but the regular American's drive for a 'race-neutral' one" (Kendi, 2019, p. 20). Teachers must engage in anti-racist teaching and not take race-neutral or color-blind approaches.

- Emancipatory: making authentic knowledge about different ethnic groups accessible to students, lifting the veil of presumed absolute authority from conceptions of scholarly truth typically taught in schools.

Similar to analyzing the normative and ethical in education, emancipatory culturally responsive teaching as it intersects with global competencies from a feminist standpoint is problematic. As previously mentioned, power (its existence or the challenging of) is not included in the global competencies. The fifth feminist standpoint claim proposes to carry a historically liberatory role, pointing toward the present. Making knowledge about ethnic groups accessible to students and even questioning the presumed absolute authority from conceptions of scholarly truth does not inevitably lead to something emancipatory. It may be a radical moment, but it does not assure further movement. Love (2020) explains that it is the educator's option in "choosing to engage in the struggle for educational justice knowing that you have the ability and human right to refuse oppression and refuse to oppress others, mainly your students" (p. 11). Educational researchers have a similar option to struggle for educational justice. It is our human right, and even our human responsibility, to refuse oppression and refuse to oppress others throughout the research process. The issue lies in our ability to be aware of how this oppression is intersecting and institutional so that our refusal results in radical action. Culturally responsive teaching is partial action because "pedagogy should work in tandem with students' own knowledge of their community and grassroots organizations to push forward new ideas for social change, not just be a tool to enhance test scores or grades. Pedagogy, regardless of its name, is useless without teachers dedicated to challenging systemic oppression with intersectional social justice" (Love, 2020, p. 19).

Ultimately, I must admit to experiencing some dissonance in completing this analysis because the elements of culturally responsive teaching center diverse students, but I found that the global competencies appear to center students in the dominant groups. I am reflecting on this troubling interpretation. Moreover, the use of feminist standpoint theory was mostly useful when attending to intersecting oppressions.

CONCLUSION

This chapter addressed the intersection and tensions between culturally responsive pedagogies and globalizing classrooms, using the lens of feminist standpoint theory. That intersection was productively complicated here with an anti-racist approach. With regard to the tensions in the above analysis, I suggest there is much work to be done. Anti-racist work and abolitionist teaching may guide our radical movement forward. Engaging in abolitionist teaching can ensure that students feel safe and protected in schools rather than experience schools as perpetrators of violence toward them (Love, 2020). I conclude with a few suggestions.

First, educators and educational scholars must choose to do the work to be anti-racist. "To be anti-racist is a radical choice in the face of this history, requiring a radical reorientation of our consciousness" (Kendi, 2019, p.23). It is a process that is both individual and collaborative, both personal and professional. And it is difficult to do in light of this country's history.

Second, engaging in abolitionist teaching and researching means allowing it to permeate all aspects of our work and our lives. It could include the following radical moves:

> Reimagining and rewriting curriculums with local and national activists to provide students with not only examples of resistance but also strategies of resistance. Protecting and standing in solidarity with immigrant children and their families. Joining pro-immigrant community organizations in the fight for rights for all. Knowing that freedom is impossible without women and queer leaders being the thinkers and doers of abolitionist movements" (Love, 2020, p. 11).

It is about being immersed in the changes we want to see and living in that hope that we are part of something larger—a radical movement.

Third, as educational researchers, we can have the courage to take a stand even when it is not popular. We cannot remain quiet or neutral in light of current educational practices. For example, "abolitionist teaching is refusing to take part in zero-tolerance policies and the school-to-prison pipeline, demanding restorative justice in our schools as the only schoolwide or districtwide approach to improving school culture" (Love, 2020, p. 11). Reevaluate what we do and why we do it. Use our power to transform the oppressive, harmful structures.

What happens in classrooms is as impactful as what happens outside of them. Educational researchers and teachers cannot limit their scope to schooling. "It is essential for educators to break down the four walls of their classrooms, addressing today's content, curricula, and pedagogy through an international lens so that they can model for students what it means to be a global citizen" (Bender-Slack, 2019, p. 21). That international lens is helpful inside and outside of the classroom, but we must also go beyond pedagogy for this to be radical. Love (2020) states:

> No type of pedagogy, however effective, can single-handedly remove the barriers of racism, discrimination, homophobia, segregation, Islamophobia, homelessness, access to college, and concentrated poverty, but antiracist pedagogy combined with grassroots organizing can prepare students and their families to demand the impossible in the fight for eradicating these persistent and structural barriers (p. 19).

As previously mentioned, after many years in the field of education, I have developed a critical eye for its injustices, a strong sense of responsibility, and enduring optimism. This chapter addressed all three of those, conceptually analyzing tools for justice and locating our responsibilities, all in the context of hope. What suffering has schooling caused in the United States? In what ways does it continue to oppress Black, Indigenous, students of Color? Love (2002) claims that if education is one of the principal tools used to maintain White supremacy and anti-immigrant hate, then teachers entering the field must learn and acknowledge this history so that they comprehend why it matters in the contemporary educational context. Rather than research and teach in denial, I will continue to confront the heartbeat of racism in how I conceptualize and utilize current educational theories and practices.

SOMETHING TO READ, DO, OR CONSIDER

Layla's Sadd's *Me and White Supremacy* was a book that not only helped me to labor along this journey in a deeply reflective way, but it also provided details to discuss structures and constructs of race with White people. When looking for something to do, I would say—harness your power by speaking up. Whether on social media, at work, or gathering with family or friends, remaining quiet and neutral is unacceptable. Lastly, consider this: In our everyday lives, we are either maintaining the structure of White supremacy or dismantling it.

REFERENCES

Banks, J. A. (2014). *An introduction to multicultural education* (5th edition). Pearson.
Beech, J. (2020). *White out: A guidebook for teaching and engaging with critical whiteness studies.* Brill.
Bender-Slack, D. (2019). Expanding our classrooms. A rationale for internationalization in education. In D. Bender-Slack (Ed.), *Internationalization in the classroom: Going global* (pp. 11–22). Lexington Books.
Bender-Slack, D. (2020). *The Nicaraguan Literacy Campaign: The power and politics of literacy.* Lexington Books.
Camangian, P. (2017). The transformative lives we lead. In B. Picower & R. Kohli (Eds.), *Confronting racism in teacher education* (pp. 29–34). Routledge.
Collins, P. H. (2000) *Black feminist thought.* Routledge.
Crotty, M. (2003). *The foundations of social research.* Sage Publications.
Cushner, K. (2012). Intercultural Competence for teaching and learning. In B. Shaklee and S. Baily (Eds.), *Internationalizing teacher education in the United States* (pp. 41–58). Rowman and Littlefield Publishers.
Deardorff, D. K. (2015). *Demystifying outcomes assessment for international educators: A practical approach.* Stylus.
Gay, G. (2018). *Culturally responsive teaching.* Teachers College Press.
Kendi, I. (2019). *How to be an antiracist.* One World.
Love, B. (2020). *We want to do more than survive: Abolitionist teaching and the pursuit of educational freedom.* Beacon Press.
Hartsock, N. (2019). *The feminist standpoint revisited and other essays.* Routledge.
Howard, T. (2017). Tales from the dark side. In B. Picower & R. Kohli (Eds.), *Confronting racism in teacher education* (pp. 35–41). Routledge.
Lorde, A. (2007). The transformation of silence into action. *Sister Outsider.* Crossing Press.
Mansilla, V. & Jackson, A. (2011). *Educating for global competence: Preparing our youth to engage the world.* The Asia Society.
NAEYC https://www.naeyc.org/resources/pubs/yc/nov2019/understanding-anti-bias
Nieto, S. (2017). Identity matters: My life as a [Puerto Rican] teacher educator. In B. Picower & R. Kohli (Eds.), *Confronting racism in teacher education* (pp. 21–28). Routledge.
New America https://www.newamerica.org/education-policy/reports/culturally-responsive-teaching/teacher-competencies-that-promote-culturally-responsive-teaching/ updated 7-23-21

Picower, B. & Kohli, R. (2017). Introduction. In B. Picower & R. Kohli (Eds.), *Confronting racism in teacher education* (pp. 1–17). Routledge.

Ramazanoglu, C. & Holland, J. (2004). *Feminist methodology.* Sage Publications.

Shaklee, B. & Baily, S. (Eds.) (2012). *Internationalizing teacher education in the United States.* Rowman and Littlefield Publishers.

Short, K. (2016). A curriculum that is intercultural. In K. Short, D. Day, and J. Schroeder (Eds.), *Teaching globally: Reading the world through literature* (pp. 3–24). Stenhouse Publishers.

Snowball, L. (2007). Becoming more internationally minded: International teacher certification and professional development. In M. Hayden, J. Levy, & J. Thompson (Eds.), *The Sage handbook of research in international education* (pp. 247–55). Sage.

Stearns, P. (2009). *Educating global citizens in colleges and universities.* Routledge.

Tichnor-Wagner, A., Parkhouse, H., Glazier, J. & J. Cain. (2019). *Becoming a globally competent teacher.* ASCD.

Chapter 13

When Silence Is Not an Option

Creating Space for Marginalized Voices

Francis Godwyll

In this chapter, I define silence, identify some of the motivating factors that produce silence as a consequence, and discuss the examples of societal disruptions and the complex responses silence evokes. In addition, societal reactions are examined, lessons learned are deduced, and then possibilities for creating spaces for empowerment are examined.

Silence results when enough symbols or information sufficient to understand something is not relayed to a potential receiver (Kostiuk, 2012). Asrifan and Ghofur (2021) viewed silence as absolute stillness or a state where there is the absence of sound or noise. They epitomized silence as muteness, absence of speech, taciturnity, forbearance from, refusal to speak, or quietness.

According to Benevene (2020) and Milliken and Morrison (2003), the choice for individuals to express themselves or keep quiet at the workplace is one of the major concerns faced in any organization. The context is characterized by the following: an organizational arrangement in which leaders detest to hear about challenges, where those in authority can penalize those who speak up, as well as a social system where speaking up has absolute undesirable norms.

Milliken, Morrison, and Hewlin (2003), Ridzuan, Abd Rahman, and Manas (2019) and Ryan and Oestreich (1991) argued that to remain silent about developing issues or problems is a fairly usual occurrence that is not surprising. The authors further accentuated that it is salient to understand the decisions to remain silent, as it may threaten the reporting of unethical and illegal operations as well as the chances of undermining efficacious organizational and societal practices (Argyris & Schon, 1978; Beer & Eisenstat, 2000; Edmondson. 2003; Khalid & Ahmed, 2016; Milliken, Morrison, & Hewlin, 2003; Ridzuan, Abd Rahman, & Manas, 2019; Ryan & Oestreich, 1991). Morrison and Milliken (2000) believe that the decision to remain silent in addition to allowing illegality and inefficiencies to occur also affect the lives of the individuals negatively. They further pointed out that risks exist with speaking up about issues and problems, but negative consequences outweigh the option of staying silent as individuals or groups. Other scholars argued that the cumulative effect of silence over time is a feeling of disenfranchisement, incapability, reduced job satisfaction and high job turnover, among other lasting outcomes (Argyris & Schon, 1978; Beer & Eisenstat, 2000; Edmondson, 2003; Khalid, & Ahmed, 2016; Morrison & Milliken, 2000).

There are many motivations for silence. Some include the fear of personal harm, isolation, disparagement, shame, criticism, oppression, misunderstanding, fear of hurting others, fear of being labeled a complainer, whiner, trouble-maker, psychological safety, and rejection, among others. Another dimension of silence that makes it lethal is what Bowen and Blackmon (2003) and Yalçın, & Baykal (2019) call "contagion" which is the phenomenon in which silence exercised over one issue spreads to a wide range of issues. Noelle-Neumann (1974) and Huang et al. (2018) further argued that there is a higher probability for an individual who is silent over one issue to spread it to other issues.

Having attempted to define silence and laid the foundations for the conditions that evoke it, I turn my attention to discuss some circumstances of societal disruptions that have evoked complex reactions including silence. Examples to be discussed in this chapter include the Holocaust, the Crisis in Darfur, the Rwandan Genocide, Slavery, the Trail of Tears, the Japanese Internment in the United States, the Flint Water Crisis, and poverty and economic disenfranchisement.

The Holocaust was based on a perception that fostered into a movement and an ideology, which took an entire world war to defeat. Human aggression has been known in history; yet, the Holocaust (1940–1945), a magnum opus of intentionally orchestrated destruction is incomprehensible. Sometimes when destructions of such unimaginable proportions occur it evokes an epic silence. The Wannsee Conference held in Germany posed these critical questions: How do we judge a people so brutalized and traumatized by the social structure? How are we to understand the psychology of the survivors when the norms of a "good-enough" society no longer applied? How realistic an assessment can we make when the structure of their society, the organization of family life, and the moral value of human relationships disintegrated under the planned extermination by the Nazis? (Bergmann, & Jucovy, 1982; Kestenberg 1980; Niederland, 1981; Ostow, 1997; Pines, 1986; Pines, 2020).

Survivors of the Holocaust were perplexed as to how to explain the circumstances to others, sometimes it is survival guilt, and sometimes the society is not ready to hear out of social guilt. Laqueur (1980) and Breitman and Herf (2019) argued that the enlightened world could not hear what had happened to the six million Jews and to the other groups who had perished in the camps and the ghettos. To hear is to know, and the knowledge imparts a demand for reflection and understanding. They questioned, what could possibly be gained by reflection, except the awareness of guilt and betrayal? Schwartz (2006) further buttressed this point by opining that in this social climate, for the survivors to talk meant the creation of another hostile environment; perhaps, inner distance is preferable to ostracism. To remain silent, not to threaten the society that offered refuge, at least provided some emotional solace; by this collusion between the individual and the society, the survivor could physically and psychologically heal. She further argued that the social corollary to individual repression is omission and distortion, all of which I would add have been experienced in societies we are familiar with through our history books, in the oral rendering of the stories and events from generation to generation. Schwartz (2006) asserted that the role of the external world as a participant in this silence and in the reinforcement of denial mechanisms is a critical component in the appraisal.

After a period of silence, it is critical to be followed by a robust education of the citizenry about the mistakes of the past and conscious efforts made to avoid future occurrences. Here are some rhetorical questions for us to ponder over; what does the average German teenager know about the Holocaust and the steps in place to correct them? How have we written or retold the stories of social disruptions to our future generations? How can future generations be assisted to examine the lessons learned?

Another circumstance of societal disruption is the Crisis in Darfur. Darfur is said to be an abode to approximately 7 million people and it has over 30 ethnic groups that are categorized into two: African and Arab. These are Muslim communities where racial distinctions are impossible due to long years of intermarriages. Yet, intense infighting continued over the years in Darfur due to factors such as fights over resources. The crisis in Darfur commenced when two rebel groups rose up to challenge the National Islamic Front (NIF) government of Darfur in February 2003. The Sudan Liberation Army (SLA) as well as the Justice and Equality Movement (JEM) asserted that the Muslim African ethnic groups in Darfur faced discrimination from the government of Sudan. This resulted in the government of Sudan designating the SLA and JEM as terrorists (Christian, 2013; Dagne, 2004). Several spectators believed that the support given to the Arab militia to suppress the non-Arabs and the policy of discrimination against the African communities in Darfur was a deliberate and systematic pursuit of the government. The conflict pitched the three African ethnic groups, the Fur, Zaghawa, and Masalit, against nomadic Arab ethnic groups. Periodic tensions between the largely African-Muslim ethnic groups and the Arab inhabitants of Darfur resurfaced in the 1980s, and it can be traced back to the 1930s. According to Oette and

Babiker (2018), the Darfur crisis was due to discrimination against a group of people, perceived government connivance, systemic deprivation of resources, abandonment by government, and denial of government services to a group of people. The question for reflection here is, are there communities familiar to you that perceive they are discriminated against and that their governments have denied them services?

The Rwandan Genocide was another instance of societal disruption. To understand the root causes of the genocide one has to revisit the time the Rwandans call "Before," which is not the focus of this section of the chapter. Several centuries ago three groups came to inhabit what is today Rwanda. There were the Twa (1 percent), Tutsi (14 percent), and the Hutus (about 85 percent). The Tutsis were cattlemen and the Hutus were farmers. The wealth gained from cattle sales propelled the Tutsi's into political prominence. The Hutus and Tutsis were defined by class and clan, not by ethnicity. After the Germans lost possession of their colonies during the First World War, the territory was placed under the Belgians. The Belgians bought into a C16th myth by explorers that based on the shape of the noses of the Tutsis, they must have some form of European ancestry which would make them superior to the other groups. Since they spoke one language and were identical in many ways they used what they called the "Nasal Index" to ascertain who was racially superior or inferior. Privileges in colonial society were then based on this division. The Belgian missionaries and Tutsi leaders collaborated to cement notions of a Tutsi aristocracy. As a result, an ethnic divide became institutionalized. Hutus were denied government jobs, higher education, and forced into labor camps, etc. Rwandans were given identity cards stating whether they were Hutus or Tutsis (Chretien, 1995; Destexhe, 1995; Gunther, 1955; Hintjens, 1999; Lemarchand, 1996; Mamdani 1996; Maquet, 1996; Mukoyama, 2018; Prunier, 1995; Reyntjens, 1995, 1996; Uwizeyimana, 2014).

Unfortunately, at independence due to the majority numbers of the Hutus, they gained a landslide victory and came into power. The system was then turned upon its head whereby the oppressed became the oppressor and retaliation against the minority Tutsis began in earnest. Many Tutsis fled the country into neighboring African states. Many of the exiles formed a rebel armed force called the Rwandan Patriotic Front (RPF) and began attacking the Hutu led government. In a gesture of goodwill and in the interest of peace, the Rwandan President went over to Tanzania to sign a peace accord with the rebels. On his way back, his plane was shot down by a rocket attack killing both Presidents of Burundi and Rwanda. Media propaganda turned the searchlight on the Tutsis and accused them of the assassination of the president and labelling them as cockroaches (Cohn, 1967; Chretien, 1995; EIU, 1994; Human Rights Watch, 1994; Mackintosh, 1996; Malvern, 2006; Manikas & Kumar, 1996; Oplinger, 1990; Storr, 1991; Yanagizawa-Drott, 2014).

It is not my intention here to reduce the complexity of the Rwandan Genocide to a simplistic analysis but to point out the disruption that occurred and the intricate responses that it evoked. Some scholars argued that the ethnic factor as a cause is exaggerated, yet others argued it was an eruption to deep-rooted crises of state legitimacy where structural violence of the state was weaponized at the state level through economic, political, and ideological spheres ((Bayart, 2009; Uvin, 1997). Irrespective of one's perspective, an estimated 5–10 percent of Rwanda's population was killed between the second week of April and the third week of May 1994. Prunier (1995) opined that from historical perspectives the Rwandan Genocide has the highest casualty rates from non-natural causes. The Rwandan genocide was a result of the following: (1) discrimination, and providing access to one group and denying another, leading to strife and anger; (2) labelling human beings tend to dehumanize him/her, providing the oppressor a moral justification for abuse; and (3) the use of Identity cards to separate groups (Uwizeyimana, 2014; Mukoyama, 2018). Do any of these ring bells on the home front? Any form of discrimination and disenfranchisement produces resentment, fear, isolation, alienation, powerlessness, and voicelessness, creating a hot bedrock of social upheaval and disruption. Some use the shapes of noses, eye color, pigmentation of the skin, language, socioeconomic status, the appearance of the teeth, size, weight, accent, ethnicity, level of education, gender, sexual orientation, religious persuasions, and zip codes to discriminate among people.

Slavery lasted over 400 years from about 1451 to 1870. It is estimated that millions of Africans were exported from Africa and imported into the Americas (Aptheker, 1951; Foner, 1983, 1986). Thorpe and Taylor (2019) and Williams (1882) summed it up in these words:

> Slavery was overall villainies, an evil that caused great suffering in the land. Humans were traded; mothers were detached from their famishing and speechless children; husbands were separated from their beloved wives; wealth was made from people who were struggling; Happy families were broken . . . yes is there anything worse? To over work people in spite of aging, to deprive them of the goodness of life, . . . to brainwash the intelligent through lethal ignorance, to seize the opportunities of sharing the gospel of love; and then when the hollow cough becomes unpleasant, when the shadows diverge, when the hand trembles, when the gait is shuffling, when the ear is deaf, the eye dim, when desire failed—then to turn that human being out to die is by far the profoundest crime man can be guilty of in his dealings with mankind. (p.255)

In 1776 when we declared these words "We hold these truths to be self-evident, that all men are created equal, that they are endowed by their Creator with certain unalienable Rights that among these are Life, Liberty and the pursuit of Happiness," it is worthy to note that not all groups were free. Slavery was still in force, it was not until 1924 that Native Americans were given the right to become citizens, women could not own property or vote. Thus, the very foundation of our nation had fractures in it right from its inception. We need to acknowledge and understand that it is critical for us to work toward a more perfect union. While reflecting on slavery, we ask ourselves these questions: Did the constitution at that time indeed include ALL humans? Who were humans? Who could vote? Who could own property?

The Trail of Tears is a term for the collective pain and suffering experienced by the forceful relocation of the Native Americans starting from 1831. The Native American tribes lived peacefully in self-governance well before the Western settlers arrived. The Native tribes inhabited the Eastern States and achieved peaceful cohabitation with the Westerners at the early stages of their settlement. The relationship between these two groups was amicable to the point the Cherokees formed alliances with the Westerners for war to defeat the Creek Indians when Andrew Jackson, seventh President of the United States was in power (Anderson, 1989).

As time went by, land cessations by the Westerners intensified. More than 100 treaties were made, which nibbled away at Native American land boundaries (Debo, 1973). Although the treaties always promised Native American sovereignty within remaining tribal areas, these cessions turned out to become the agenda of gradual invasion by the Westerners and the beginning of one of the most tragic gentrification and coerced migration that happened in the history of the United States. On May 28, 1830, the Indian Removal Act was passed. The forceful migration lasted between 1831 and 1842. The native nations from which the removals happened were Choctaw, Creek, Chiksaw, Cherokee, and Seminole. The estimated number of people forcefully removed is around 59,000 people plus 2,000 Black slaves owned by the Cherokees. Estimated number of deaths due to diseases and the weather are said to be between 8,000 and 16,300 Native Americans (Anderson, 1989; Britannica, 2018; Debo, 1973; Magliocca, 2003; Satz, 1975; Schlesinger, 1945).

Reflecting on the Trail of Tears, one can conclude that oppressors can strategically plan to befriend the group they plan to oppress in the future. In this case, the Westerners were able to establish some form of relationship with the Natives and then through coercion, subtle and overt force began a process of displacement and takeover. In addition, the Westerners had weapons and arms that were far more advanced which made them advantageous not only in wars but to convince the oppressed group to acquiesce, silence, and oppress them. Stripping a group of people of language and ethnic pride are powerful and essential strategies to colonize, oppress, and silence them.

The Japanese Internment in America is another case of societal disruption that I explore in this section. An Executive Order was issued by President Franklin Roosevelt on February 19, 1942, 10 weeks after Pearl Harbor was bombed. This order was to remove every person of Japanese ancestry from the west-coast region of the United States. Over 110,000 Japanese Americans were unfairly considered as potential traitors (Nagata, Kim, Wu, 2019). People of Japanese descent from the first to the third generation were forced to migrate to isolated camps in desert and swampland where they were constantly under surveillance by armed guards (Nagata et al., 2019). This lasted for roughly three years. Even though two-thirds of those imprisoned were American-citizenship holders, it did not matter. The basis of internment was solely on whether a person was of Japanese descent or not.

According to Rodriguez (2017), it is of importance to note that even though Japanese Americans were labeled as potential traitors, no evidence of betrayal or lack of Japanese American loyalty to the United States were found. Furthermore, two-thirds of the interned population owned an American citizenship. Their fundamental rights of due process, freedom from unreasonable search and seizure, and the freedoms of speech, religion, and press were stripped off. Chew (2018) opined that people of Japanese heritage in Latin America also experienced forceful removals. In the name of national security, over 2000 people of Japanese heritage were transferred to internment camps in the United States as illegal aliens, first the males, followed by their women and children. In 1988, the United States offered reparations to all the victims that survived the internment camps, paying $20,000 per person to Japanese Americans whereas only $5,000 was paid to Latin American Japanese survivors. Despite the reparation and apology offered by the United States government to Japanese descent individuals in 1988, the three-year-long event can be identified as a profound racial trauma in the history of America and the Japanese Americans. Lessons learned from the Japanese Internment in America include war hysteria that brought citizens into a state of uncontrollable panic that took over people and led to the failure of political leadership. Racial prejudice rooted in the strict separation of citizenship and ethnic origin stripped the rights of Japanese Americans allowing racial trauma to be inflicted upon Japanese Americans.

The next societal disruption to be explored is the Flint Water Crisis in the United States which was an environmental hazard that occurred in the city of Flint, Michigan. This crisis was an incident in which it was estimated that 140,000 humans were poisoned by lead and other pollutants in drinkable water (Ruckart et al., 2019). In April 2014, the city of Flint temporarily redirected the source of its drinking water from Lake Huron which had phosphate inhibitors to the Flint River water that had no corrosion control implemented (Pieper et al., 2018). This resulted in lead leaching from plumbing. The unfortunate part of this incident is its connection to structural racism. In order to understand how this environmental crisis is connected to structural racism, it is important to know the city of Flint in its context. Flint's white population declined from 162,128 in 1960 to 38, 328 in 2010. Meanwhile, the population of black people grew from 34,521 in 1960 to 57,938 in 2010 (Bernstein, 2016; Bosman, 2016; Coyne, 2016).

Not only does the racial demographics between these two locations cited below differ, but so is the distribution of wealth. The median household income in 2010 was $28,384 for residents in Flint, while it was $41,586 for those in Genesee County. Moreover, Flint City's is an example of the economy plummeting due to deindustrialization. General Motors (GM) had employed 80,000 city residents in 1978, and that number decreased to 23,000 in 1990, and further came down to 8,000 people in 2006. Furthermore, 40 percent of people lived below the poverty line by 2016 and one in five people in the city did not have access to a car. This economic isolation causes a great amount of mental and emotional health, even inflicting negative effects on the physical body due to the disparity in access to medical health and nutritious food. Lessons learned from the Flint Water Crisis include injustice done through deliberately causing disparity according to race and socioeconomic status, social engineering, and systemic oppression resulting in health deterioration and other forms of damage-inflicting procedures deliberately done to gradually inflict harm on someone without their knowledge physically, mentally, emotionally (Bosman, 2016; Darden 1992; Hurley, 1988; Michigan State Housing Development Authority, 1986; Ruckart et al., 2019).

Socio Economic Status/Poverty and economic disenfranchisement: Poverty is another factor of disruption, alienation, and disenfranchisement. In the introduction to my earlier book on Poverty, Education and International Development in 2008 I posited that:

> poverty is regarded as a violation of human rights. Granted that there are more than 1.3 billion people according to the United Nations (UN) living in extreme poverty then poverty could be regarded as the most widespread human rights abuse the world is witnessing. . . . That poverty is not merely a statistic but impacts the lives of real people who live on less than a dollar a day. (pp. vii-ix)

I strongly contended in this book that poverty in itself is disempowering. In addition, it creates the bedrock and the fertile ground for the cultivation of all forms of disempowering spaces. These disempowering spaces manifest themselves in phenomena such as but not limited to social, political, economic and cultural inequalities, violence, rape, torture, culture of silence, war, hunger, deprivation, racism, sexism, ethnocentrism, ableism, linguicism, sizeism, ageism, nativism, colonialism, classism, lookism, exploitation, marginalization, and powerlessness, all of which are dehumanizing. Borrowing from the ideas of Freire (1993) and Vlieghe (2018), dehumanization makes those who become victims of dehumanization as well as those who perpetuate both less human. Freire further argued that:

> To surmount the situation of oppression, people must first critically recognize the causes, so that through transforming action they can create a new situation, one which makes possible the pursuit of a fuller humanity. . . . Although the situation of oppression is a . . . dehumanizing totality affecting both the oppressors and those whom they oppress, it is the latter who must, from their stifled humanity, wage for both the struggle for a fuller humanity; the oppressor, who is himself dehumanized because he dehumanizes others, is unable to lead the struggle . . . . As long as they live in the duality in which *to be is to be like, and to be like is to be like the oppressor*, this contribution is impossible. The pedagogy of the oppressed is an instrument for their critical discovery that both they and their oppressors are manifestations of dehumanization. (pp. 47–48)

Thus, the task of empowerment has a dimension that involves the role of the victim to arrive at a critical self-consciousness of the unacceptable nature of the disempowering space and begin to adopt counter-hegemonic paradigms to liberate not only himself but to dismantle the pillars that prop up the unacceptable conditions. In doing so if a paradigm shift is desired then the perpetrators of the disempowering spaces need to be assisted to swim up with the high tide.

How do we create the spaces for those who were not in the position to enjoy life, freedom and the quest of well-being? We certainly need to create empowering spaces to heal the fractures. In the introductory section of my book on Perspectives of Empowering Education, I have argued that an empowered person believes that he or she possesses the required skills contextually relevant as well as the potential of altering the balance of scales. Thus, an empowered person chooses to go against the tide with a sense of purpose with the view to altering outcomes believing that he or she possesses the skill and oomph to undertake the task. On the other hand, to use the ideas of Al-Ababneh, Al-Sabi, Al-Shakhsheer, and Masadeh (2017) and Spreitzer (1995) an empowered individual does not see his or her situation as already carved out but rather something able to be shaped by acting on it.

Aloisio et al. (2019) and Chamberlain (1997), in their attempt to define the concept of empowerment, acknowledge the multiple perspectives and therefore chooses to describe the term by providing 15 characteristics that are indicative of empowerment:

- Possessing power to make decisions
- Possessing access to knowledge and resources
- Having multiple options in order to make choices (not limited to yes/no, either/or)
- Assertiveness
- A feeling of autonomy to make a difference (being hopeful)
- Ability to see things from different perspectives by learning to think critically and unlearning stereotypes
- Learning to redefine our personality (speaking in our own voice)
- Learning to readdress our ability
- Learning to readdress our relationships to institutionalized power
- Learning the manner to express anger
- Feeling as part of a group; Not feeling secluded
- Understanding the rights of people
- Making difference in one's life and one's community
- Learning skills as prioritized by the individual (e.g., communication)
- Redirecting peoples' notion of one's competency and capacity to act
- Breaking out of the shell
- Autonomous growth and change that is never ending
- Increasing one's positive self-image and overcoming stigma. (p. 44)

Even though Chamberlain's characteristics are framed within the mental health field, they are fairly representative of the feelings and meanings projected through the use of the word "empowerment." An assessment of the meaning of empowerment discloses both diversity and commonality. Among the factors explicated in these definitions are access; awareness of causes of structural inequalities and how they impact social groups; power to make decisions; authority over economic resources; incorporating a sense of assertiveness and capacity; ability to bargain and influence decisions through interpersonal skills; opportunities to indulge in matters that involve the least privileged; access to resources and agency; and freedom for individuals to make diverse choices and get varying results (Albertyn, 2001; Baiocchi, Heller, Chaudhuri & Silva, 2005; Biggs, Gurung & Messerschmidt, 2004; Daniele, 2017; Foucault, 1980; Kabeer, 1999; Kaufmann, Kraay & Zoido-Lobatón, 1999; Mosedale, 2005; Narayan-Parker, 2005; Rowlands, 1997; Sen, 1999; UNDP, 1995).

In conclusion this chapter defined silence and discussed the conditions that evoke the phenomenon. It also explored different historical events that created societal disruptions and the complicated responses that resulted as a consequence. It also interrogated the possibilities of creating spaces for empowerment. It is my considered opinion that to make room for marginalized voices one has to respect the individual and uphold their fundamental human rights and distinctiveness. This distinctiveness is expressed through their race, gender, religious orientation, sexual preference, physical status, SES status, and intellectual disability among others. Disregarding this distinctiveness would be comparable to destroying the essence of their being and undermining their humanity. Thus, to find common ground one should not vilify the messenger and the message, we do not dismiss claims of voices but listen, communicate, and dialogue, as well as open the channels of communication about the perceptions of groups and individuals in honest and authentic discourses.

REFERENCES

Al-Ababneh, M., Al-Sabi, S., Al-Shakhsheer, F., & Masadeh, M. (2017). The influence of employee empowerment on employee job satisfaction in five-star hotels in Jordan. *International Business Research*, *10*(3), 133. https://doi.org/10.5539/ibr.v10n3p133

Albertyn, R. (2001). Case Study: Increased accountability through empowerment assessments. *People Dynamics*, *19*(2), 20–23.

Aloisio, L. D., Baumbusch, J., Estabrooks, C. A., Bostrom, A. M., Chamberlain, S., Cummings, G. G., ..., & Squires, J. E. (2019). Factors affecting job satisfaction in long-term care unit managers, directors of care and facility administrators: A secondary analysis. *Journal of Nursing Management*, *27*(8), 1764–1772. https://doi.org/10.1111/jonm.12871

Anderson, W. L. (1989). The Trail of Tears through Fictional Reminiscence. *The Georgia*

Aptheker, H. (Ed.). (1951). *A Documentary history of the Negro people in the United States, Volume 1*. Citadel Press

Argyris, C., & Schon, D. (1978). *Organizational learning: A theory of action perspective*. Addison-Wesley.

Baiocchi, G., Silva, M., & Heller, P. (n.d.). *Measuring and Evaluating Empowerment: Participatory Budgeting in Brazilian Municipalities*. https://businessdocbox.com/78895606- Government/Measuring-and-evaluating-empowerment-participatory-budgeting-in-brazilian-municipalities-03-21-05.html.

Bayart, J.-F. (2009). *The State in Africa: The politics of the belly* (2nd. ed.). Longman.

Beer, M., & Eisenstat, R. A. (2000). The silent killers of strategy implementation and learning. *IEEE Engineering Management Review*, *28*(4), 35–45. https://doi.org/10.4135/9781446250228.n9

Benevene, P. (2020). Managing silence in workplaces. *Journal of Workplace Learning*. https://doi.org/10.1108/jwl-02-2020-157

Bergmann, M. S., & Jucovy, M. E. (1982). *Generations of the Holocaust*. Columbia University Press.

Biggs, S. D., Gurung, S. M., & Messerschmidt, D. (2004). An exploratory study of gender, social inclusion and empowerment through development groups and group-based organizations in Nepal: building on the positive. *Report Submitted* to the *Gender and Social Exclusion Assessment (GSEA) Study National Planning Commission, The World Bank and DFID. Version, 2.* https://documents1.worldbank.org/curated/en/201971468061735968/pdf/379660Nepal0GSEA0Summary0Report01PUBLIC1.pdf

Bosman, J. (2016, February 5). *Many Flint Residents Are Desperate to Leave, but See No Escape.* The New York Times. http://www.nytimes.com/2016/02/05/us/many-flintresidents-are-desperate-to-leave-but-see-no-escape.html

Bowen, F., & Blackmon, K. (2003). Spirals of silence: The dynamic effects of diversity on organizational voice. *Journal of Management Studies, 40*(6), 1393–1417. https://doi.org/10.1111/1467-6486.00385

Breitman, R., & Herf, J. (2019). Obituary: Walter Ze'ev Laqueur. *Holocaust and Genocide Studies, 33*(1), 172–173. https://doi.org/10.1093/hgs/dcz020https://www.muse.jhu.edu/article/726089.

Britannica, T. Editors of Encyclopedia (2018, May 11). Creek War. *Encyclopedia Britannica.*

Chamberlain, M. (1997). Power in action: Empowerment of Indigenous communities. A midwifery run birthing centre in the Canadian Arctic. *The Truth, Virtue and Beauty of Midwifery,* 85–93. https://doi.org/10.1016/s0266-6138(97)90061-9.

Chew, P. (2018). *For Others,* World Scientific 56–59. https://doi.org/10.1142/9789813231016_0014

Chretien, J.P. (1995). Rwanda: les medias du genocide. Paris: Karthala. *civil war* (Vol. 2). Greenwood Press.

Christian, P. J. (2013). Darfur—Ground zero for Africa's crises of identity: A Psychohistoriography of tribes in conflict. *African Security, 6*(1), 1–37. https://doi.org/10.1080/19392206.2013.759457

Cohn, N. R. C. (1967). *Warrant for genocide: The myth of the Jewish world-conspiracy and the protocols of the elders of Zion* ([1st U.S. ed.]). Harper & Row.

Coyne, C. (2016, January 20). Flint, Michigan's water crisis: what the national media got wrong. *Vox.* http://www.vox.com/2016/1/20/10789810/flint-michigan-water-crisis

Dagne, T. (2004, June). Sudan: The Crisis in Darfur. Library of Congress Washington DC Congressional Research Service.

Daniele, L. (2017). Discourses on empowerment in adult learning: A view on renewed learning. *IAFOR Journal of Education, 5*(2), 49–64. https://doi.org/10.22492/ije.5.2.02

Darden, Joe T. (1992). *Residential segregation of Blacks in metropolitan areas of Michigan, 1960-1990. The state of Black Michigan.* East Lansing: Urban Affairs Programs, Michigan State University.

Debo, A. (1973*). And still the water runs: The betrayal of the five civilized tribes* (Vol. 287). Princeton University Press.

Destexhe, A. (I995). *Rwanda and genocide in the twentieth century.* Pluto Press.

Economist Intelligence Unit ([EIU], I994). *Rwanda country report*; *1st Quarter March.* Economist Publications.

Edmondson, A. C. (2003). Speaking up in the operating room: How team leaders promote learning in interdisciplinary action teams. *Journal of management studies, 40*(6), 1419–1452. https://doi.org/10.1111/1467-6486.00386

Foner, P. S. (1986). History of Black Americans: From the Emergence of the Cotton Kingdom to the Eve of the Compromise of 1850 [History of Black Americans: From the Emergence of the Cotton Kingdom to the Eve of the Compromise of 1850 by J.D. Smith]. *Journal of American Ethnic History, 5*(2), 110.

Foner, P. S. (1983). *History of Black Americans: From the Compromise of 1850 to the End of the Civil War.* Greenwood Press.

Foucault, M. (1980). Empowerment on employee job satisfaction in five-star hotels in Jordan. In C. Gordon (Ed.). *Power/knowledge* (p. 90). Pantheon.

Freire, P. (1993). *Pedagogy of the oppressed:* Anniversary edition (M. B. Ramos, Trans.). *Continuum.* (Original work published 1970)

Gunther, J. (1955). *Inside Africa.* Hamish Hamilton.

Hintjens, H. (1999). Explaining the 1994 genocide in Rwanda. *The Journal of Modern African Studies, 37*(2), 241–286. Retrieved July 21, 2021, from http://www.jstor.org/stable/161847 *Historical Quarterly, 73*(3) 610-20. https://www.jstor.org/stable/40582019 https://www.britannica.com/event/Creek-War

Huang, J., Qiu, Y., Ye, M., Yu, P., & Zheng, H. (2018). Online opinion expression and me-too movement: testing spiral of silence under social media context. http://dspace.cityu.edu.hk/handle/2031/9134

Hurley, S. (1988). Home mortgage lending patterns in Genesee County from 1981 to 1986. *Journal, 53*(3), 875–965. http://www.jstor.org/stable/1373221.

Kabeer, N. (1999). *The conditions and consequences of choice: reflections on the measurement of women's empowerment* (Vol. *1*(108), pp. 1–58). Geneva: United Nations Research Institute for Social Development UNRISD.

Kaufmann, D., Kraay, A., & Zoido-Lobatón, P. (1999). Aggregating Governance Indicators. ‖ World Bank Policy Research Working Paper No. 2195. Washington, DC. https://doi.org/10.1596/1813-9450-2195

Kestenberg, J. S. (1980). Psychoanalyses of children of survivors from the Holocaust: Case presentations and assessment. *Journal of the American Psychoanalytic Association, 28*(4), 775–804. https://doi.org/10.1177/000306518002800402

Khalid, J., & Ahmed, J. (2016). Perceived organizational politics and employee silence: supervisor trust as a moderator. *Journal of the Asia Pacific Economy, 21*(2), 174–195. https://doi.org/10.1080/13547860.2015.1092279

Kostiuk, D. D. (n.d.). Silence: the reasons why people may not communicate. https://doi.org/10.32469/10355/15006

Kumar, K., (ed.). (1997). *Rebuilding Societies after Civil War: Critical Roles for International Assistance.* Lynne Rienner.

Laqueur, W. (1980). Hitler holocaust-who knew what, when, and how. *Encounter, 55*(1), 6–25. https://doi.org/10.1515/9783110968705.60

Lemarchand René. (1996). *Burundi: Ethnic Conflict and Genocide.* Cambridge University Press.

Mackintosh, A. (1996). International aid and the media. *Contemporary Politics, 2*(1), 37–55. https://doi.org/10.1080/13569775.1996.10382949

Magliocca, G. (2003). The Cherokee removal and the fourteenth amendment. Duke Law Journal, 53, 875–965 Available at: https://scholarship.law.duke.edu/dlj/vol53/iss3/1

Mamdani, M. (1996). From conquest to consent as the basis of state formation: reflections on Rwanda. *New Left Review*, 216, 3–36.

Manikas, P. M., Kumar, K. (1996). Protecting human rights in Rwanda. In K. Kumar (Ed.), *Rebuilding Societies after Civil War* (pp. 63–83). Lynne Rienner.

Maquet, J. J. (1961). *The Premise of Inequality in Ruanda: A Study of Political Relations in a Central African Kingdom* (1st ed.). Routledge. https://doi.org/10.4324/9780429488160

Melvern, L. (2006). *Conspiracy to Murder: The Rwandan Genocide*. Verso Books.

Milliken, F. J., Morrison, E. W., & Hewlin, P. F. (2003). An exploratory study of employee silence: Issues that employees don't communicate upward and why. *Journal of Management Studies*, *40*(6), 1453–1476. https://doi.org/10.1111/1467-6486.00387

Morrison, E. W., & Milliken, F. J. (2000). Organizational silence: A barrier to change and development in a pluralistic world. *Academy of Management Review*, *25*(4), 706–725. https://doi.org/10.5465/amr.2000.3707697

Mosedale, S. (2005). Assessing women's empowerment: towards a conceptual framework. *Journal of International Development*, *17*(2), 243–257. https://doi.org/10.1002/jid.1212

Mukoyama, N. (2018). Causes and consequences of third-party intervention in disputes over history: Recognition of the Armenian massacre as genocide and relations with Turkey. *World Political Science*, *14*(1), 101–122. doi:10.1515/wps-2018-0006

Nagata, D. K., Kim, J. H. J., & Wu, K. (2019). The Japanese American wartime incarceration: Examining the scope of racial trauma. *American Psychologist, 74*(1), 36–48. https://doi.org/10.1037/amp0000303

Narayan-Parker, D. (Ed.). (2005). Measuring empowerment: Cross-disciplinary perspectives. *World Bank Publications*. https://doi.org/10.1037/e597202012-001 Nebraska Press.

Niederland, W. G. (1981). The survivor syndrome: Further observations and dimensions. *Journal of the American Psychoanalytic Association*, *29*(2), 413–425. https://doi.org/10.1177/000306518102900207

Noelle-Neumann, E. (1974). The spiral of silence a theory of public opinion. *Journal of Communication*, *24*(2), 43–51. https://doi.org/10.1111/j.1460-2466.1974.tb00367.x

Oette, L., & Babiker, M.A. (2018). *Constitution-making and Human Rights in the Sudans* (1st ed.). Routledge. https://doi.org/10.4324/9781315624075

Oplinger, J. (1990). *The Politics of Demonology: The European Witch Craze and the Mass Production of Deviance*. Associated University Press.

Ostow, M. (1997). *Judaism and Psychoanalysis* (1st ed.). Routledge. https://doi.org/10.4324/9780429476310

Pieper, K. J., Martin. R., Tang, M., Walters. L., Parks, J., Roy, S., Devine, C., & Edwards, M. A. (2018). Evaluating water lead levels during the flint water crisis. *Environmental Science Technology*, *52*(15), 8124–8132. https://doi.org/10.1021/acs.est.8b00791

Pine, L. (2020). The Experiences and Behavior of Male Holocaust Victims at Auschwitz. In Krondorfer, B., & Creanga, O. (Eds.). *The Holocaust and Masculinities: Critical Inquiries into the Presence and Absence of Men* (p. 77). SUNY Press.

Pines, D. (1986). Working with women survivors of the Holocaust: Affective experiences in transference and countertransference. *International Journal of Psychoanalysis, 67*(3), 295–307. https://psycnet.apa.org/record/1987-04755-001

Prunier, G. (1995). *The Rwanda Crisis 1959-1994: History of a Genocide*. Hurst.

Reyntjens, F. (1996). Rwanda: Genocide and beyond, *Journal of Refugee Studies, 9*(3), 240–51. https://doi.org/10.1093/jrs/9.3.240

Ridzuan, M. R., Abd Rahman, N. A. S., & Manas, N. H. N. (2019). The effects of organizational commitment and status of wrongdoer on external whistleblowing intention among same day staff. *Journal for the Social Sciences, 22*(00), 117–123.

Rodriguez, R. A., Green, M. T., Sun, Y., & Baggerly-Hinojosa, B. (2017). Authentic leadership and transformational leadership: An incremental approach. *Journal of Leadership Studies, 11*(1), 20–35. https://doi.org/10.1002/jls.21501.

Rowlands, J. (1997). *Questioning empowerment: Working with women in Honduras*. Oxfam.

Ruckart P. Z., Ettinger, A. S., Hanna-Attisha, M., Jones, N., Davis, S. I., & Breysse, P. N. (2019). The flint water crisis: A coordinated public health emergency response and recovery Initiative. *Journal of Public Health Management and Practice, 25*(Suppl 1, Lead Poisoning Prevention), S84–S90. https://doi.org/10.1097/PHH.0000000000000871

Ryan, K. D., & Oestreich, D. K. (1991). *Driving Fear Out of the Workplace: How to Overcome the Invisible Barriers to Quality, Productivity, and Innovation*. Jossey-Bass.

Satz, R. N. (1975). *American Indian policy in the Jacksonian era*. University of Oklahoma Press.

Schlesinger, A. M. (1945). *The Age of Jackson*. Little, Brown and Company.

Schwartz, S. (2006). A theory of cultural value orientations: Explication and applications. *Comparative Sociology, 5*(2–3), 137–182. https://doi.org/10.1163/156913306778667357

Sen, A. (1999). *Commodities and Capabilities*. Oxford University Press.

Spreitzer, G. M. (1995). An empirical test of a comprehensive model of intrapersonal empowerment in the workplace. *American journal of community psychology, 23*(5), 601-629. https://doi.org/10.1007/bf02506984

Storr, A. (1991). *Human Destructiveness: The Roots of Genocide and Human Cruelty* (2nd ed.). Routledge.

Thorpe, K., & Taylor, N. A. (2019). *Fannie C. Williams (1882–1980). Unsung Legacies of Educators and Events in African American Education*. Palgrave Macmillan, Cham, 23. https://doi.org/10.1007/978-3-319-90128-2_4

UNDP, U. (1995). WHO special programme for research, development and research training in human reproduction. World Bank: IUD Research Group. *Contraception, 52*, 77–83. https://doi.org/10.1016/s0010-7824(95)00140-9

Uvin, P. (1997). Prejudice, crisis and genocide in Rwanda. *African Studies Review, 40*(2), 91–115. https://doi.org/10.2307/525158

Uwizeyimana, D. E. (2014). Aspects and consequences of the Rwandan law of genocide ideology: A comparative analysis. *Mediterranean Journal of Social Sciences*, 5(23), 2363–2363. https://doi.org/10.5901/mjss.2014.v5n23p2370

Vlieghe, J. (2018). Rethinking emancipation with Freire and Rancière: A plea for a thing-centered pedagogy. *Educational Philosophy and Theory, 50*(10), 917–927. https://doi.org/10.1080/00131857.2016.1200002.

Williams, G. W. (1882). *History of the Negro Race in America from 1619 to 1880: Negroes as Slaves, as Soldiers, and as Citizens; Together with a Preliminary Consideration of the Unity of the Human Family, an Historical Sketch of Africa, and an Account of the Negro Governments of Sierra Leone and Liberia* (No. 289). GP Putnam's Sons.

Yalçın, B., & Baykal, Ü. (2019). Development and psychometric testing of the organizational silence behavior scale for healthcare professionals. *Nursing & Health Sciences, 21*(4), 454–460. https://doi.org/10.1111/nhs.12619.

Yanagizawa-Drott, D. (2014). Propaganda and conflict: Evidence from the Rwandan genocide. *The Quarterly Journal of Economics, 129*(4), 1947–1994. https://doi.org/10.1093/qje/qju020

Index

ability, 24, 31, 62, 65, 100, 115, 148, 154, 155, 160, 163, 195, 218
abolitionist (teaching), 4, 21, 23, 24, 123, 135, 136, 201, 204, 205
absolute authority, 195, 203
abuse, 213, 216
academic achievement, 60–63, 105, 107, 108, 116, 118
academic competence, 194, 200
adversity, 141, 142, 147
affinity groups, 90, 136
African, 15, 78, 95, 150, 197, 211–13
alienation, 132, 213, 216
anecdotal feedback, 92, 95
anger, 75, 78, 79, 81, 213, 218
anti-immigrant, 18, 205
anti-racist pedagogy, 25, 37, 44, 48, 51, 83, 143, 203, 205
anti-racist practices, 123, 124, 129, 201, 204
anti-racist professional discernment, 4, 37–39, 41, 44, 45, 47, 49, 51
authentic knowledge, 195, 203

Black Lives Matter, 57, 69, 71, 102, 144, 152, 156, 201
Blackness, 61, 63, 64
Black women, 192, 197

catalyst, 125, 143, 144, 151, 153, 154
citizenship, 41, 65, 193, 215
class (economic), 1, 3, 5, 6, 17, 103, 106, 163, 216
classroom climate, 194, 201, 202
classroom management, 130, 194, 201, 202
climate, 194, 202, 211
co-conspirator, 34, 189, 197
colonize, colonial, colonialism, 41, 49, 197, 212, 216
comprehensive, 34, 187, 194, 197
consciousness, 4, 9, 46, 58, 61, 62, 73, 105–8, 112, 114, 116, 118, 134, 136, 204
counter-hegemonic paradigms, 217
critical educators, 40, 44, 195
critical literacy, 45, 46, 48, 162–64
critical media literacy, 126, 127
Critical Race Theory, 4, 9, 73, 82, 125
cultural awareness, 103, 111, 171
cultural barriers, 193, 197
cultural competence, 27, 61, 62, 105–9, 111–12, 114, 116–18
cultural knowledge, 4, 30, 45, 58, 61, 62, 67, 80, 106, 177, 178, 184, 194, 198

deconstruct, 74, 84, 106, 108, 179
dehumanize, 60, 95, 213, 217
democracy, 10, 163
democratic, 1, 9, 10, 15–17, 66, 67, 164, 194, 225
demographics, 177
denial, 42, 77, 176, 189, 190, 205, 211, 212
difficult conversations, 30, 32, 65, 96, 130
dignity, 195, 201
disability(ies), 24, 161, 164, 168, 171, 178, 181, 219
discourse, 1, 4, 5, 10, 38–40, 42, 44, 50, 51, 73–75, 83, 84, 104, 106, 118, 125, 127, 128, 132, 135, 136, 164, 194, 195, 219
discrimination, 22, 29, 59, 60, 101, 129, 132, 135, 137, 141, 178, 181, 202, 205, 211–13
disenfranchisement, 132, 210, 213, 216
displacement, 202, 214
dispositions, 31, 33, 73, 78, 175–77, 186, 193
disruption, 6, 209–13, 215, 216, 218
diverse audiences, 193, 197, 201
diverse classrooms, 6, 26, 104, 116, 119, 175, 183, 185, 191
diversity, 1, 10, 11, 17, 22, 25, 26, 28, 33, 38, 51, 57, 77, 79, 80, 84, 91, 100, 103, 107, 109, 110, 114, 117, 118, 127, 130, 153, 160, 162, 164, 165, 171, 176–78, 185, 186, 194, 195, 197, 202, 218, 225
domination, 22, 192, 197–99, 203
duality, 146, 202, 217

economic, 16, 24, 49, 59, 78, 106, 116, 123, 129, 148, 160, 164, 181, 190–92, 197, 202, 213, 216, 218
educational justice, 39, 203
elementary, 4, 37–39, 77, 81, 148, 150, 177
emancipatory, 195, 196, 201, 203

empathy, 25, 91, 92, 95, 97, 99, 107, 110, 130, 160
empowerment, 6, 177, 180, 192, 209, 217, 218
epistemological, 4, 45, 189, 191, 196, 198, 201
equity, 2–4, 6, 9, 11, 23, 25, 33, 40, 44, 80, 81, 83, 89, 91, 98, 99, 106, 111, 114, 117, 124, 126, 134, 162, 163, 186, 194, 198
ethical, 39, 44, 49, 195, 196, 201–3, 209
ethnically diverse, 61, 62, 178, 183–85, 191, 194, 195, 198, 202
ethnicity, 103, 106, 160, 163, 171, 175, 176, 194
ethnic studies, 4, 9, 11–13, 15–19, 42, 143
Eurocentric, 39, 59, 67, 186, 200
exploitation, 197, 216

family, 4, 6, 27, 29, 30, 66, 81, 104, 129, 141, 142, 146–49, 152–55, 161, 169–71, 206, 210
fear, 6, 13, 18, 27, 37, 40, 47, 78, 81, 90, 106, 130, 159, 169, 175–79, 182–86, 210, 213
feminist, 6, 136, 137, 189–93, 195–99, 201, 203–5
Freire, Paulo, 14, 45, 46, 48, 50, 63, 66, 67, 112, 131, 163, 217
frustration, 79, 153

gender, 5, 6, 22, 24, 31, 93, 100, 103, 104, 106, 109–11, 113, 115, 116, 118, 125, 128, 132, 155, 160–64, 166, 168, 169, 171, 178, 181, 183, 184, 191, 192, 195, 197–99, 202, 213, 219
genocide, 210, 212, 213
geographic, 96, 191, 193
global, 5, 6, 82, 104, 106, 113, 118, 123, 124, 136, 162, 164–66, 189–93, 196–205

global competence(ies), 6, 189, 192, 193, 196, 197, 201–4
globalizing classrooms, 6, 189, 204
government, 9, 10, 13, 16, 192, 211, 212
grassroots, 98, 204, 205

healing, 6, 9, 123, 135
health, 3, 37, 47, 51, 63, 66, 75, 130, 192, 202, 216, 218
Holocaust, 210, 211
homophobia, 185, 186, 205
housing, 192, 202, 216
humanizing, 2, 38, 39, 44, 45, 47, 51, 217
humanistic, 195, 201
humanity, 66, 67, 115, 201, 217, 219

identity, 5, 15, 31, 41, 58, 59, 63, 65–67, 77–81, 83–85, 100, 103, 106, 109–11, 113, 116, 118, 125, 130, 133, 141, 143, 145, 146, 148–52, 154, 160–62, 167, 184, 195, 212
ideological, 38, 47, 163, 193, 197, 199, 213
images, 25, 126–28, 162, 165, 170, 218
immigrant, 13, 15, 18, 42, 204, 205
implicit bias, 25, 27, 101, 133
inclusion, 1, 10, 11, 25, 26, 28, 33, 100, 162, 185
inclusive, 2, 18, 25, 105, 165, 167, 171, 179, 180, 183, 194, 197
inequality(ies), 1, 3, 23, 24, 31, 57, 59, 94, 106, 131, 194, 216, 218
inequity(ies), 1, 2, 23, 30, 33, 34, 39, 41, 61, 62, 67, 82, 90, 106, 195, 197
injustice, 1, 33, 78, 94, 96, 106, 119, 130, 136, 165, 170, 189, 202, 205, 216
Instagram, 124–28
institutionalized power, 202, 218
instructional techniques, 194, 201, 202
intentionality, 103, 104, 118, 119, 171
internalized racism, 124, 128, 130, 132, 133

interracial marriage, 141–43
intersecting oppressions, 192, 199, 203, 204
intersectional justice, 6, 124, 204
Islamophobia, 97, 101, 205

joy, 6, 30, 124, 135

Kendi, Ibram, 2, 3, 23, 190, 199, 203, 204

language barriers, 96, 225
language learners, 13, 175, 182, 183, 185
leadership role, 21, 89, 153, 154
learning differences, 5, 58, 103, 106, 109, 110, 113, 116, 118
liberatory role, 6, 46, 47, 51, 189, 200, 203
linguicism, 216
linguistic diversity, 51, 164, 177, 185, 194, 197
literacy instruction, 38, 39, 45, 47
literacy practices, 45, 51, 164, 171
love, 6, 15, 33, 43, 49, 60, 77, 104, 124, 130, 135, 159, 168, 213
Love, Bettina, 1, 6, 23, 30, 33–35, 38, 51, 54, 112, 121–24, 135, 136, 138, 169, 201–6

marginalization, marginalized, 3, 6, 9, 11, 13, 15, 22, 23, 25, 30, 32, 39, 43, 47, 60, 73, 82, 83, 93, 103, 148, 163, 191, 192, 202, 209
Marxists, 192, 198
material realities, 39, 59, 198, 199
math, 27, 65, 133, 134, 136
microaggressions, 31, 33, 59, 60, 143
monoracial, 143, 144, 146, 151
multicultural education, 11, 22, 24, 28, 103, 104, 108, 110, 118, 176, 180
multiculturalism, 45, 107, 123, 162
multicultural literature, 164–67, 171–73
multidimensional, 194, 196, 201, 202

nationality, 5, 31, 103, 106, 109–11, 113, 116, 118, 161, 171, 195
National Reading Panel, 37, 38, 44
neutrality, 2, 73, 198
No Child Left Behind, 38, 39

oppressed, 9, 11, 14, 73, 125, 199, 200, 212, 214, 217
oppression, 26, 29, 46, 58, 60, 77–79, 81, 83, 116, 124, 130, 132, 162, 163, 191, 192, 195, 199, 202–4, 210, 216, 217
oppressor, 212–14, 217
outsider, 2, 94, 200

pandemic, 58, 64, 95, 97, 123, 124, 128, 192
partnership, 5, 29, 98, 104, 118
pedagogical strategy, 61, 66, 177, 202
perpetrators, 204, 217
political claims, 189, 196
political climate, 94, 101
poverty, 27, 205, 210, 216, 225
powerlessness, 213, 217
power dynamics, 90, 98, 202
psychological, 38, 75, 110, 145, 146, 154, 210, 211
public education, schools, 1, 3, 9, 10, 15, 18, 22, 30, 57, 58, 104, 148, 149, 151, 194, 201

queer studies, 4, 126, 204

race-neutral, 2, 73, 198, 203, 206
racial inequity(ies), 2, 23, 33, 39, 82, 90, 195, 197
racial purity, 144, 145
reflexivity, 33, 83, 189, 195, 198
reimagining, 124, 204
rejection, 42, 51, 151, 153, 210
religion, 3, 5, 22, 100, 103, 106, 109–11, 113, 116, 118, 160–63, 169, 171, 176, 178, 181, 215
resentment, 13, 213

resistance, 27, 43, 60, 77–79, 82, 107, 108, 145, 176, 197, 200, 204
restorative justice, 108, 130, 205

school-to-prison pipeline, 57, 205
science of reading (SoR), 37, 40, 41, 50, 51
segregation, 12, 17, 60, 78, 94, 107, 205
self-awareness, 124, 129, 130, 135, 165
self-determination, 5, 59, 110, 141, 143, 146, 151
sexual identity, 5, 103, 106, 109–11, 113, 116, 118, 184
sexuality, 31, 115, 163, 192, 195, 229
sexual orientation, 164, 177, 178, 181–86, 213, 219
shame, 75, 210
silence, 6, 22, 32, 60, 80, 130, 197, 209–11, 214, 216, 218
slavery, 49, 60, 144, 145, 210, 213–14
social disruptions, 6, 209–11, 213, 216
social identities, 58, 63, 89, 90
social media, 64, 98, 124, 133, 136, 152, 206
societal disruptions, 6, 209–12, 215, 218
socioeconomic, 106, 116, 160, 164, 181, 213, 216
sociopolitical, 46, 58, 59, 61–63, 105, 106, 108, 109, 112–14, 116, 200
solidarity, 11, 13, 34, 128, 132, 136, 189, 201, 204
stakeholders, 38, 62, 113, 117
status quo, 1, 4, 33, 62, 202
structural racism, 24, 59, 76, 81, 82, 117, 130, 198, 205, 216
student-centered instruction, 58, 177
student engagement, 17, 22, 24, 63–65, 68, 69, 110, 112, 113, 127, 130, 131, 135, 136
survival, 46, 151, 200, 210
systemic oppression, 26, 77, 79, 195, 216

systemic racism, 22, 28, 29, 31, 81, 94, 106, 116, 123, 131, 135, 151, 152, 155, 186, 216

teacher candidates, 4, 5, 24, 26, 73–85, 90, 91, 110, 128, 129, 132, 135, 136, 175, 178
tension, 6, 13, 38, 44, 90, 141, 151, 185, 189, 193, 204, 211
third spaces, 3, 5, 89–91, 93, 95, 98, 99
tolerance, 59, 83, 180, 202, 205
Trail of Tears, 210, 214
transformation, 5, 33, 46, 67, 83, 103, 108, 117, 118, 160, 164, 180, 192
transforming silence, 197
trauma, 30, 202, 210, 215
Twitter, 126, 127, 132–36

undermining, 40, 209, 219
Universal Design for Learning (UDL), 24, 31, 32
urban, 74, 84, 107, 191, 194

values, 16, 17, 27, 45, 61, 62, 67, 100, 111, 112, 117, 133, 154, 160, 161, 165, 166, 169, 171, 182, 183
violence, 9, 61, 123, 191, 202, 204, 213, 216
vision, 19, 51, 82, 91, 99, 110, 197–200
voluntary, 5, 90

Whiteness, 3, 4, 29, 43, 75, 77, 79, 81, 83, 107, 124, 135, 194, 199, 203
White privilege, 3, 10, 18, 77–79, 124, 125, 146
White supremacy, 3, 4, 9, 19, 39, 45, 48, 51, 78, 129, 130, 135, 152, 194, 195, 203, 205, 206
worldview, 31, 159, 163

xenophobia, 14

youth, 18, 45, 59, 60, 63, 65, 67, 194

zero-tolerance, 59, 205

About the Editors

Delane A. Bender-Slack is a professor of literacy and the program director for both reading and TESOL in the School of Education at Xavier University. She is a teacher educator, teaching courses in English Language Arts methods, middle childhood, adolescent, and multicultural literature, content area literacy, process writing, and reading theories. She has been published in a variety of journals and has published two books. She has been involved in coordinating and implementing international experiences in Peru and Nicaragua. Her research interests include social justice teaching, global issues/perspectives, critical literacy, curriculum studies, study abroad, and adolescent literacy. She is president of the Midwestern Educational Research Association.

Francis Godwyll obtained his master's in education at the University of Cape Coast, Ghana, where he also received a bachelor's honors degree in education concurrently with a diploma (associate degree in religions). He went on to study for a doctorate degree in education from the University of Education at Heidelberg in Heidelberg, Germany. He has taught in seven different institutions including two in Ghana, two in Germany, and four in the United States. His higher education career spans 27 years with rich international/multicultural experiences. He has been a social justice activist since high school. He has taught courses in educational leadership, social foundations, cultural studies and international studies. His major research interests include, among others, leadership applied to marginalized populations/voices and the use of education as a tool for empowerment, diversity issues, poverty education and development, language issues, children's rights and communication barriers. He has authored and co-authored books, journal articles and book chapters. His leadership is embedded in a strong philosophy of teamwork, democratic/

shared governance, and social justice. Previously, he was a full professor of education and served as the chair of the Department of Educational Research and Administration, the EdD program director for curriculum and instruction in the College of Education and Professional Studies, and the faculty administrative fellow at the graduate school at the University of West Florida in Pensacola, FL, USA. Currently, he is the dean of the College of Education and Human Services at Western Illinois University in Macomb and the Quad Cities.

About the Contributors

Kerry Alexander is a doctoral student in language and literacy studies at the University of Texas at Austin. She is interested in the pedagogical implications of, and alternatives to, white language ideologies in elementary writing instruction. She asks how teachers can expand critical linguistic consciousness by learning with and from their students in community and, in particular, how race, racism, and language are intertwined in neoliberal ethics of care and success.

Lauren Angelone is an assistant professor of science education and instructional technology at Xavier University in Cincinnati, Ohio. She is a former middle school science teacher and technology coach/consultant with a PhD in cultural foundations, technology, and qualitative inquiry from Ohio State University. Lauren has published several book chapters and articles in journals such as *Science Scope*, *The Ohio Journal for Teacher Education*, and *The Ohio Journal of English Language Arts* on the topic of science and technology in education. Her research interests include blended learning, science teacher preparation, and cultural studies in education.

Joanne Baltazar Vakil has a PhD in STEM education. She has been a classroom educator for 17 years and an online adjunct instructor for 6 years. Her research interest lies in the intersection of online STEM teacher education programs with the support of bilingual learners and students with disabilities. Her work critically examines how multimedia tools support collaborative learning, knowledge co-construction, as well as the access and equity of STEM education among all learners.

About the Contributors

K. Milam Brooks is a co-founder of Roots & Legacy™, a web-based platform designed to help students steward information about their family and cultural history. She is the co-author of the published article, "School as Solution to the Problem of Urban Space: Student Migration, Perceptions of Safety, and Children's Conception of Community." She previously served as the assistant editor for *Children's Geographies* and student editor of *Social Problems* journals.

Dominique M. Brown is a holistic educator cultivating collective well-being with historically oppressed peoples. She is committed to dismantling systemic oppression by pursuing systems of care. This ethos is carried into her facilitation practice and community work with 10-year experience teaching social change frameworks and facilitating critical dialogues. She is currently a doctoral candidate at Miami University in the educational leadership, culture, and curriculum program. Her research is rooted in womanist spirituality and contemplative practice.

Brett A. Burton is an assistant professor at Xavier University's educational administration program focusing on school leadership and preparing future principals, assistant principals, and athletic directors. Dr. Burton has over 20 years of experience in school administration from Suburban Chicago. His experience includes elementary teacher, serving as an elementary principal, middle school principal, assistant principal at the middle and high school levels, high school athletic director, and assistant professor in education administration at Xavier University. Dr. Burton holds multiple licenses as a teacher and school administrator, including a superintendent endorsement from Illinois.

Sara Fitzgerald is a lecturer in education with expertise in English language and literacy at Mary Immaculate College, Ireland. Fitzgerald has experience working on postgraduate and undergraduate degree teacher education programs specializing in literacy education. She graduated from the University of Limerick with an MEd. Prior to lecturing in Mary Immaculate College, she worked as a primary school teacher, teaching various class levels, and has gained experience in different leadership and management roles including principal and deputy principal. Her research interests include children's literature, teaching methodologies, writing development; writing and reading motivation; reading comprehension and digital literacy.

Helene Arbouet Harte is an associate professor of education at the University of Cincinnati, Blue Ash College. She earned her doctoral degree in special education and master's degree in early childhood education from The

University of Cincinnati. She has worked in the community as a classroom teacher, center director, coach, content expert and consultant. Her research interests include family engagement, engagement of young children in inclusive settings, engagement of students in the college classroom and equity in early childhood education.

Romena M. Garrett Holbert is an associate professor of teacher education at Wright State University where she teaches courses in foundations of education, assessment, and research. Building classroom community and effectively responding to needs emergent from diverse life experiences focus her work.

Jody Googins is an assistant professor of secondary education at Xavier University where she teaches education methods and foundation courses at the undergraduate and graduate level. She received her PhD in educational leadership, with a focus on leadership, culture, and curriculum, from Miami University in Oxford, Ohio. She has an MEd in athletic administration from Xavier University, an MEd in secondary education from Miami University, and a BA in political science from Xavier University. Before moving to higher education, Dr. Googins taught high school English and a teaching professions course for eighteen years in Southwest Ohio. Her research interests include culturally responsive pedagogy, curriculum, and critical discourse analysis.

Jimmy McLean is a doctoral student in language and literacy studies at the University of Texas at Austin. A former public school teacher, he is interested in the ways that children negotiate their identities through their in-school and out-of-school multimodal literacy practices. He is especially interested in the ways that queer knowledge and queer subject positions are made available (or not) in literacy curriculum and instruction. This includes troubling scripted literacy curricula and test-centered literacy pedagogies in order to disrupt the narrowly defined gender and sexuality norms in school and society.

Angela Miller-Hargis is a licensed educator and reading specialist with more than eighteen years of teaching experience in reading, literacy, and the English language arts. She is an associate professor at the University of Cincinnati Blue Ash, teaching coursework in educational foundations and literacy that includes an emphasis on cultural awareness, cultural competence, and differentiated instruction. Dr. Miller-Hargis' current research interests include critical literacy, diversity and equity in early childhood classrooms, and the integration of analytic phonics in ECE reading curricula.

Vanessa M. Rigaud is an assistant professor and Montessori elementary program coordinator of the Montessori Institute in the School of Education at Xavier University. Rigaud received her EdD in executive leadership at St John Fisher College in Rochester, NY. She has an MS in elementary education from Hofstra University and a BA in international relations and political science from the Long Island University/C.W. Post. Her research interests are in the areas of culturally responsive pedagogy in curriculum design, the intersections between Montessori-based research and curriculum pedagogy, and building teacher capacity in curriculum and pedagogical framework. Rigaud has presented at various conferences nationwide and internationally. She is currently a guest peer reviewer for the *Journal of Montessori Research*. She also serves on the board of the American Montessori Society Research Committee.

Jennifer K. Shah is an assistant professor in the Department of Education and Health Sciences at North Central College. Her current research focuses on creating third spaces for BIPOC students and she is the faculty sponsor for Project LEAD (Leaders in Education Advocating for Diversity), a state-wide initiative to recruit and retain a diverse teaching force in addition to a move toward anti-racism. Dr. Shah teaches courses that include topics of cultural relativity and inclusion and she enjoys working with preservice teachers. She lives in Naperville, Illinois with her husband, Birav, and two children, Sofia and Dilan.

Amari T. Simpson is a co-founder of Roots & Legacy™, a web-based platform designed to help students steward information about their family and cultural history. He is also a doctoral student in education policy, organization and leadership in the College of Education, University of Illinois at Urbana-Champaign. He is the co-author of the published article "Understanding early research experiences through the lens of connected learning."

Winston Vaughan is an associate professor in the School of Education at Xavier University where he teaches courses in cultural diversity and adolescent development. His research interests are culturally responsive teaching and learning, multicultural education, and adolescent development.

Nicole V. Williams is an associate professor in the College of Education at the University of Findlay in Findlay, Ohio. She teaches courses in the dissemination of research, educational technology, and educational psychology. Dr. Williams' dissertation research published under the title "Anti-Racist Teacher Education: Toward a Reconceptualization of the Racial Framework of Prospective Teachers" won the 2011 James T. Sears Award from the Curriculum and Pedagogy Group.

Teresa Young is an associate professor at Xavier University, Childhood Education and Reading/TESOL programs and is currently the faculty director of assessment. Young has many years of experience working with preservice and graduate students in the areas of teacher preparation, early childhood education, and literacy. She earned her EdD from the University of Cincinnati in literacy. Prior to earning her doctorate, she was a teacher for elementary students. She has published as well as presented in the areas of literacy, children's literature, and teacher development. She continues to focus her interests on the education of students in literacy and early childhood.

www.ingramcontent.com/pod-product-compliance
Lightning Source LLC
Chambersburg PA
CBHW061711300426
44115CB00014B/2647